MY
WONDERFUL WORLD
OF SLAPSTICK

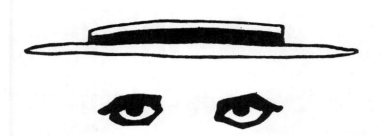

MY
WONDERFUL WORLD
OF SLAPSTICK

BUSTER KEATON
WITH CHARLES SAMUELS

with a new introduction by
DWIGHT MACDONALD
and a new filmography compiled by
RAYMOND ROHAUER

A DA CAPO PAPERBACK

Library of Congress Cataloging in Publication Data

Keaton, Buster, 1895-1966.
  My wonderful world of slapstick.

  (A Da Capo paperback)
  Reprint. Originally published: 1st ed. Garden City, N.Y. : Doubleday, 1960.
  Filmography: p.
  1. Keaton, Buster, 1895-1966. 2. Comedians — United States — Biography. 3.
Moving-picture actors and actresses — United States — Biography. I. Samuels,
Charles. II. Title.
PN2287.K4A3 1982   791.43′028′0924   [B]   82-9952
ISBN 0-306-80178-7 (pbk.)   AACR2

This Da Capo Press paperback edition of *My Wonderful World of Slapstick*
is an unabridged republication of the first edition, here supplemented
with a new introduction by Dwight Macdonald and a new filmography by
Raymond Rohauer. It is reprinted by arrangement with Charles Samuels
and the Estate of Buster Keaton.

Published by Da Capo Press, Inc.
A Subsidiary of Plenum Publishing Corporation
233 Spring Street, New York, N.Y. 10013

Manufactured in the United States of America

For Eleanor

Adapted from an article first published on October 9, 1980 in *The New York Review of Books,* with whose permission these portions have been reprinted.

INTRODUCTION

I think that during the Seventies Buster Keaton replaced Charlie Chaplin as the master of movie comedy most admired by Americans seriously interested in cinema. The reasons are aesthetic and historical. *College* (1927) is generally considered the weakest of the twelve feature-length comedies Keaton made in the Twenties, his creative period. But it is superior to *The Gold Rush* (1925), much the best of the four long comedies Chaplin made in the Twenties. *College* is superior in photography, casting, plot continuity, and consistency of style, for Keaton's aim—though he would never have admitted it—was to make a work of art. Chaplin didn't bother with such trivia; he had in mind not art but himself.

Keaton's comedies were all of a piece while *The Gold Rush* is five or six disparate shorts (one, the long sequence in the cabin, brilliant) Scotch-taped together with barely a stab at a plot line. The whole thing is rigged up, with plentiful close-ups, to show the comic expressiveness of every muscle in the great clown's face and body. So hack photography, scripts, direction, and the cheapest stock sets satisfied Chaplin, who was thinking not of making a work of art but rather of displaying himself as one.

"In retrospect," Kevin Brownlow writes in *The Parade's Gone By,* his fascinating history of American silent movie-making, "Buster Keaton was probably the best comedy director in the business." Not only did he understand "story construction" but also his features were delightfully free of the sentimentality that blights Chaplin's. The late James Agee has called Keaton "the only major comedian who has kept sentiment almost entirely out of his work." The opposite is true of Chaplin. One reason, besides structure, that Chaplin's shorts are so much better than his features is their comparative freedom from sentimentality—indeed, they often go too far the other way, becoming heartless.

History may also have something to do with the present taste for Keaton. Perhaps the World War II horrors have changed our cultural climate. Perhaps in this postwar age of disillusion, one feels more responsive to Keaton's gentle "coolness"—in McLuhan's terms—and deadpan bewilderment than to Chaplin's "hot" certainties, his stance of the wise guy who is one up on the yokels, including God, to Whom, in *Monsieur Verdoux* (1947), as he struts to the gallows as a mass-murderer, he gives, via the prison chaplain, some suggestions on how He might order His world better. Keaton is the fall-guy, puzzled but not helpless, and always courteous, who wins or loses without hurting anybody else; while Chaplin is the aggressive, know-it-all, take-charge type. In this somber period, when confusion invades us, with which comedian can we identify more easily?

❂   ❂   ❂   ❂

At present the Keaton vogue is limited to an elite (ghastly word!) that is as small as the general public is large. This is a familiar situation that's never bothered me because I know it won't last. *Time*'s jocose sneers in its first issue (March 3, 1923) at *Ulysses* and *The Waste Land* as "incomprehensible" nonsense were followed presently by two respectful "cover stories" on Joyce and one on Eliot. So, too, the conventional wisdom of my boyhood was that Cézanne and Van Gogh "didn't know how to draw."

In fact, the pendulum of taste among the advanced *cinéastes* who initiate vogues may now be swinging too far against Chaplin. After all, he was the greatest of all movie clowns and "Charlie" is still the best-known twentieth-century personage to everyone, from Argentine gauchos to left Bank *Cahiers du Cinéma* types, outstripping Churchill, Einstein, Freud, Stalin, and both Roosevelts. He was a pantomimic genius to whom Buster in single combat, *mano a mano*, is not just inferior—he isn't even in the same league. That Buster doesn't try to compete, that he has his own Little League, so to speak, in which he wins every game against the great Charlie, this is one of the many curious aspects of his genius.

Despite the usual assumption that Keaton's career ended with his silent comedies, his gravelly monotone on the sound track was matched to his image on the screen. What destroyed his creativity wasn't sound but what came with it, the taking over of movie-making by big capital and a consequent "rationalization" (cost-accounting, efficiency rating, tight budget control) that couldn't afford maverick geniuses like Keaton, who was instantly and permanently reduced from director to actor.

Although he never made another film of his own, Keaton was profitably employed in every sense, throughout the latter half of his life, as actor, gag writer, circus clown, and, above all, consultant. Keaton had perfect pitch, so to speak, about what would and what wouldn't "go" in any form of comedy—TV, movies, stage, night club—and in his later years became a kind of sage of comedy whose laconic wisdom, or savvy, was respected and sought after, especially in France, which became his second homeland.

My own conversion to Keaton came embarrassingly late. Perhaps I was too young for the subtler artistry of Keaton; perhaps, like many adult moviegoers of the Twenties, I found his unsmiling, frozen face boring or repulsiye or even scary compared to Chaplin's lively clowning. Or perhaps by the time I entered Yale in 1924, Chaplin had become the only movie comedian the intellectuals paid attention to, with disastrous effects on his ego and his work. And I was ever the culture-snob.

By the Thirties I had grown up to Keaton and was delighted when the film department of Alfred Barr's newly founded Museum of Modern Art began showing *The General* and *The Navigator* every now and then without causing excitement except among a few of us who longed for more. But there weren't any more, it seemed, because the careless and hard-drinking Buster had mislaid them or Metro-Goldwyn-Mayer had scrapped them or something.

So everybody assumed, until one night in 1955 Keaton dropped into a showing of *The General* at the Coronet Theatre in Los Angeles and the owner, Raymond Rohauer, recognized him. As he was leaving, Rohauer asked him, on a hunch, if he still had any of his old films and Buster answered, casually, that he had a few to show to friends and, when Rohauer asked if he might duplicate negatives of them, said sure why not? That was the first step. The next was to acquire. with Buster's absent-minded blessing, after complex negotiations with the trustees of the long-defunct Buster Keaton Productions, Inc., the rights to the first eight of the shorts and most of the features. Further inquiry revealed that they had been right next door in MGM's vaults all the time and. by mistake, had been treated just as if they belonged to MGM, which they didn't. unlike Keaton's sound films. which did. So MGM kept renewing their copyrights and preserving them along with the sound films they did own.

Another source was the British actor James Mason, who had rented in the fifties the big Italianate villa where Buster had thrown famous parties thirty years before. (He was a celebrated barbecuer and a genial host so long as the subject of conversation wasn't himself.) Poking around in the private projection room one day, Mason was startled to find in a corner several dozen cans containing prints of high quality that Buster had stashed away and forgotten when he moved out. These, too, were added to Rohauer's hoard. The first thing he did, as always, was to transfer them from the perishable old nitrate stock onto modern safety stock. The Paris *Cinémathèque* probably filled in some other gaps, for the French, unlike his compatriots, have always admired Keaton and his work.

In the late Sixties Rohauer began releasing Keaton films that had not been seen for forty years and the foundations were laid for the Keaton Vogue—or rather, since "vogue" implies a passing fashion and I think Buster is here to stay, the Age of Keaton.

—DWIGHT MACDONALD
New York City

THE THREE KEATONS

Down through the years my face has been called a sour puss, a dead pan, a frozen face, The Great Stone Face, and, believe it or not, "a tragic mask." On the other hand that kindly critic, the late James Agee, described my face as ranking "almost with Lincoln's as an early American archetype, it was haunting, handsome, almost beautiful." I can't imagine what the great rail splitter's reaction would have been to this, though I sure was pleased.

People may talk it up or talk it down, but my face has been a valuable trade-mark for me during my sixty years in show business. Sixty years is right, for it was in 1899, when I was not quite four years old, that I officially joined my parents' vaudeville act.

And if you think sixty years is a long time in your life you should be in show business. Last Wednesday is a long time ago to most actors. The young ones talk of the great vaudeville days at the

Palace as though these came at the dawn of theatrical history. When I started, vaudeville was just beginning to replace the minstrel show as the country's favorite entertainment. The Palace was not even built.

If I say I "officially joined" my folks' act in 1899 it is because my father always insisted that I'd been trying to get into the family act unofficially—meaning unasked, unwanted, and unbilled—practically from the day I was born.

Having no baby sitter, my mother parked me in the till of a wardrobe trunk while she worked on the stage with Pop. According to him, the moment I could crawl I headed for the footlights. "And when Buster learned to walk," he always proudly explained to all who were interested and many who weren't, "there was no holding him. He would jump up and down in the wings, make plenty of noise, and get in everyone's way. It seemed easier to let him come out with us on the stage where we could keep an eye on him.

"At first I told him not to move. He was to lean against the side wall and stay there. But one day I got the idea of dressing him up like myself as a stage Irishman with a fright wig, slugger whiskers, fancy vest, and over-size pants. Soon he was imitating everything I did, and getting laughs.

"But he got nothing at all at the first Monday show we played at Bill Dockstader's Theatre in Wilmington, Delaware. Dockstader told me to leave him out of the act. But he had a special matinee for kiddies on Wednesday and suggested that children, knowing no better, might be amused by Buster's antics."

On Wednesday Bill noticed that their parents also seemed amused and suggested I go on at all performances. Pop said he didn't want to use me in the night show as I had to get my rest like any small child. Dockstader then offered to pay the act ten dollars a week extra. My father agreed to try it. I had no trouble sleeping through the morning and played night and day with the act from then on.

Even in my early days our turn established a reputation for being the roughest in vaudeville. This was the result of a series of interesting experiments Pop made with me. He began these by carrying me out on the stage and dropping me on the floor. Next

THE THREE KEATONS

he started wiping up the floor with me. When I gave no sign of
minding this he began throwing me through the scenery, out into
the wings, and dropping me down on the bass drum in the orchestra pit.

The people out front were amazed because I did not cry. There
was nothing mysterious about this. I did not cry because I wasn't
hurt. All little boys like to be roughhoused by their fathers. They
are also natural tumblers and acrobats. Because I was also a born
hambone, I ignored any bumps or bruises I may have got at first
on hearing audiences gasp, laugh, and applaud. There is one more
thing: little kids when they fall haven't very far to go. I suppose
a psychologist would call it a case of self-hypnosis.

Before I was much bigger than a gumdrop I was being featured
in our act, The Three Keatons, as "The Human Mop." One of the
first things I noticed was that whenever I smiled or let the audience suspect how much I was enjoying myself they didn't seem to
laugh as much as usual.

I guess people just never do expect any human mop, dishrag,
beanbag, or football to be pleased by what is being done to him.
At any rate it was on purpose that I started looking miserable,
humiliated, hounded, and haunted, bedeviled, bewildered, and at
my wit's end. Some other comedians can get away with laughing
at their own gags. Not me. The public just will not stand for it.
And that is all right with me. All of my life I have been happiest
when the folks watching me said to each other, "Look at the poor
dope, wilya?"

Because of the way I looked on the stage and screen the public
naturally assumed that I felt hopeless and unloved in my personal
life. Nothing could be farther from the fact. As long back as I can
remember I have considered myself a fabulously lucky man. From
the beginning I was surrounded by interesting people who loved
fun and knew how to create it. I've had few dull moments and
not too many sad and defeated ones.

In saying this I am by no means overlooking the rough and
rocky years I've lived through. But I was not brought up thinking
life would be easy. I always expected to work hard for my money
and to get nothing I did not earn. And the bad years, it seems

13

to me, were so few that only a dyed-in-the-wool grouch who enjoys feeling sorry for himself would complain of them.

My parents were my first bit of great luck. I cannot recall one argument that they had about money or anything else during the years I was growing up. Yet both were rugged individualists. I was their partner, however, as well as their child. And from the time I was ten both they and the other actors on the bill treated me not as a little boy, but as an adult and a full-fledged performer. Isn't that what most children want: to be accepted, to be allowed to share in their parents' concerns and problems? It is difficult, of course, for a man of my age to say with certainty what he felt and thought and wanted as a little kid. But it seems to me that I enjoyed both the freedom and privileges of childhood, certainly most of them, and also the thrill of being treated as full grown years before other boys and girls.

Neither Mom nor Pop was demonstrative, but not many children expected that of their parents in those days. You were supposed to please them. When I disobeyed orders I got a good clout over the backside. Nobody expected me to like it, or cared whether I did or not. The clout told me in the one way a normal and mischievous boy understands to behave myself. When I failed to get the point I got another clout.

After I was seven, Pop would punish me for misbehaving while we were working on the stage. He knew I was too proud of being able to take it to yell or cry. I don't think my father had an ounce of cruelty in him. He just didn't think it was good for a boy as full of beans as I was to get away with too much. And nothing that I have observed since gives me reason to think he was wrong.

For my last off-stage licking, by the way, I can thank Elsie Janis, then a child performer herself. At this time Elsie was thirteen, a half-dozen years older than I. Our act and hers were playing at a Midwestern summer-resort theatre that week. One day she suggested stealing some corn from a farm close by.

Neither of us knew how to cook corn, and we made so much smoke when we tried that the farmer caught us and reported the crime to my father and Elsie's mother, Mrs. Bierbower. Pop sure whacked me good that day, but I never found out whether or not Elsie's mother punished her.

Even at thirteen, Elsie's talent made it obvious that she would quickly reach the top of our profession which she did just four years later when she was starred in the Broadway hit, *The Vanderbilt Cup*. Incidentally I have seen stage mothers who were furious, hysterical, given to lioness-like rages and ear-bending tantrums but never another like Mrs. Bierbower for do-or-die energy in putting a daughter over. Even then, when Elsie Janis sang on the stage, Mrs. Bierbower, watching from the wings with a hypnotized look on her face, sang every note with her as though transported.

My own mother, Myra Cutler Keaton, was four feet eleven inches tall, weighed ninety pounds, and was born into show business, being the daughter of F. L. Cutler, one of the owners of the Cutler-Bryant 10-cent Show, a traveling tent outfit. Before my mother was eleven she could play the bull fiddle, the piano, and the cornet. Later on, she became the first woman stage performer in the United States to play a saxophone. But Mom could take show business or leave it alone. Due to traveling with her father's carnival-on-wheels as a girl, then later as Pop's partner in their vaudeville act, she never learned to cook until she was almost thirty years old. Then she did all right by us in the kitchen. But all of her life Mom preferred playing auction pinochle to any other occupation, sport, amusement, employment, or, as we say in show business, divertisement.

My father, Joe Keaton, was five foot eleven, a natural comic and a fine eccentric and soft-shoe dancer. He was the most gifted man at taking a fall I ever saw in action. He was also one of the country's best rough-and-tumble fighters. Unlike my mother, he was not born to show business. He had to fight, wisecrack, and hoof his way into it. But once there, he counted himself a man who had made it all of the way to the Promised Land.

Yet, as much as he loved being an actor, tasting the applause, and listening to the laughter he created, it was not the main thing in life for him. Above all else, Pop was a convivial soul, and he sure was in the right business for it. Traveling from city to city almost every week meant constant and pleasant surprise encounters with his pals, actors we'd worked with on bills in Seattle, Boston, Louisville, New Orleans. Every week was old home week for my Pop. Every town we played was, for him, like being back in his home town of Terre Haute, Indiana.

Pop knew Will Rogers in Oklahoma. Harry Houdini was his first business partner. He was the pal and admirer of Fred Stone, George M. Cohan and his jovial father, Jerry, Billy B. Van, Jack Norworth, Al Jolson, McIntyre and Heath, Gus Edwards, the Avon Comedy Four, Doyle and Dixon, and just about everyone else who was around and up and doing in the old two-a-day days. In each town we played he would have reunions with some of these talented men. There would be long nightly sessions of drinking beer, eating free lunch, and swapping hilarious reminiscences. And if by some horrible accident everybody on the bill was a stranger Pop belonged to the Elks and a dozen other fraternal organizations whose members everywhere welcomed him at their clubhouses with open arms and free-flowing beer spigots.

Pop was named Joseph after his father, grandfather, and great-grandfather. Like each of them he was the first son of a first son. But the three earlier Joe Keatons were honest, hard-working Midwestern farmers and millers. Pop's personality was so unusual even as a boy that before he was twelve my grandfather gave up all hope of starting a flour-mill dynasty. By that time Pop had run away from school to become a bootblack and poolroom habitué in the downtown section of Terre Haute. My father got so many black eyes fighting with bigger boy bootblacks for the best street corners that he soon was nicknamed "Dick Deadeyes."

When he got too big to shine shoes for a living Pop returned to the family mill—but not to work. He spent most of his time entertaining the hired help and the farmers who were waiting for their corn to be ground. His repertory included songs, witty sayings, making funny faces and doing flip-flaps, as back somersaults were then called.

Grandpa Keaton was amused, but not enough. Pop was just over voting age in 1889 when Oklahoma Bill, a promoter with a long beard and a longer imagination, came to Terre Haute and told of the great fortunes homesteaders could make in that new territory. His listeners ought to get some money together, he said. If they followed him he would show them how to conquer the elements, outwit any shifty characters who tried to rob them, and help them cope with various other problems the hardiest of pioneers had to face.

My father was intrigued, and Grandpa Keaton didn't have to be coaxed very much before he agreed to back the plan. He gave Pop one hundred dollars in cash and handed over his trusty Winchester rifle.

"If Oklahoma Bill is what I think he is," he told Pop, "you'll need that gun more than I do around here in Terre Haute."

Despite Grandpa Keaton's skepticism, Pop did obtain possession of a quarter-section of virgin land and managed to hold onto it long enough to sell it for $1,000.

"I used this money to get to California," he said, "with the intention of joining some show. But no one appreciated my talent. There was talk in the air about a gold strike, but like a lot of other people I got there too late. Time passed, and so did my money. When it was almost all gone I headed back to Oklahoma where the Cherokee Strip was being opened up."

Pop made the last lap of this trip straddling the top of a wood-burning locomotive, clinging for safety to the smokestack. The train stopped every time the locomotive ran out of wood. Pop and the other passengers had to get off and gather up more fuel before they could proceed. When he finally approached his destination he had only Grandpa's trusty Winchester and eight dollars in cash. Knowing from his previous experience as a pioneer what slippery customers and greedy varmints he was likely to encounter he spent seven of the eight dollars on bullets for his rifle, using the remaining dollar for bacon and beans. Though they were charging a dollar a quart for water on the Cherokee Strip and everything else was expensive, Pop managed to survive and hold onto some of the land the generous Government had allotted him. Then it was that his destiny, disguised as the Cutler-Bryant 10-cent Medicine Show, caught up with him. Pop who was twenty-six, took one look at Mom, then sixteen, and applied for a job.

Her father, Frank Cutler, was a typical traveling showman who worked the small towns in the Midwest. I don't think he ever saw Chicago, to say nothing of New York. He came originally from Council Bluffs, Iowa. Grandpa Cutler liked to write verses, and later on, one-act plays. The verses concerned everything from politics to the Sullivan-Corbett fight at New Orleans. When he could afford it, Grandpa Cutler had his verses printed and wrapped them around the Kickapoo Elixir which for some years had been the show's only source of revenue. He and his partner, Mr. Bryant, started charging ten-cents admission on discovering that even the small-town hicks of the Middle West didn't believe that entertainment was any good when you got it free.

Pop once wrote a letter to his home-town paper in Terre Haute describing his entry into show business together with his and my mother's romance.

"I could talk show shop," the letter explains, "even if I couldn't do much on the stage except for my few flip-flaps. However, I was hired at $3 a week, plus board and transportation. Nobody mentioned it, but I soon found out I was supposed to be a general utility man, which meant I was expected to do everything else, including driving in stakes with a mallet, distributing the hand-bills, posting up two-sheets and four-sheets, and to come in with fists flying at the cry of 'Hey, Rube!' the carnival man's call for help when the local yokels become resentful at being bilked and try to take it out on the troupe. Being a sort of forgetful chap at the time, and in love besides, I often used my mallet to drive away the indignant customers.

"While developing into a good rough-and-tumble fighter, I was also learning to augment my few flip-flaps with a blackface monologue, songs, and real good eccentric dancing. I called it eccentric because neither the audience nor Myra, who was accompanying me on the piano, ever knew which way my feet were going next. Neither did I, because I never made up my mind about that until the last possible moment.

"Now Mr. Cutler never denied I was earning my $3 plus board, lodging, and transportation. But he didn't like me paying attentions to his daughter. He may have been holding out for a son-in-law with an earning capacity of at least $5 a week.

"At any rate, he kept firing me every time he saw us holding hands. Myra and I exchanged more tearful good-bys than a dozen Romeo and Juliet teams. But I had an ace in the hole: my minute wages. Search as he would, Mr. Cutler never could find anyone love-smitten or stupid enough to work as hard as I did for such small wages. So he also kept re-hiring me.

"One day, when the Cutler-Bryant 10-cent Show was playing Lincoln, Nebraska, Myra and I slipped off to the home of a Justice of the Peace to get married.

"He knew his lines perfectly. But a crisis developed after he had united us in holy matrimony. He told me, 'That will be $2, sir.' After I looked in all my pockets I could produce only $1.90. Myra, being only seventeen and the impractical type, had nothing to contribute except a bewildered smile.

"While I was squirming and sweating, the Justice of the Peace said with a grin, 'Okay, Joe, I'll split the $1.90 with you.' On the ninety-five cents I gave him he bought a big wedding breakfast, ham and eggs, rolls and coffee, for the three of us."

After the wedding my parents went to work for a medicine show at seventeen dollars a week. Again Pop had to drive in stakes, put up the tent, pass handbills and post up two-sheets and four-sheets. They put on three acts—his song, dance, and flip-flap specialty, Mom's saxophone solos, then both of them together, Mom at the piano and Pop doing more songs, dances, and flip-flaps. Many a time, Pop said, he had to take a club along to collect their seventeen dollars.

After a few months of this, Pop and Harry Houdini, who was also just making his start in show business, became partners in their own medicine show. Pop did his dances and flip-flaps, Mom played her saxophone solos, and Houdini did a few card tricks and astonished the customers by getting out of the local sheriff's handcuffs with the greatest of ease. In her memoirs, Mrs. Houdini years later told how indignant Pop became when the magician laughed uproariously at his antics, spoiling the joke, while they were on the stage together. Houdini was also the "doctor" who sold Kickapoo Elixir for a dollar a bottle, or six for five dollars. It was good, to hear Dr. Houdini tell it, for everything from the barber's itch to galloping consumption.

To prove it, he had a Kickapoo squaw on one side of him, a Kickapoo brave on the other. They grunted approvingly and nodded whenever he asked them to confirm his statement that the secret prescription for this marvelous medicine had been passed down to them by their ancestors.

About two months before I was born my mother was in an accident. Pop was driving her to their boardinghouse in a small Iowa town but got out of the buggy to buy something at the general store. Startled by a flash of lightning, the horse bolted. He raced around the corner at such speed that the carriage went over on two wheels, throwing my mother out on the ground. When Pop reached her side, she looked up and smiled.

"Did they catch the horse, Joe?" she asked.

My birth, in Pickway, Kansas, on October 4, 1895, was comparatively uneventful, though Pickway itself soon afterward was blown away during a cyclone.

In addition to the humiliation of having my birthplace blown right off the map, I had to share Mom's milk with the papoose of the Kickapoo squaw who had none of her own.

When I was six months old, I fell downstairs and burst into tears. Houdini, who was nearby, picked me up, and said, "My, what a Buster!"

Pop there and then decided I should be called that. As far as I have been able to learn I was the first man given that nickname. Even Buster Brown, the character in R. F. Outcault's comic strip, was born a few years after I came into the world. Everybody, including each of my three wives, always called me Buster.

The one time having that nickname worried me was when I was about eleven. "It is all right for me to be called Buster now," I complained to my mother, "but what will it sound like when I'm an old man and have grandchildren?"

"You have a point," she said, but suggested I wait till I had my first grandchild before troubling myself too much about it. (Mom was right. I now have six grandchildren who call me Grandpa Buster—and I like it fine.)

If neither Mom nor my father ever worried about my getting hurt on the stage it may have been because of a rather full day I put in while we were in some little Kansas town. I was not yet three, so it was just about the time they were quitting the medicine-show business for vaudeville.

On this particular morning I wandered out into the back yard of the boardinghouse where we were staying. The hired girl was wringing out the clothes. The wringer fascinated me, and I stuck my index finger in it, crushing it, so that the doctor summoned cut off the finger at the first joint. After he bound it up, I cried myself to sleep. When I woke up I once more went adventuring in the back yard. This time I saw a peach I wanted. But it was too high for me to reach. Being a resourceful little chap, I managed to find a brick to throw at it. I missed the peach, but the brick fell on my head, splitting it open. The doctor was summoned again, this time to sew three stitches in my scalp.

Again I was put to bed. This time I was awakened by the noise of a Kansas twister. Getting up I went to the open window to investigate the swishing noise. I didn't fall out of the window, I was sucked out by the circling winds of the cyclone and whirled away down the road. I had rolled and revolved about a block from the farmhouse when a man saw me, rushed out, scooped me up, and carried me to the safety of the nearest storm cellar.

A pretty strenuous day, as anyone will admit. But superb conditioning for my career as "The Human Mop." In my sixteen years in vaudeville I missed but one performance because of an injury sustained during our wild and rowdy roughhouse act.

Once, it was true, Pop threw me into scenery that had a brick wall right behind it. None of us had noticed the wall until then. I got a big lump on my head from that, but the lump went down quickly enough for me to appear at the evening performance.

I was about eight the day I missed the show I mentioned. This happened at Poli's Theatre in New Haven, a date every act looked forward to playing because of the superb plank steaks they served in the hotel across the street from the theatre.

We had just invented the half-strangling routine which hundreds of comics have been using ever since. In this I went behind a door and stuck out my head. A hand was around my throat and apparently choking me. Pop rushed over to fight my unseen assailant, kicked at him above my head. But when he pulled me from behind the door the audience discovered that it had been my own hand which had been gripping my throat. I'd created the illusion merely by bending my arm back from the elbow.

At this matinee Pop misjudged the distance when he kicked, and caught me in the head, knocking me cold. I fell backward, headfirst. There was a loud thump, but Pop was so accustomed to me making loud noises with my fist that he didn't realize at first what had happened. When the truth dawned on him he picked me up and carried me out of the theatre and across the street to our rooms in the hotel.

I was unconscious for eighteen hours, causing The Three Keatons to miss that night's performance. The doctors never stopped working on me until the next morning when they managed to revive me.

After examining me they told me I was a lucky boy because the base of my brain was uninjured and my skull was intact. If I rested quietly in bed for a couple of days, they said, I would be perfectly all right.

After they left I sent downstairs for some food, and at 1:30 in the afternoon I started to dress. Mom, on seeing me, said, "Where do you think you're going?"

"It's time for the matinee, isn't it?"

"You think you should . . ." she started to say.

"Sure, I feel all right."

She sighed. "Well, for the love of Mike, take it easy. At least for the first couple of shows."

"Sure, Mom, sure."

When Pop saw me walk into our dressing room he could hardly believe his eyes. As I sat down and started putting on my make-up I said, "I just won't take any tough falls today, Pop. I'll just take them easy." And then I thought I might as well tease him a little. "I'll be all right if you just make sure you don't kick me in the head again today."

There were no aftereffects. But I did take it easy. What got my goat was that when I finally did get knocked off for a few days it was due to an accident outside the theatre.

One night while playing a date at the Majestic, in Chicago, I was delayed and had to rush to the theatre. As I raced down the stage-door alley in the dark I stepped on a board with a rusty nail in it. The nail went through my shoe and deep into my foot. I was able to pull off the board but not the nail. The Majestic's prop man had to use a pair of pliers to get it out. I doused the wound with iodine and bandaged it. But next day the foot was still sore, and I limped through both shows.

Next day we took a train for Milwaukee, our next stop. On the train I ran a high fever. The doctor in Milwaukee, whom we consulted, said I was on the verge of lockjaw. He slit open the wound and put a drain in it; he warned me to keep off my foot for the next few days.

He must have guessed that I had no intention of doing that, for he told me, "If you don't, I won't be responsible. There is still a great danger of you getting lockjaw."

That caused me to drop the idea of getting up as soon as he left. The theatre got a replacement for us. It was the first and last time The Three Keatons laid off for a whole week because of illness.

Like all real troupers it was a matter of pride with us to work whenever it was possible at all.

If Pop or I had a sprained ankle we worked despite advice of doctors "to keep off of it for the next few days." All we did was tie it up crisscross with webbed bandage as tight as we could. That hurt a little, but far worse was taking falls with a stiff neck. That was agony.

Some of the stage floors we worked on were tough on our act because they were full of splinters. One time Pop fell off the table we used in our act. A thick splinter four inches long and about a half-inch wide was driven into his head. It pinned his fright wig to his head so tightly he couldn't get the wig off. I finally managed to pull it out for him. As usual when he had such accidents we washed out the wound carefully with soap and water, squeezed some blood out of it, and applied iodine.

The one time Pop missed a couple of performances was when he got ptomaine poisoning in Boston. "I never did like New England cooking," he groaned, "but I never thought I'd be *poisoned* up there in the land of the bean and the cod."

Mom was the champion trouper of us Keatons. Except for the time out for having her babies she never missed a show.

Mom also never complained about anything. Pop ran the act's necessary business, and she was supposed to take care of the money. Like every other woman in vaudeville she carried the act's cash in a grouch bag. This was a chamois purse which hung under her dress from a string round her neck.

Because Mom only weighed ninety pounds this presented her with a little difficulty back in 1901 when our act traveled to the Coast for the first time. At each city west of Kansas City we were paid off in gold.

Mom did all right with the grouch bag during the first three stops we made after that. These were Denver, Salt Lake City, and Vancouver. But soon after we started down the West Coast the grouch bag was so full of ten-dollar and twenty-dollar gold pieces that Mom had to buy a money belt. The reason was that our act was then getting $225 a week with our expenses very small. The best American-plan hotels, where we stopped, charged only $1.25 per day per person for room and board, which came to $26.25 a week for the three of us. All of our other living expenses, including tips, Pop's beer, and other modest luxuries ran no more than fifty dollars a week, and traveling expenses averaged thirty dollars a week. So Mom was stashing away almost $120 a week. By the time we started back East she was carrying about $1,600 on her gold-lined person. I understand that this much money in ten-dollar and twenty-dollar gold pieces weighs almost seven pounds. Mom could be described as truly loaded when she got back where Uncle Sam's folding money was recognized as valid currency.

Thinking over that exciting childhood of mine, I must admit that one thing I missed while growing up was an ordinary school education. I was so successful as a child performer that it occurred to no one to ask me if there was something else I'd like to do when I grew up.

If someone had asked me I would have said, "Civil engineer." I imagine I would have been a good one. But even fifty years ago you could not qualify for a degree with a one-day school education.

That's all I ever had: one day in school. This, when I was six years old and we were playing the Bon Ton Theatre in Jersey City. The night before we opened another actor on the bill asked my father if he didn't think it was time I started going to school.

"Of course it is," said Pop, but pointed out that I'd have to attend a school in a different city almost every week.

The other actor, a man who obviously had truant officer's blood in his veins, said that school principals would co-operate in every way they could to help me get an education.

"What about matinees?" asked Pop. "As you know we're on some afternoons before three o'clock, and that's when school gets out." His friend also had the answer to that one. He said my teachers would let me leave before school was dismissed.

"All you'll have to do is send a note explaining the situation," he said. "This would give Buster a full morning in school and also a half hour to an hour of the afternoon session."

Next morning Pop roused me at the ungodly hour of 8 A.M., to hustle me to the public grammar school closest to the Bon Ton. The principal could not have been more gracious. By nine-fifteen I was at a desk with other little boys my age and fascinated by everything I saw and heard.

Unfortunately, I knew some jokes I'd heard in the Avon Comedy Four's school act and decided to bring joy into the classroom by telling them. The teacher called the roll:

"Smith?"

"Here!"

"Johnson?"

"Here!"

"Keaton?"

"I couldn't come today."

That sent the class into an uproar and even won an appreciative smile from the teacher. Enchanted that going to school meant only putting on an extra show each day, I could hardly wait for the next opportunity to spin my fellow scholars out into the aisles. During our geography lesson our teacher asked: "What is an island?"

Up shot my hand. When the teacher gave me the nod, I said, "An island, ma'am, is a wart on the ocean."

Though that brought only a wry smile from her, my classmates rocked the room with their guffaws and shrieks of delight. Next came grammar. One of the questions was: "Give me a question with the word delight in it?"

25

Once again my hand was up first. My answer was: "The vind blew in the vindow and blew out de light."

The next thing I knew the teacher was marching me, by the scruff of my neck, down to the principal's office. On hearing the evidence against me, he sent me home with this note: "Do not send this boy to our school any more."

After that Mom attended to the job of teaching me the three 'Rs'. Instead of formal schooling I did get the best catch-as-catch-can education from my profession anyone could have wanted. As I've mentioned before, I was a natural mimic and could imitate everything from sword-swallowing to playing a musical saw. I also got instruction in soft-shoe dancing from George Primrose, the famous old minstrel man, and Bill (Bojangles) Robinson taught me soft-shoe and tap dancing, Herb Williams gave me piano lessons between shows, and Houdini showed me a few of his sleight-of-hand tricks. That greatest of all stage magicians never told me his real secrets; how he managed to escape from "escape-proof" prison cells, from bank safes tied with strong ropes, or from strait jackets. He could do this last trick while hanging upside down from Brooklyn Bridge, or even while under water.

Oddly enough, I cannot remember Pop teaching me anything. I just watched what he did, then did the same thing. I could take crazy falls without hurting myself simply because I had learned the trick so early in life that body control became pure instinct with me. If I never broke a bone on the stage it is because I always avoided taking the impact of a fall on the back of my head, the base of my spine, on my elbows or my knees. That's how bones are broken. You also bruise only if you do not know as I do which muscles to tighten, which ones to relax.

Once Pop made an arrangement with Papa Dollar, the head of a famous German acrobatic troupe, to teach me some tumbling tricks. That course of instruction was even more brief than my schooling in Jersey City.

My father had never been told that European performers encourage their youngsters to learn routines rapidly by smacking them good each time they fail to do a trick perfectly. Papa Dollar slapped me once with his huge hand, and Papa Keaton had to be restrained from showering him with hooks and right uppercuts.

"No one hits Keaton's children but Keaton," he kept yelling.

Yet Pop, always the impulsive type, did not hesitate on one occasion to throw me at a young man out in the audience who insulted Mom.

This happened when we were booked into Poli's Theatre at New Haven the week after four hundred Yale students were enraged because Gaby Deslys, the French charmer who was advertised as the headliner, had not appeared. They tore up the seats and threatened to lynch the manager. They were suspended by the university. But most of them came to catch the show the following week, possibly to prove that Ivy League undergraduates could behave as well as so many well-bred truck drivers.

After our first roughneck routine my mother, as usual, played a saxophone solo. This day the Yale students applauded her modest effort vigorously enough to rock the theatre. After she took about six bows Pop stepped to the footlights and told them with a wink, "Don't *spoil* her, boys. She's hard enough to handle now."

Whereupon one of the Old Eli cutups, sitting in the first row, yelled, "I agree with you, friend. She stinks!" My infuriated father promptly picked me up and threw me at the young man with unerring accuracy, hitting him in the stomach and breaking three of his ribs. My slap shoes socked the Yale man next to him in the face, breaking two of *his* front teeth. I was uninjured, which surprised neither Pop nor me. It never occurred to either of us that I could get hurt no matter where he threw me.

Once Pop accidentally wrecked another act by tossing me into the backdrop curtain. This was the turn of Madame Herrmann, the widow of Herrmann the Great, one of the most popular magicians. She was working some of his simpler tricks. At the finish of her act she had dozens of white doves flying to her from every corner of the stage.

She was to close the show right after our turn. I suspect that Madame Herrmann had never seen our act. If she had, she hardly would have waited until we were actually on to start stuffing her little feathered friends into boxes all over the back stage. Madame Herrmann's stage costume, by the way, was a quaint colonial dress with a hoop skirt.

In those days, all vaudeville theatres had a house drop (or curtain) which was used by acts like ours who carried no drop of their own. On this were local ads and invariably a painting of a waterfall, a lake, or a river. Pop used this toward the end of our act. He would saunter to the footlights and, pretending it was the brass footrail of a saloon, would put his foot on the curved metal guard over the footlights. I would do the same thing. As we stood there, each resting an elbow on a knee, he would ask: "What will you have, scotch?"

I would shake my head.

"Rye?"

"No."

"Gin?"

"No!"

"What do you want then?"

"Water!"

Grabbing me by the back of the neck he would turn me around and walk me toward the curtain, meanwhile grumbling, "So it is *water* you want?" Then he would hurl me into the painted water scene. As I hit the curtain, it would give quite a bit. While sliding to the floor, the drop's wooden strip sometimes would flap up, and I would be trapped in it. The stagehands then would pull up the curtain a few inches to help me free myself.

That Monday matinee at the Bon Ton everything went off as usual until I was sliding down the curtain. Near the bottom I felt a bump as I hit some object of substantial proportions that I couldn't see.

The stagehand pulled up the drop dumping me on the stage. This revealed the highly respectable Widow Herrmann in the most exposed position of her stage career. She had been bending over to stuff the last of her doves in a box near the curtain when knocked flat. The startled birds promptly flew out of their boxes going in every direction. Sitting on the stage, as ribald laughter erupted in the audience, I looked around and saw that the lady magician's hoop skirt had been thrown over her head, displaying her bottom which, even by the standards of that well-padded era, was enormous.

I BECOME
A SOCIAL ISSUE

Pop made me the featured performer of our act when I was five. There were dozens of other popular family acts in vaudeville at the turn of the century, but none of the children in them was featured as early as that. Many of those kids were very talented, and their parents were as eager as mine to give them the same headstart in show business that I was getting.

The reason managers approved of my being featured was because I was unique, being at that time the only little hell-raising Huck Finn type boy in vaudeville. The parents of the others presented their boys as cute and charming Little Lord Fauntleroys. The girls were Dolly Dimples types with long, golden curls.

Reformers in New York, Massachusetts, and Illinois, among other states, were tireless in their efforts to stop us all from going to hell via the stage. I guess they meant well, but like so many other sincere do-gooders they were a pain in the neck, particularly to those they were attempting to rescue. I doubt that any kid actor had more attempts made to save him than did our Little Buster. The reason, of course, was our slam-bang act. Even people who most enjoyed our work marveled that I was able to get up after my bashing, crashing, smashing sessions with Pop. The Three Keatons were always better received in the big cities than in the smaller ones, and by an annoying coincidence it was in these cities that the most persistent efforts were made to save me from the stage. The New York Society for the Prevention of Cruelty to Children started its campaign the day I made my debut at five at Tony Pastor's Theatre. The New York law then barred child actors under seven years old. The benevolent Tony Pastor got around that problem by blithely signing an affidavit swearing I was already seven. Incidentally, at our next appearance at Pastor's, a skinny East Side youth named Izzy Baline was paid five dollars a week to sing ballads from the gallery during our act. He was, of course, the same Izzy Baline who later changed his name to Irving Berlin.

Undiscouraged by Pastor's perjured affidavit the Gerry Society, as the S.P.C.C. was then called, accused my father of mistreating me on the stage. They made such an issue of it that Mayor R. A. Van Wyck, a Tammany man, ordered me brought to his office and stripped so he could see for himself if I had any bruises or black and blue marks.

"Why he is as free of hurt as one of my own boys," said his honor, dismissing the charges.

That summer the S.P.C.C. once more tried to stop me from working when we were booked into Steeplechase Park, Coney Island. The Society's Superintendent Wilson asserted that Coney Island was no place for a child of my tender years, because it was full of pickpockets, streetwalkers, and other riffraff.

Though this was true, the Mayor resented these aspersions on a section that voted Democratic every Election Day and considered all Republicans demented.

"I have been to Coney Island frequently of a Sunday on my bicycle," he declared. "I have seen 50,000, even 60,000 people there and have never noticed any disorder. Those people are entitled to amusement as well as the rich. The permit is granted."

"I have never seen any disorder there either," happily chimed in Mom. Mayor Van Wyck turned and gave her an owlish stare.

"Madam," he said, "take my advice: when you've won a case don't say another word."

The undiscouraged child-savers continued their battle. When Seth Low, a reform mayor, succeeded Van Wyck, they brought me before him to be stripped and examined, also before one New York governor. They had the age limit raised. But our lawyer beat them in court by pointing out that the law barred children only from performing on a high or low wire, a trapeze, bicycle, and the like. There was not one word that made it illegal for my father to display me on the stage as a human mop or to kick me in the face.

What most burned up Pop was that there were then thousands of homeless and hungry abandoned children of my age wandering around the streets of New York, selling newspapers, shining shoes, playing the fiddle on the Hudson River ferryboats, and thousands of other small children working with their parents in the tenement sweatshops on the Lower East Side. Pop couldn't understand why the S.P.C.C. people didn't devote all of their time, energy, and money to helping them.

Some theatre managers advertised me as a midget to avoid trouble with the do-gooders and got my parents to dress me as one. But Pop wanted to make sure that all show people, at least, realized I was his little boy. He put ads in the theatrical trade papers that said I was not a midget and added modestly, "but a revelation in eccentric juvenile talent, properly directed to produce the lasting comedy effects. The most unique character in vaudeville. A miniature comedian, who presents irresistible comedy, with gigantic effects, making the ladies hold their sides too."

As you can see, no adjective—not even gigantic for a miniature comedian—was too much for my Pop to roll off his old Blickensderfer, the antique typewriter he hauled all over the country with him.

Meanwhile, as I grew older, our act became progressively rougher. For one thing, we never bothered to do the same routines twice in a row. We found it much more fun to surprise one another by pulling any crazy, wild stunt that came into our heads.

The act started with Pop coming out alone and announcing that he would recite. Sometimes he said he would sing a beautiful song. He had hardly started on "Maud Muller" or "Where Is My Wandering Boy Tonight?" when I'd come out and fastidiously select one of the thirteen or fourteen old brooms that were on the end of the battered kitchen table we used in our act.

Ignoring him, I would carefully sweep off the table, then appear to see something that wasn't there. Picking up this imaginary object with my cupped hand, I examined it and then put it down on another part of the table. This distressed Pop. Stopping his singing or reciting, he moved the invisible thing back to the place where I'd picked it up. I'd move it to where I wanted it, he'd move it back. That went on with our rage mounting until we were fighting wildly, blasting, kicking, punching, and throwing one another across the table and all over the stage.

But our most popular fighting routine was one in which I whaled away at him with a broom while he retaliated by skidding his hand off my forehead. We started with tiny taps exchanged in fun. These were followed by harder blows, then slams to which we gave our all. In the middle of this fight the orchestra leader, reacting as though all this had never happened before, got to his feet, tapped his baton, and had the orchestra start playing "The Anvil Chorus," to which we kept time by hitting one another.

In another routine we used the house set. Every vaudeville theatre also had one of these which represented usually a room in a farmhouse. Mom came out in front of this and played the saxophone. She continued this, ignoring the chaos which erupted behind and all around her. As she played on, Pop hung a mirror on the corner of the house set, lathered his face, and started to shave himself with a straight, old-fashioned razor. I tied a long, thick rubber rope on a hook above the mirror. This was attached to a basketball which I carried to the opposite corner of the stage. With each step I took, the audience screamed, expecting the rubber rope to break and snap against his head.

When the rubber rope was stretched as tautly as possible, I let it go. As Pop was shaving his throat with his old-fashioned open razor, the basketball would sock him on the head and push his lathered face into the mirror. With the audience shrieking, Mom placidly continued playing her saxophone.

In 1910 when Annette Kellerman, the Australian aquatic star, created a sensation with her one-piece suit, we got Mom to put on one under a breakaway dress. She wore a big picture hat with the outfit. For a finish Pop pulled a string that stripped off the dress, leaving Mom playing the saxophone in a tight-fitting bathing suit and that large, dressy hat.

Before long there were four Keatons. Then there were five. My brother, Harry Stanley Keaton, better known as Jingles, was born when I was nine, my sister Louise two years later.

For a time Pop had wistful dreams of competing with "Eddie Foy and the Seven Little Foys." A great moment in that act was when Eddie, Sr., stepped to the footlights and confided to the audience: "It took me a long time to put *this* act together."

For a start Pop tried to bill us as "The Four Keatons," but we were too well known an act, it turned out, to change our billing. Pop had to satisfy himself with the billing he gave us on hotel registers. Using up an entire page, he checked us in this way:

Joe and Myra   K
                  E
Buster   A
Jingles   T
                  O
Louise   N

He had, of course, lost no time in getting both my little brother and sister into the act. When Jingles was only a week old Pop was wheeling him on stage in a baby buggy. As soon as the young man could stand up unassisted Pop figured out a way of using him for a laugh finish to our act.

He put Jingles into the same Irish workingman's outfit we were wearing, then for our new finish stripped him down to *his* Kellerman. Being a true Keaton, Jingles reveled in the applause. He even liked it when Pop held him by the leg upside down, and Pop and I used the leg as though it were a baseball bat on which to choose up sides for a scrub ball game.

When Jingles was thirteen months old Pop, with the connivance of the press agent of the Keith Theatre, in Portland, Maine, pulled off a fake kidnaping stunt that he hoped would get us nation-wide publicity.

The plot was simple. He left Jingles on the street in his baby carriage while he went into a grocery store. Then "the kidnaper," a prop man who traveled with another act on the bill and was allowed to say a couple of lines as part of his pay, drove up in a hired carriage, snatched the child from its little buggy, and hurried to the Boston and Maine Railway Station. The prop man was given candy to keep Jingles quiet. His instructions were to leave the baby on a bench in the station and then disappear.

The schemers made one mistake: not casing the scene of their crime. If they had they would have gone somewhere else with their shenanigans. For on the chosen day the street before the grocery was being ripped up by twenty Italian laborers, who were eating their lunch, sitting on the curb, when the snatch took place.

They saw the prop man-kidnaper jump from the carriage, grab Jingles, jump back, and drive off. Family men all, they were outraged and pursued him down to the B. and M. Station. By that time the prop man was scared witless. He hastily put down Jingles, and then streaked for the men's room. From this he presumably escaped the wrath of the Italian ditchdiggers by climbing out of the window. I say presumably, because the unfortunate man was never seen again. Apparently, he was completely intimidated, for he did not even come back to the theatre to get his pay.

Mom quit the act shortly before Louise was born. For a while Pop toyed with the idea of continuing in vaudeville anyway as The Three Keatons, using Jingles as the third member of the trio. But someone convinced him that managers would resent having a baby palmed off on them during Mom's absence from the act. When I suggested that he and I could work together, he said, "But it wouldn't be The Three Keatons, would it?"

In the end he decided that we'd become the "special added attraction" that most touring stock companies hired to appear between acts or after the regular show. When Mom got strong enough to join us we'd go back into vaudeville for the rest of the season.

After much dickering, Pop made a deal with the Fenberg Stock

Company which traveled through New England offering such sturdy melodramas as *Beware of Men!, Grit, the Newsboy,* and *In a Woman's Power.*

There was one disturbing thing about working with the Fenberg outfit. Mr. Fenberg insisted on putting us on between the last acts of whatever play he was doing that evening. This wasn't too bad when the show was *Grit, the Newsboy,* but when it was one of the tear-jerking operas it was asking an awful lot of an audience to cry compassionately one moment, laugh at our roughhouse capers for a few minutes, then go back to its crying during the last weepy act of the play.

Sometime during the seventeen or eighteen weeks we played with that troupe Pop got the notion that I should be given a whack at dramatic work in addition to my job as a human projectile. He felt the experience would help me become an all-around performer. With little difficulty Mr. Fenberg was talked into the idea of adding a couple of plays to his company's repertory that had good parts for me. His choices, of all things, were *Little Lord Fauntleroy* and *East Lynne.* I was to play the title role of Fauntleroy and "Little William" in *East Lynne.*

When we got the script for *Little Lord Fauntleroy* we discovered the part had seventy-five sides, which made it the longest role, except Hamlet, in the English-speaking theatre.

After learning all of those lines, doing "Little William" seemed just a bit. There was a difficulty here also though, because of Mr. Fenberg's spotting us between the two last acts of the show. This because "Little William" dies at the end of the fourth act of *East Lynne.* That meant I had to put on my slap shoes and my comic Irishman's costume before getting into bed to die. The moment the curtain hit the floor I leaped up, wiped off the white powder suitable to a dying boy, hurriedly put on my fright wig and whiskers and raced on stage with Pop.

Everything worked out well enough until a highly emotional actress was hired to play my mother in *East Lynne.* Determined to outshine Sarah Bernhardt she played the scene where I die with everything she had, including her elbows.

The script called for her to fall on my bed just as I passed away. But swept away with emotion she landed square on my stomach with both elbows. That brought dead "Little William" back to life violently. Howling with pain, his feet went up, exposing the fact that he was wearing slap shoes and baggy pants as he passed on.

The audience, crying until then, became hysterical with laughter. They laughed at the grotesque incident all through our act, and through the play's final act in which the poor Bernhardt had her own death scene. They were still laughing, uncontrollably, when the final curtain came down.

As soon as he could manage it Pop had Louise in the act with the rest of us. He put her in the breakaway dress and the Kellerman. I guess she had just learned to talk when he gave her a line in the show. We were playing that week on the same bill with Robert Hilliard, the Broadway matinee idol, who had a sketch in which a deputy sheriff repeatedly muttered, "Law's Law!" as though that were the answer to everything.

Pop thought it would be cute if Louise repeated this line in our act. But at one matinee Jingles beat her to it and said, "Law's Law!" before she could get her mouth open.

Thereupon Louise, a girl of spirit, hauled off and hit Jingles in the face, causing him to burst into tears. As Pop wiped off Jingles's face with a corner of his shirt, he told the audience in a stage whisper, "This family doesn't wait to get to the dressing room to settle their quarrels." And the folks out front roared.

With Mom doing double duty, taking care of little Jingles and Sis, I helped when I could by taking the children out for an hour or two on sunny mornings. I did that one day when we were playing at Keith's Boston. Jingles was then five, Louise three, and neither could work in the act because of the local laws. But we brought them to the theatre.

This day I took them to the Common where I sat them on a bench and bought them bags of peanuts so they could feed the pigeons. There were a great many things nearby to fascinate a fourteen-year-old boy, including the show windows of a candy store and a firehouse where you could see the horses in their stalls, waiting to dash out when the gong rang.

Suddenly I noticed a crowd of people standing around a police wagon. As the wagon started I saw Jingles's head and little red cap inside. I ran after it all the way to the police station.

As I was claiming Jingles, a policeman walked in, holding Louise by the hand. "Here's another lost kid," he told the desk sergeant.

"That's my sister, Louise," I explained.

"Oh, it is, is it?" asked the desk sergeant. "First you lose your brother, then you lose your sister. Now, are there any more little ones that you have left scattered around the city to be brought in by my already overworked men?"

"No, sir," I said. Then I glanced at my watch and whistled. "I'm in trouble," I told the desk sergeant. "I have a matinee to do at Keith's theatre, and I'll never get there in time."

That police sergeant was a goodhearted man. He had his police wagon rush us to the theatre just in time for the show. A few years later so many states had passed laws against stage appearances by minors that Pop entirely gave up the idea of using Louise and Jingles in the act. We put them into good schools near Muskegon, Michigan, where for some years we'd had our summer home. Both protested furiously, but my parents were firm, and Pop saw whatever hope he had of outdoing Eddie Foy's family act die right there.

The best summers of my life were spent in the cottage Pop had built on Lake Muskegon in 1908. This was in Bluffton, a summer colony on a bluff just across Lake Muskegon from the town and located on a mile-wide strip of sandy land between that lake and Lake Michigan. Ours was a small place without modern plumbing, or even medieval plumbing. But it was just right for us, had three bedrooms, and in the kitchen the gasoline stove on which Mom learned to cook.

Having seen values skyrocket in the Oklahoma territory, Pop was convinced that real estate was the one safe investment. This despite a previous purchase of five water-front lots in Galveston, Texas. These five lots were condemned soon afterward when the city fathers decided to build a sea wall across them. The city paid Pop only a fraction of what the property cost, but when he complained he was told that it was a valuable lesson to him and should teach him to make more intelligent investments in the future.

Bluffton was perfect for us for another reason: there were about eighteen or twenty vaudeville actors living there with their families. That meant Mom could play all the pinochle her heart craved and Pop would not run out of fellow performers to swap yarns with. There was a bar in Pasco's Tavern and a club to which all the actors belonged. As for me and the younger children, we just got into bathing suits each morning on getting up and never took them off until we went to bed.

The Bluffton Club members had a bamboo fishing pole set in a prop on the clubhouse porch which overlooked the lake. On its line was a floating cork which obligingly bobbed the moment a newcomer stepped out there to admire the view across the lake.

When the visitor took the pole off its cradle, he would give it a jerk, starting what proved to be the fish-fighting battle of his life. Meanwhile, his cries and those of the people on the porch with him had attracted the attention of the people in the nearby houses. They would run up with gaffs and small and large fish nets.

"Jerk him to the left!" they would cry encouragingly; also, "Let out your line!" and "My God! Don't let this big fellow get away. You'll never forgive yourself!"

When the visitor neared hysteria or exhaustion the fish would dive five feet down, then reverse itself and come back up, as no fish had ever done.

That was usually the first hint the buoyant fisherman got that something might be amiss. At the proper moment someone in the room behind him would say, "For the love of Mike will you let go of that pole so I can tie off this thing!"

After the guest put back the pole in the cradle, the gimmick would be explained to him. The line from the bobbing cork went through a pulley weighted down by a big rock, from there under the clubhouse and up through a small hole in the main room of the club.

We fooled a lot of funny men with that gimmick, including Bernard Granville, Harry Fox, and Frank Tinney, whom many theatrical people considered the greatest natural comedian of his day.

I tried occasionally to contribute a thrill for visitors to Bluffton. If I saw anyone I didn't know sitting on the clubhouse porch while

I was riding by on my bicycle I would race down the dock there and go off, bicycle and all, into the water. If strangers rowed past our house they sometimes saw something that made their eyes pop. Below the house there was a hill of soft sand which slanted down for twenty or thirty feet to the edge of the water. Looking up from their boat, the strangers would see pots and dishpans being thrown off the porch, then the two children, Jingles and Louise. Before they got over the shock, I myself would come flying out. By going to the back of the house I'd get a running start that enabled me to leap high in the air and come down headfirst, landing on all fours. The innocent observers had no way of knowing, of course, that the sand on that hill was too soft to hurt either the kids or myself when we landed.

By that time, anyway, they were rowing madly to the nearest house, eager to locate a telephone and notify the police that some madman had just thrown kitchen utensils and two children off his porch, and then had leaped to destruction himself.

Like so many other American boys I was "mechanically inclined." I spent a lot of my time tinkering, grinding the valves, taking apart and putting together again the motors of our car and the 25-foot cruiser boat Pop bought and modestly named *Battleship*.

One of the cottages near ours was owned by Ed Gray, a big, fat and very lazy monologuist. The general opinion was that he was still a bachelor because he was too lazy to get married.

He complained of having to make any unnecessary move, and when the weather was hot he considered all moves unnecessary. It distressed him even to fan himself.

I liked Ed Gray and worked on several devices to save him the agony of having to stir. One of the worst trials of his life, he said, was having to get up in the middle of the night to close the window when it rained. He was most grateful when I rigged up a contrivance that enabled him to close or open the bedroom window without leaving his bed.

Ed had only one clock in the house and no watch. But he complained that he had to change the position of the clock on the mantel in the hall each time he went into another room. He couldn't thank me enough when I rigged up a turntable for the clock with strings attached. By pulling one of the strings he could turn its face to whichever room in the house he was in.

"Now there is just one more thing, Buster," he said one day, "that somebody could do for me that would make my life a complete delight. But I'm afraid not even you can help me solve this problem."

On being pressed, Ed Gray said the problem concerned his outhouse which sat on the top of a hill commanding a view of both beautiful lakes.

Picnickers who came to the vicinity either for an afternoon in the country or to pick the wild grapes and berries which grew in the sandy soil in profusion were forever using his outhouse.

"And at the most inconvenient times," he said. "Warnings on signs reading 'Private' or 'Personal Outhouse,' 'Watch Out for Gnats!' and 'Beware! Giant Bulldog at Large!' have not stopped these—shall I say—squatters."

To stop this abuse of his facilities I bought some spring hinges and cut his outhouse's four walls into separate panels. I also cut the roof of this refuge into two, and nailed each half to opposite sides of the outhouse. I put a long pipe under the outhouse and attached a bolt. From the bolt I ran a line to Ed's kitchen window, hanging on it some red flannel underwear and old shirts to make it look like a clothesline.

With all of that done Ed merely had to sit by a window and wait. If any trespasser—stranger or friend—had the audacity to use his outhouse, Ed jerked the clothesline causing all four sides of the outhouse and the roof of it to fall outward. The helpless intruder was then revealed in the same position as Whistler's Mother but sitting on a less dignified perch.

This was a good many years before Chic Sale wrote *The Specialist*, but when that curious little book became a best seller, Chic came to Bluffton just to see Ed Gray's outhouse and graciously put his stamp of approval on it. He said it was a masterpiece of its kind, and he regretted that modern plumbing would one day make it obsolete.

Whenever a standard act like ours had a few free weeks during the winter it moved to New York, generally to one of the theatrical boardinghouses that lined West 38th Street in those days.

These were within walking distance of both the Broadway offices of America's greatest showmen and of the theatres housing the new shows which the vaudevillians were eager to see.

There were a lot of good boardinghouses on that street, but our favorite was the Ehric House which was run by a German family. The food was good, the atmosphere was friendly, the rooms were large and comfortable, with lots of storage space in case you wanted to leave a couple of trunks behind while you went on the road. There were good boardinghouses for actors, of course, in the other big cities. Two I remember with particular fondness are Zeiser's in Philadelphia and Mother Howard's in Baltimore.

It was in Ehric's on a freezing night that a long series of disasters, including fires, train wrecks, and other accidents began to imperil the lives and property of us bewildered and innocent Keatons. With the temperature one below zero and the streets outside covered with ice and snow a fire started in the cellar. At two o'clock that morning smoke started billowing up through the floors of the house. We had a large room on the second floor rear, but the smoke was so thick by the time we were awakened that we didn't even have time to dress. "Where's your father?" asked Mom. I knew he was at the saloon at the corner of Eighth Avenue and 38th Street, but I just shrugged, knowing what she'd say if I told her. There was no time to dress, so I grabbed Jingles and Mom grabbed Sis. We managed to make our way safely to the street with the other boarders. The neighbors took in all of us, wrapped us in blankets, and gave us coffee. As soon as Mom and the kids were taken care of, I tore down to the corner saloon to tell Pop about the fire. He had seen the engines but didn't know the Ehric House was their destination.

Shouting to the bartender to wrap me in warm clothing, he rushed out. As it turned out we had lost nothing. Thanks to the firemen the flames never reached above the ground floor. The dining room furniture was destroyed, and Mrs. Ehric's silverware, stored in the top drawer of the bureau, had melted into one vast lump of metal.

Not long after this fire broke out in the cellar of a Chicago theatre while we were working on stage. This was not too long after the heartbreaking Iroquois Theatre fire there which cost hundreds of lives. The audience remembered that holocaust only too well. From the moment smoke started curling up from the floor, they seemed on the verge of panic. But at the last moment the theatre manager was able to convince them that the fire was under control and could not spread.

That summer we were in two more boardinghouse fires. One was at the Canobie Lake Hotel, near Salem, New Hampshire. The theatre was close to the hotel, and when Pop heard the fire engines he raced straight to the hotel and up two flights of stairs. He managed to gather up the clothes and get them into wardrobe trunks which he threw down the stairs. Our losses were small compared to those of the other actors living at the hotel.

"I have a strange feeling that this can happen again any time," said Pop when he rejoined his admiring family, "but next time I'll be prepared for it."

Later he explained to Mom and me how he planned to cope with smoke, fire, and flame. A scarf (he pointed out) was always on the bureau in the rooms wherever we stayed. He would pick up the four ends of this and everything on the bureau top and dump it all on the bed. Next he would throw everything in the bureau drawers on the bed. Finally, he would go into the bathroom, gather up everything there in a large Turkish towel and get that stuff on the bed.

All he then would have to do was tie up all of this and throw it out of the window. "After that," he concluded triumphantly, "I will throw out our trunks and other luggage."

At our next fire it worked splendidly—except for a couple of details. This fire occurred later that summer at the Lake Hotel, just outside of Toledo, Ohio. One detail was an ink bottle which turned out to have him bewitched. He picked it up from the mantel and, handling it as though it were a gem, put it down on a table, picked it up, put it down on the bureau. The third time he picked it up he threw it out of the window and broke the spell. The second detail was his forgetting that the wardrobe containing our clothes was detachable. When Pop fought his way to the wardrobe he made a wild swipe, hoping to grab all of the clothes with that one swing. He managed to disengage every hanger but one. Unable to see what he was doing, he yanked away. The one hanger remained caught on the hook with the result that he dragged down the whole wardrobe on top of himself.

Then he had to fight his way out of that and all of the clothes as well. With the smoke thickening and choking him more by the minute, Pop managed to throw the clothes out of the window, dashed downstairs, and joined us on the lawn. But when he did he said, "Damn it, I forgot my typewriter."

Though the smoke was thicker than before Pop dashed back into the burning hotel and picked up the typewriter. But he couldn't walk straight because of the dense smoke, he couldn't bend down or even do a Russian Kazatsky. He came out dragging his precious typewriter with one hand and with his nose an inch from the floor. As he got out of the building this time the second floor collapsed with a terrible crash. Pop would have been killed if he had delayed a moment longer.

Two weeks after leaving Muskegon that fall it happened again, while we were playing Sioux City, Iowa. Our room this time was on the third floor.

When that fire broke out, Mom was taking a bath and Pop was down at the post office getting our mail. The first he knew about a blaze was when he saw the red fire engines racing past him on their way to the scene.

"I bet it's the damned hotel," he yelled to nobody in particular.

It was. Everybody did the usual. I grabbed Sis, and Mom climbed out of the bathtub and got Jingles. The firemen had just put up their ladders to the roof of the store on the hotel's ground floor, but Pop clambered up one of these ahead of them while they yelled their brains out at him. He got to the room in time, gathered up our stuff and threw it out of the window and saved everything. That was the last of the fires.

But beginning with that same season we started getting involved with train wrecks. Our first one occurred while we were traveling on a Lehigh Valley train from Albany, New York, to Scranton, Pennsylvania. We were sitting in reversible seats except for Jingles who was lying asleep on a seat. Mom, Louise, and I were on the other seat. Pop, as usual, was in the smoking car gabbing happily away about the five Keatons.

Suddenly, there was a jolt and an ear-splitting crash. The train had plowed right into a freight train, derailed two cars, and climbed on top of the freight train's caboose. Jingles was jarred right over to the other seat, flying across the aisle just as the seat backs reversed. He rolled under the moving seat backs without even being touched. He did not even wake up, thus winning the undisputed title as the sleeping champion of all the Keatons.

The following spring, while on our way to Norfolk, Virginia, we were rolling through the Blue Ridge Mountains. For three days it had been raining heavily. We were at a point on a side of a mountain with a 200-foot drop on one side and craggy mountains towering on the other side.

Once again there was a jolt as the engineer braked the train. But this time there was a different noise. He had stopped less than a dozen feet from a landslide. On inspection, this proved to be twenty-five feet high and a city block long.

After some consultation with the other trainmen the engineer decided to back up. Just then there was a landslide in the rear which didn't miss the end car by more than thirty feet. But we all got our hand luggage and climbed over the muddy rubble, tree roots, and rocks that covered the tracks. By the time we reached the other side a relief train was being rushed to our rescue.

Not long after that, while on the New York to Pittsburgh express, our sleeping car was dropped off at Harrisburg where we were playing a week. The porter woke us at nine.

All of us were about half-dressed when another train crashed into ours. Jingles and I were sent tumbling into the lower berth, and the typewriter along with Mom's saxophone and music case all crashed around us and to the floor. Nobody was hurt except Pop, who was just fixing his tie and was in perfect position with the chin lifted to mash his face against the mirror.

We were so mixed up with the luggage that we required the help of the porter and two other trainmen to extricate ourselves.

We had hardly gathered our wits when a claim agent rushed in. "Hurt?" he asked. Pop said slowly, "Well, not too bad."

Without waiting for further details the claim agent eagerly offered to pay $250 in exchange for a release. When Pop accepted and signed the release the claim agent seemed delighted to pay over the money.

After that night's show this man came to our dressing room.

"You people ought to be arrested for taking $250 of my company's money," he spluttered.

"What are you talking about?" demanded Pop.

"I thought you were hurt in that railway accident today. But not after seeing you and that son of yours throw each other all over the stage. You ought to be arrested, I tell you!" and he left.

"Next time you get that urge to force money on people," Pop yelled after him, "wait till you catch their act."

All of these near catastrophies and accidents occurred, as I say, within two years, and we were in no other fire or train wreck during the other sixteen years The Three Keatons were in vaudeville.

When Louise was only thirteen months old she proved that she was indestructible as the rest of us. We had just moved into our second floor room at the Ehric House in New York when she walked out of a french window, cutting her mouth practically from ear to ear, gashing her tongue, and throwing both her jawbones out of their sockets. Mom carried her to the street where she commandeered a horse and buggy and rushed her to the hospital. The doctors massaged her jawbones back into their sockets and sewed up her tongue which had been all but cut in two. Louise came through that dreadful accident without a lisp, any other speech impediment, or even a scar.

THE KEATONS
INVADE ENGLAND

During my vaudeville years I never enjoyed anything more than doing burlesques of the other acts on the bill. The first I ever tried was one of Houdini getting out of a strait jacket. I was then about six. I just put on my own jacket backward, held the sleeves together, hiding my hands, then wriggled, writhed, and grimaced as the audience had seen him do a few minutes before.

No one, by the way, ever worked harder than I did to figure out Houdini's tricks. I watched him like a hawk every chance I got. I studied his act from all parts of the theatre, from both wings of the stage, from the orchestra and both sides of the balcony and gallery. I even climbed high up in the flies so I could look straight down on him as he worked.

I found out nothing, and the man who once was my father's partner and had given me my nickname told me nothing. He delighted in baffling me along with everyone else. I recall taking a walk with him one day to a small-town post office. We found a big lock on the telephone there. As always, whether he was off or on the stage, I was watching him every second. But he made a single pass at that lock and had it off. I still can't explain how he did it.

Until William Lindsay Gresham's recent book, *Houdini, the Man Who Walked Through Walls* was published, no one ever explained his never-duplicated escapes from strait jackets, strong boxes, bank vaults, and "escape-proof" prison cells while handcuffed and tied up from head to foot. But a great many rumors were circulated about Houdini's extraordinary gifts. His brother, a physician, was said to have taught him to dislocate his shoulders at will, enabling him to get out of any strait jacket. He was supposed to conceal in his mouth a key that unlocked any handcuffs put on him.

I know just one thing about Houdini: he was not a contortionist. His unique trickery was no simple matter of having flexible muscles and bones. But that is all I know about it.

The burlesques of ours that audiences seemed to enjoy most were those we did of the dramatic sketches and one-act plays the Barrymores and other Broadway stars used in their vaudeville appearances. An example is the one we did of *The Yellow Jacket*, a one-act version of a popular Broadway melodrama.

The scene was a curio shop in Chinatown. It opened with a young white couple walking in. When the shop's proprietor looked at the white woman it was a case of lust at first sight. He had one of his coolies stab her husband to get her into his power. As the poor chap's body was dragged out of sight another coolie banged a big Chinese gong to announce that death had come to the house. As he did, he loudly wailed a prayer in Chinese. The curtain went down, then rose on the same curio shop twenty years later. The white woman, now middle-aged, has long since become resigned to remaining the shopkeeper's concubine until the end of her days. But when a young couple walks in she recognizes the wife as her daughter whom she hasn't seen since the girl was an infant. But her Chinese master is also staring at the pretty young customer, and the concubine knows what's on his mind. She kills him, then rings the Chinese gong as the curtain comes down.

For our burlesque of this act I attached a washtub under our table, planning to use it during a rough-and-tumble routine Pop and I had been doing for some time. While he was singing I lined up our thirteen or fourteen short-handled alley brooms along the side of the table, with the handles jutting out over the edge. Getting up on the table, I began whirling the basketball around my head, letting out a bit of the rope at a time. The circling basketball kept coming closer and closer to Pop, who continued to sing, until I took off his hat with the basketball. Then he took it on the run, chased by the basketball. Still on the table I cornered him near the backdrop and coiled the rubber string around his neck. It kept coiling, and at the end the basketball smashed him in the face, and he fell, battered and helpless, into the backdrop. For the finale I jumped on the brooms, so they fell on him in a shower.

When we were on the bill with *The Yellow Jacket*, I followed this up by jumping to the stage and banging on the washtub hard with one of the brooms, meanwhile jabbering away in my best imitation Chinese. This simple little stunt got such a laugh that we got ourselves booked on the same bill with the sketch as often as possible.

None of the other actors enjoyed this sort of spoofing more than those in the turn burlesqued. They recognized it for the flattery it was. For you cannot burlesque a bum act, only a good one, and almost all performers realize this.

Being freewheeling clowns we were delighted to have the other acts watch us work. But once Pop did complain about it. This was during a week that Alla Nazimova, the great Russian dramatic actress, was headlining the bill. On Monday we tried to catch her act from the wings but were ordered away. "Madame Nazimova," we were told, "is unable to perform while people are milling about in the wings."

We went out front and saw her from there. Nazimova, who later became a popular silent movie star, was a woman with great burning eyes and possessed great emotional power. You had to respect her first-rate talent and concentration on her work.

We were not really offended. We knew that unlike ourselves the people in the dramatic acts depended a great deal on everything being quiet backstage while they were on. Some of them even carried slippers in their trunks for the stagehands to wear while their act was on.

But a day or two after we were chased from the wings by Nazimova's order Pop caught her, of all people, watching our roughhouse act from there.

"Please clear the wings," he called to a stagehand. "How can we do our work while the wings are cluttered up with other acts studying our technique and the secrets of our success?"

Pop was sorry the moment he said it. Nazimova's huge brown eyes filled with tears, and she turned away. Being a foreigner, she didn't understand that Pop was only kidding.

He felt terrible about it. And that night he got out his old Blickensderfer typewriter and issued this invitation:

PROFESSIONAL MATINEE
For Madame Nazimova,
Supreme Stage Queen of All the Russians,
This Thursday Afternoon
Please Attend Promptly
As Both Wings May be Crowded
(signed) *The Three Keatons*

He had a Morris chair put in the wings for Nazimova. She came for our "professional matinee," used the Morris chair, and laughed at our low comedy antics until tears again filled her soulful brown eyes.

Most of the top women stars of vaudeville, like the men, as I said, could laugh at themselves. The tempestuous Nora Bayes was one of these good-humored sports. Everybody loved her for her cheerfulness and boundless generosity. But she had a raging temper as well. For several years she and Jack Norworth, whom she married and teamed up with, had the greatest man-and-woman act in the business. But once Nora became so incensed on hearing he was taking more than a fatherly interest in a certain young chorus girl that she changed their billing to:

NORA BAYES
Assisted and Admired by Jack Norworth

Marie Dressler, of course, had a magnificent sense of humor along with the fighting heart of a crusader. Long after she became a great stage and screen star she continued to resent the small pay she'd got as a young Broadway chorus girl. It was just like Marie to undertake a one-woman campaign to do something about the chorus girls who were still underpaid. In 1918 she insisted that Equity, the just-formed stage actors' union, protect the chorines as well as more important performers, and kept fighting until she won.

Putting on airs was what old-timers most ridiculed. And they would rib the hell out of a woman as well as a man. Fritzi Scheff, the dainty Viennese singer, learned that the hard way. We were at the Grand Theatre, Pittsburgh, the week Fritzi, following a great Broadway triumph in one of Victor Herbert's operettas, was headlining there. She had made Herbert's "Kiss Me Again," her theme song, and she sang it at all performances.

Fritzi traveled in the style of a Russian Grand Duchess. Nothing like her vaudeville tour had been seen since Sarah Bernhardt's last farewell visit to the United States. If Fritzi didn't pretend to sleep each night in a coffin as Bernhardt did, she did everything else. This little lady carried thirty-six pieces of luggage with her and an entourage consisting of a pianist, a chauffeur, a footman, and two French maids. One maid served her at the theatre, the other at her hotel suite. A week before Fritzi arrived in each city, an interior decorator redecorated and refurnished her dressing room and hotel suite. Her dressing room's décor featured magnificent mirrors with gold-leaf frames and drapes suitable to one of the fabulous boudoirs at Versailles.

She traveled in a private railway car. Attached to this was a flat car on which her Pierce-Arrow limousine rode. She used the Pierce-Arrow only for travel between her hotel and the theatre. Or when it was only a short jump to the next city where she was booked to play. She made the longer jumps by train. This wasn't stupid considering what travel over our rough roads was like then.

The air in Mlle. Scheff's dressing room was kept freshly perfumed with a delicate scent. And over the door of her dressing room a stagehand fastened an illuminated sign, reading "Fritzi."

She also had a red velvet carpet laid from the door of her dressing room to the stage.

I promptly got into the spirit of things by nailing a cigar box over our dressing room. I cut the letters—B-U-S-T-E-R—out of it, and for illumination stuck a small lighted candle in the box so the light would shine through.

Bernard (Bunny) Granville, the comedian who did the best "drunk" act ever seen in vaudeville, was dressing with Pop and me that week.

"Why should I let Fritzi put me in the shade?" he demanded. "I might not have red carpet, but I have something that is a lot more useful at times." As he talked Bunny got out a roll of toilet paper and rolled it from our dressing-room door to the stage. Within minutes the house manager was in our dressing room.

"Fellers!" he said. "What are you trying to do to me? If she finds out about any of this she'll throw a fit. I think she'll walk out. Then where will I be?"

To avoid his having a heart attack, we took down the cigar-box sign and picked up the toilet paper. But as we waited to go on next day we heard that one of the stagehands had fixed Fritzi's wagon.

All of us were told, "Just stand in the wings and catch Fritzi's first show today and watch how she behaves."

Fritzi made her usual entrance waving a little fan. Leaning against the grand piano she sang her opening number, with the little fan resting against her hip. As she sang the first few notes she seemed to be twisting and squirming. The smile with which she bewitched audiences was half grimace. And whatever was troubling her got worse as she continued. Again and again she twisted away from the audience to scratch her tightly-corseted side with the fan here, there, and everywhere.

All of us immensely enjoyed this weird performance. We might have enjoyed it even more if we had known what was making majestic little Fritzi Scheff twist, turn, squirm, wriggle, and scratch. That morning a stagehand had sneaked into her dressing room and sprinkled itching powder lightly everywhere in that elegant room that the great woman could possibly sit down.

Occasionally a little backstage joke got out of control. This happened to a young English monologuist who was making his American debut at Proctor's Twenty-third Street Theatre, in New York. He was sharing a dressing room with Pop, me, and a popular turn-of-the-century minstrel man named Press Eldridge.

Before the Monday matinee, Press told the Englishman, "You know, there are a great many of your British expressions that Americans just do not understand. Why don't you go over your material with me right now so we can see if you should change anything you may be using?"

The monologuist was most grateful. Press, Pop, and I listened gravely, making no comment until he described his main bit. In this, dressed in a bride's wedding outfit, he sang "Waiting at the Church!" the song later rendered so effectively by Gracie Fields.

When the Englishman sang the tag line, "When I found he left me in the lurch, Lord! how it did upset me!" Press held up his hand. "I'm glad you went over this with me, my good fellow. American audiences just do not like the word 'Lord.' I don't know why exactly, but you must use another word there."

"But what would you suggest?" asked the Englishman.

"*Christ!*"

The surprised Englishman looked at Pop for confirmation which Pop gave him with a sage nod. None of us dreamed for a moment that the Englishman would take Eldridge's advice as even the word "damn" was taboo then in theatres all over America.

We watched the young Englishman from the wings. And when he came out with the line "Christ! how it did upset me!" there was one of those blood-chilling dead silences in the theatre. Next thing anyone knew the lights went out, the unfortunate Englishman was smuggled off the stage, and the orchestra was playing the next act's introductory number. Meanwhile, Press Eldridge had streaked for the street. When we went back to the dressing room, the poor Englishman was still in his bride's costume, trying to explain to the irate and red-faced house manager how he had happened to utter the shocking word. "One of the men I dressed with told me to say it instead of 'Lord.'" he said. The house manager demanded, "Which man was it?"

The Englishman shook his head, and replied in a broken voice, "I can't remember."

Neither could we. Nor could Press Eldridge when he returned to the dressing room. I never saw nor heard of that unlucky English actor again.

Pop believed that whatever harm Press and we had done him was more than repaid when The Three Keatons invaded the 'alls of the man's native land in the summer of 1911.

"I always thought I would enjoy the quaint charm of London," Pop often said, "right up until the very moment I went over there."

Though our stay in London was brief, Pop ever afterward would spend whole hours relating the misfortunes that befell us there. His Anglophobia became so complete that he didn't even like to mention that one of his very best pals, Walter C. Kelly, had talked him into going there. Pop seemed to feel it was a terrible charge to make against anyone, no less vaudeville's famous "Virginia Judge." Pop preferred people to think that Alfred Butt, the distinguished manager of the Palace in London had enticed us there. But it was Kelly who suggested to Butt that he make us an offer.

On our return home Pop described in a long letter to *Variety*, the theatrical weekly, the humiliations and exasperations American artists could anticipate in London. His letter is longer, I think, than the Bill of Rights, the Declaration of Independence, and Lincoln's Gettysburg Address combined.

Our misfortunes started, Pop revealed in this document, when he made the distressing mistake of buying four steamship tickets for his family instead of three. It was only after he had paid half fare for Jingles and Louise that he learned that they could have traveled free.

Unable to get his money back, Pop said he rushed home and announced that the trip was off, but changed his mind when both Mom and I burst into tears. Nevertheless he made one last desperate attempt to get out of the adventure.

"I started a fuss when we got on board," his letter continued, "anything to be thrown off. I even auctioned off Louise. Jumping on a box, I yelled, 'Before the ship sails I am authorized to sell this two-year-old orphan child.' The bids opened well, and I sold the baby to a bright-looking little boy. But when I demanded cash his father told the youngster I was only fooling. Instead of us being put off the ship, one of the officers told me that if I tried to auction off any more of my children they would put me in irons."

Kelly's idea that The Three Keatons would be highly successful in London was logical enough, being based on his own popularity there, in the provinces, and such far-flung British outposts as Johannesburg and Hong Kong. For his humor was as typically American as baseball or George M. Cohan's slang. Yet Britishers everywhere laughed at such classic jokes of his as the one about Mandy, the Negro laundress who came to his imaginary court for a divorce. It went like this:

"Does he beat you, Mandy?"

"No."

"Does he support you?"

"Yes, sir, he brings home his $1.75 wages every Saturday night."

"Well, then, Mandy, why do you want to divorce him?"

"I guess, your honor, I just lost my taste for him."

Kelly, a kindhearted man, met our boat train in London. He had already obtained accommodations in a boardinghouse for us.

Pop had no English money so Kelly gave him a handful of coins for tips and wrote down the address of our boardinghouse. "You get your luggage," he said, "and I'll take Myra and the kids to your rooms. They look tired."

"How do I get my baggage when nobody gave me any claim checks," said Pop. Kelly explained that claim checks weren't used in London. Pop need only go and point out his trunks and the table we used in our act which Pop had insisted on bringing along. Kelly didn't explain that there were no redcaps at Victoria Station. So after seeing us off, Pop had to cope with a mob of Whitechapel Willies, Lambeth Louies, and other men who looked as though they had been sleeping on the Embankment.

Though unable to understand these chappies' Cockney, Pop selected a half dozen of them. They found a one-horse cab for him, helped him into it, then piled all of our luggage and the table on both sides and on top of him, accepted the tips he gave them.

On the way there, Pop looked back through the rear window and saw the men who had helped him trotting after the cab. Believing himself pursued he asked the cabbie to whip up the horse. Unfortunately, the driver obeyed with such alacrity that the top-heavy cab took the next corner on two wheels, toppling over on its side.

As Pop unscrambled himself from the debris, he said to the driver nervously, "Let's get going. Those men are still chasing us."

"Good show!" said the driver. "They'll be able to help us right the rig here."

"I don't think that's why they are chasing us. Maybe I did something wrong. Maybe I said something that offended them."

"Not likely, sir," said the cabbie. "If you don't mind me saying so, I think you must have tipped them most liberally." When Pop pleaded ignorance of British currency, the man said, "When we arrive at your boardinghouse, sir, I will instruct you concerning what constitutes a fair tip."

The six men caught up with them and cheerfully helped right the cab and get the horse back on his hoofs. They rearranged the luggage and the table around and on top of Pop. The cab started off again, with them trotting after it. At the boardinghouse they helped unload the cab and carry the luggage and table up to our lodgings on the third floor. After obtaining the tipping instructions from the driver, Pop distributed some more largesse and took all hands to the nearest pub for a round of drinks.

We were delighted with the family-type boardinghouse the Virginia Judge had found for us. We all went to bed early and in the morning were served with a regular London boardinghouse breakfast, consisting of porridge, bloaters, boiled eggs, muffins, and tea.

Kelly was living at the Queen's Hotel on Leicester Square just around the corner from us. That evening he took Pop to a theatrical club in London. Coming up the stairs at one o'clock in the morning, Pop observed sailors coming out of various rooms, buttoning up their coats.

He hurried to our rooms, woke us up, and insisted we move without waiting for morning. He whispered, to Mom "We are in a house of ill fame" and within an hour we were installed in the Queen's Hotel where Kelly was staying.

At the time the Palace Theatre in London was the world's most elegant vaudeville house and the only one with a royal box. It occupied a whole block, full dress was obligatory in the stalls, tuxedos in the balcony. On Pop's first visit he found that The Three Keatons weren't even billed on the posters that announced the following week's attractions.

Pop's next unpleasant surprise came when we went to the theatre to rehearse our act's music with the orchestra. He had brought special orchestral arrangements with him. Fred Heff, the New York music publisher who supplied these, had told him to give these to Fink, the Palace's orchestra leader, and to be very deferential about it.

The thoughtful music publisher had even rehearsed Pop in the polite speech he made. This went: "Is this Mr. Fink? Allow me on behalf of Mr. Fred Heff, the American music publisher of New York City, to offer you this set of orchestrations with his compliments."

"What has this to do with the act?" demanded the unfeeling Mr. Fink. "Let's get on with it, man."

The rehearsal's first number went off smoothly. But when Mom got out her saxophone the whole orchestra pit started grumbling. "What the blooming hell!" exclaimed one flute player. "Is she going to play *that?*"

The trombonist next to him moaned, "Never heard one that was in tune."

I got on guard in case Pop grabbed me and threw me at the carping musicians, but he restrained himself.

There were matinees only on Wednesday and Saturday at the Palace, which meant we opened on Monday night. Arriving at the theatre, Pop was depressed to find the long line of waiting people, seated on camp chairs, being entertained on the street by buskers, including a juggler, a troupe of three acrobats, who carried their own rug to work on, and a singer with a guitar accompanist.

"Why should they go inside where they have to *pay?*" grumbled Pop. From the first performance we were handicapped because the stage floor was warped and full of splinters. Pop couldn't use me as a human mop, but he had his usual fun throwing me into the scenery and out through the wings.

We did get a few titters from the gallery, but the stalls, the boxes, and balcony greeted us with absolute silence. Even Pop's best lines fell flat. When I swatted him violently he said, "He has a mind." Later when he threw me into the back curtain, he told the audience, "Children should be taught to respect their parents." Even when Pop, in desperation, said after a bit of hurly-burly, "It loses a bit in the translation, doesn't it?" he was greeted by the same blood-chilling silence.

When we came off, Kelly and Blanche Ring, who were also on the bill, both advised Pop to tone down on the rough routines.

"You actually scared the audience," Kelly said. "They think you are hurting Buster. The act is too brutal for them."

Next day Alfred Butt told him the same thing, to tone down the "brutality." As Pop was leaving, Butt said, "Isn't that an adopted boy you use in your act?"

"Who, *Buster?*" exclaimed Pop. "Of course not. He's my son."

"Judging by the way you threw him around," said Butt, "I thought he must be adopted and that you didn't give one damn about him."

Pop went straight from Butt's office and booked passage home for us on the following Wednesday.

Meanwhile, we continued to ease up on our roughhouse routines at each performance, and by Wednesday and Thursday we were going good. By Friday and Saturday we were doing great.

Toward the end of the week Alfred Butt congratulated Pop on the reception we were now getting and said, "Now you will have no trouble at all in getting forty weeks of straight booking in the provinces, and when you are finished that tour, you can play here in London for me again."

But Pop had made up his mind to leave.

Pop never would admit the British had a sense of humor. His experiences in the pubs there had poisoned his mind against the entire United Kingdom. He even refused to laugh at what an Englishman had said about the American monologuist, Marshall P. Wilder, who was a dwarf whose face was not unlike a monkey's.

The week we arrived, Peter the Great, the smartest chimpanzee I ever saw on a stage, was headlining the bill at the Palace. He seemed almost human as he took off his hat, coat, and gloves, ate at a table with a knife and fork and napkin, roller-skated, rode a bicycle, then took off the rest of his clothes and went to bed.

Wilder came into the Palace the following week. Londoners then had the habit of dropping in at vaudeville houses just to see again a favorite act, and one particular Palace patron that week seemed not to have known that Peter the Great had concluded his engagement. In any event, one Englishman, arriving in the middle of Wilder's act, took a quick look and groaned, "My God! Now they have him *talking*."

That story quickly went around the world and for a time threatened Wilder's career in vaudeville. Wherever he walked on a stage somebody out front was sure to say quite audibly, "My God! Now they have him talking."

But it was the eating and drinking situation that most distressed Pop. No one had tipped him off that there were barmaids in the pubs. He spent half of one night in London wandering around from place to place in hope of discovering a man behind a bar. Pop liked telling slightly off-color stories almost as much as he liked beer. But he was incapable of telling one of these before a woman. On top of the deprivation of being unable to indulge in his favorite indoor sport Pop could not drink the warm beer they served in the pubs. He ordered ale but gave that up on finding it the same temperature. Though at the time he drank nothing stronger than beer he ordered a Manhattan cocktail in sheer desperation.

Cocktails were then unknown in London, and the barmaid, determined not to be kidded, said, "Oh yes, and do tell us about your skyscrapers?"

He also could not endure the uninteresting English food. "They do not even season it," he kept groaning. His whole attitude was that of a man who was discovering himself surrounded by Bronze Age savages. But Mom and I liked it fine, urged him to stay on. Mom pointed out that if we once established ourselves as an attraction we could always return if we did not care to accept the salary or working conditions American managers tried to impose on us. It would be our ace in the hole. But Pop would not listen.

"I'm homesick," said my Pop who had had no home for over twenty years.

BACK HOME AGAIN IN GOD'S COUNTRY

Pop did not mention in his long letter to *Variety* one of the reasons for taking the family to England in the first place. A short while before, thanks to the indefatigable Gerry Society, we had been barred for two years from playing the New York theatres. The irony of this was that the do-gooders got us in the end, because we'd played a benefit show for a charity. The manager of the Grand Opera House in Manhattan had asked Pop to put on the act with all five Keatons appearing.

Pop agreed on condition that the manager guaranteed that we would have no trouble with the Gerry Society. The manager gave the guarantee, but we were served with a summons just the same. Still counting on the manager's word, Pop did not even bother to bring a lawyer with him when he appeared in court and explained about the manager promising to assume responsibility.

However, the manager double-crossed him by taking the stand and denying he had made any such promise to Pop. We were fined $250 and The Three Keatons were banned from the New York stage. The ban remained in force for two years and was a cruel setback for our act because it kept us off the stage of Hammerstein's Victoria along with New York's other vaudeville houses.

By that time Hammerstein's Victoria had long been recognized as America's greatest vaudeville theatre. That grand old showcase, located at 42nd Street and Broadway where the Rialto Theatre now stands, was in its day everything—and perhaps a little more —than the Palace became later. As any old-timer will tell you, Hammerstein's Victoria was vaudeville at its all-time best. I suppose the greatest compliment we Keatons were ever paid was being booked there four to six times each season. Most acts were happy when they got one date a year there. Favored acts usually got two.

The original Oscar Hammerstein built the Victoria, but it was run by his son Willie, a master showman and the father of Oscar II, the creator, with Richard Rodgers, of "Oklahoma!", "South Pacific," and a few other theatrical tidbits.

Willie Hammerstein would try anything—and did. Willie reveled in such capers as booking Paul Swan, the classical dancer, and advertising him as "the world's most beautiful man" and giving a big publicity build-up to something he called "a wrestling cheese." This stood seven feet high, was two feet broad, and no human wrestling champion could make it stay on the floor. The indomitable cheese, of course, was so heavily weighted at the bottom that it righted itself automatically.

Willie also filled his big playhouse with other freak attractions. When Ethel Conrad and Lillian Graham were arrested for shooting W. E. D. Stokes, a millionaire hotel owner and prominent social figure, Willie bailed them out and put them on as "The Shooting Stars." He also booked Nan Patterson, the Floradora girl, who was acquitted of murdering her lover, Caesar Young. He could even fatten the box office with the Cherry Sisters, who were so bad that a screen had to be put up in front of them to intercept the vegetables and rotten eggs audiences bombarded them with. And Willie Hammerstein, knowing showman that he was, increased the fun of his customers by having his ushers pass out artificial fruit and vegetables to those who had not brought any with them.

Vaudeville is variety entertainment, and Willie tried to give his customers everything in the world that could possibly amuse, charm, bewilder, baffle, amaze, or enchant them. And I do mean everything from "Sober Sue, the Girl Who Never Laughed" to "Don, the Talking Dog," fire-eaters, jugglers, clowns, men who could add and subtract backward, horses that could count, melodramas, comedies, high divers, ice skating and bicycle-riding basketball teams.

Besides the prestige of appearing so often in American vaudeville's most esteemed showcase, Hammerstein's was the most fun to play. This was because it attracted the most show-wise crowd in the country, for other performers attended in droves. And there is no applause so sweet to hear as that which comes from other actors. They really know whether you are any good or not, whether the entertainment you are selling is the real thing or phony.

Nobody who saw one matinee we played at Hammerstein's ever forgot it. Pop stayed that day at Dowling's bar just down the street several minutes too long. On looking at his watch, he slapped his head and ran for the stage door. In his hurry he forgot to put on the felt pad he had been wearing under his trousers ever since I had got strong enough to hurt him when we did our anvil-chorus work on each other with the brooms. His own right arm, by the way, had swelled to twice normal size because of the years he'd been throwing his growing boy around the stage.

That afternoon, as usual, we were working before an audience that had seen our act so often they knew the routines as well as we did. The first time I whacked Pop good that afternoon the broomstick made a different sound than the usual muffled one. Pop turned green with pain and jumped about three feet in the air.

"Christ," he groaned, "I left the pad off!"

I have mentioned, I think, that as far as my father was concerned there was no such thing as a stage whisper. But the whole house roared and rocked as they heard him say the word that was still forbidden and would have shocked a less worldly crowd.

"Are you going through with it?" he asked.

"Sure," I said, as he winced, "it's part of the play."

I socked him again. "Going through with it?" he asked once more.

"Yes," I said. This time he gave me an appealing look, and remarked, "But remember I'm your father."

And Pop did go through with it, although I showed him no mercy. At the end of the act Joe Keaton, black and blue, made one of his best ad libs. Stepping to the footlights, he told the audience, in one of his confidential stage whispers, "This is the last time I let George M. Cohan write anything for me."

Pop was always there with the right line. Once when an audience was slow to laugh Pop told them in a sad tone, "You're not taking this production seriously enough. It is every bit as important as *Ben-Hur* ever thought of being."

These ad libs were best appreciated, of course, at Hammerstein's. I often think of how ecstatically that sophisticated Broadway crowd would have greeted the wildest fight Pop and I ever put on in public. This took place at the Grand Theatre in Pittsburgh, the same theatre where Fritzi Scheff was introduced to itching powder. The fight was over my smoking. I was seventeen, but like most of the fathers of that era Pop believed that smoking stunted a youth's growth and should not be indulged in until one was twenty-one.

Pop and Mom both smoked themselves. Pop always rolled his own cigarettes out of Bull Durham tobacco. He kept the little white bag Bull Durham came in and the packet of brown cigarette papers attached to it in the right hand pocket of his jacket.

On that particular day, Pop and I were wearing blue serge suits which we had hung next to each other in the dressing-room closet. While we were making up he went to get some tobacco from his pocket and by mistake fumbled for it in the pocket of my jacket. In my make-up mirror I saw him come up with the bulldog pipe I had bought myself a few days before. He studied the pipe for a moment, put it back into my pocket without saying anything to me. He said nothing to me about the pipe as he got his tobacco and cigarette papers from his own suit, rolled one for himself and smoked it while he finished putting on his make-up.

When the call came for us to get on stage, I let Pop leave first, then I told Bernard Granville, "I'm in for it tonight, Bunny."

I was in for it but so was my old man. Our routine now had me hitting him as often and as hard as he hit me. I did not neglect my duties that day particularly after he threw me around so hard that he knocked down the house set.

This broke the batten. Pop also broke two kitchen chairs on me. I retaliated by breaking three brooms on him. I also knocked him over the footlights with the aid of my whirling basketball. We also dropped the kitchen table on one another.

There was a typical high-class audience at the Grand that afternoon, and they enjoyed it with the uninhibited abandon of orphans turned loose in an ice-cream plant.

After we staggered back to the dressing room, Pop got my bulldog pipe and smoking tobacco from my suit and slapped them on the table. It was his way of acknowledging that I had won his permission to smoke in his presence or behind his back.

That afternoon it took two doctors and two masseurs to get us back into good enough shape to work the evening performance.

I have often wondered what Pop would have done if he had learned that same year that I had taken my first drink of whiskey. That had happened during our summer vacation at Muskegon. Even as a babe-in-arms I had been given sips of beer. Most people in those days thought of beer as a health drink, something between a tonic and medicine. They even endowed it with an integrity all its own, spoke of the "honest glass of beer." But whiskey was different. Whiskey, as the ministers and newspaper editorials told us, was pure evil, apparently being distilled in hell itself.

That first drink of mine was taken with a Bluffton pal, Lex Neal, who was nineteen, two years older than I, who later became a song writer, and a gag man for me. He had just been given the brushoff by the town beauty, an indignity that angered me more than it did Lex himself. But I no longer remember her name. All I now recall about her is that she was the daughter of the Commissioner of the Muskegon County Water Works.

"I'll prove I am your true friend," I told him, "by not letting you get soused alone. I'll get drunk too."

It seemed a perfect day for it. In addition to Lex's love tragedy, our baseball team had just lost another game.

Neither Lex nor myself had the nerve to ask for a bottle of whiskey at the one place in Bluffton you could, Pasco's Tavern. We asked Mr. Feeney, who ran a tourist camp, to buy it for us which he did. The errand entailed a little difficulty as his camp—really a few shacks and tents for campers and picnickers—was situated on a bluff about ninety feet high. You could only get to and from Feeney's camp by climbing a rickety wooden ladder. When the obliging Mr. Feeney came back with the whiskey that afternoon, Lex and I drank the bottle between us while exchanging philosophical reflections on the perfidious nature of women. We also promised each other never to marry no matter how beautiful the girls were who attempted to trap us. When darkness fell I was blotto. But Lex, having had some slight previous whiskey-drinking experience, was in somewhat better shape.

He did his best to help me down Feeney's rickety ladder. But it was a moonless night, and before I took more than a step or two I fell to the bottom—without being hurt though, as the sand there was very soft and covered by thick clumps of grass. But my fall awoke Lex to the fact that I was in no shape to go home. Instead he took me to his own house where his mother, a frail old Southern woman who smoked a corncob pipe, put me to bed and nursed me through my terrible hang-over the next morning. After that experience I never took another drink of whiskey until I became a soldier in World War I years later.

For about ten years my life followed that same pattern of dreamlike Booth Tarkington summers, with the winter months spent clowning our way around the country. I always liked performing. But it was hard work, and there were occasions when it was not exactly fun. There was, for example, the Monday matinee we had to stretch out our seventeen-minute act for more than an hour and a half while waiting for the act scheduled to follow us to assemble its equipment backstage.

That equipment was something to put together, for the act was a daredevil turn called "Dr. Clark's Globe of Death." This was an immense sphere made of crisscross strips of steel placed inches apart from one another. A motorcyclist got inside this, started riding slowly around the lower part of it, increasing his speed as he made the roaring motorcycle travel higher and higher around the sides. The climax of the act came when he started doing loop the loops, riding upside down, inside the big globe.

We were already on stage that Monday afternoon when the house manager signaled to us to keep going as long as possible. Dr. Clark's massive equipment, it appeared, had not even arrived at the theatre. When it did it would take quite a long time to set up and bolt together.

Pop stepped to the footlights. "The next act is a great act," he said, "but it takes a long time to assemble, so if any of you want to go home and wash those dishes you left in the sink, we'll understand."

Nobody left.

After we finished all our routines, Pop said, "Buster, recite something."

I recited *The Boy Stood on the Burning Deck.*

"Recite something else," Pop said.

I did. When he asked for a third bit of elocution I told him, "I've run out of recitations. I do know a parody, but it doesn't belong to me. It belongs to Hoey and Lee, and we have to get their permission before I can sing it."

"They'll not sue you or kill you either if you send them royalties," said Joe. "I give you permission. I'll take the responsibility."

All very cute, and I sang the song. But how long can you keep on being cute on the stage? After a while the house manager signaled us that the sections of the Globe of Death had at last arrived. We could hear the stage crew starting to assemble it backstage. But that would take a good deal of time. When we couldn't think of one more thing to do, Pop yelled, "Pull up the curtain."

Back there they were still trying to put the Globe of Death together. Pop and I went to work with a ready will, helping the crew but really hampering them by getting our pants and other bits of clothing riveted to the big globe. Despite our assistance, they finally put together the thing, which was propped up on all sides by steel girders.

By that time we had been on the stage for an hour and thirty-five minutes. It was the one time that I wished I was Al Jolson who could hold any audience spellbound for hours whenever he felt like it.

An even tougher assignment came one night when we had to compete with a freshly killed corpse. This also happened at the Grand Theatre in Pittsburgh where Pop and I had staged our biggest fight and watched *l'affaire* itching powder. This time Ethel Levey, recently divorced from George M. Cohan, was the headliner. She went on just before us. In the middle of her second song a maniac in a box stood up, drew a revolver and pointed it at her. When she ran screaming off the stage the man turned the gun on himself and blew his brains out. He had not even known Ethel Levey.

Though still half hysterical, Miss Levey was coaxed into coming back to finish her act. Then The Three Keatons went on and did their hilarious act.

P.S. The corpse won.

Oddly enough, the clowning of other acts gave us other very tense moments on the stage. None of this was ill-intentioned. It was natural for them to do everything they could think of to throw into a panic any act like ours which prided itself on being impossible to upset.

Most of these capers were inspired by a change we'd made in one routine. Now, when Pop recited his "beautiful poem," I would come out behind him and make a terrible racket by banging a broomstick on the floor. I continued slamming the broom on the floor. The audience realized what I was doing when the stick went through a hole. This upended me, and when I hit the floor I made another terrible noise. Exasperated, Pop would kick me out of his way and grab the business end of the broom. On pulling this up with my unwanted assistance, he would throw it away and then calmly continue his recitation just where he'd left off. That was supposed to be the end of the routine.

But the Katzenjammer spirit of the other acts on the bill inspired them to contribute new plot turns and complications.

When we were playing Keith's Colonial Theatre in New York, a couple of those fellows sneaked down to the basement under the stage and tied a rope exactly 175 feet long to the end of the broomstick when it came through the hole. When Pop and I, singing "The Volga Boat Song" complete with gestures, eventually got all the rope up a dirty, tiny American flag was tied to it. The quick-witted orchestra immediately swung into "The Star Spangled Banner." But we were relieved when we finished that week at the Colonial. However word had got around, and new crazy tricks awaited us in the other theatres.

The next week an act put a ladder under the hole. When the broom stick went down they were on the ladder and quickly covered the stick with fresh mustard. At the next theatre we played, two guys on the bill hung onto the broomstick while Pop tugged away like mad. They let go suddenly, and Pop went about three feet in the air as it came up.

Once when the broom came up it had our two weeks' closing notice on it. At still another show they took the trouble to put a huge slingshot below the hole. When they let this go the broom shot away into the flies. It traveled so fast that Pop didn't even see it rocket past him. He saw it come down though a few minutes later. We were arguing, as part of the act, with our angry faces very close together when the broom whizzed down between our noses at terrific speed. It came down, of course, stick first, like an arrow. Neither of us would have needed to fake a fall if it had hit.

When we were playing Keith's Alhambra, also on Upper Broadway, the other acts went down to the Battery and got an eel several feet long from the Aquarium. This they brought up to the theatre on the subway in a five-gallon can filled with water. When this came up on the end of the rope, Joe Keaton turned green under his make-up, believing it was a snake. The eel wriggled away across the stage with the broom still tied to it.

The comical trick played on us by another act, The Three Leightons, that same season in Ottawa, Canada, easily might have had tragic results.

It was 1915, the second year of World War I, and all Canada was in mourning for its crack regiment, The Princess Pats, which recently had been all but exterminated at Ypres. So the Leighton Brothers, who did a song, dance, and comedy turn, got us very nervous when they kept threatening to tie a German flag to our broom. Naturally we pretended to take this as a joke, but each time Pop pulled up the broom I tried to peer down the hole to see if a flag was on it.

One day I did see a flag fluttering on the end of the broom. As it came up, I slashed away at the string. In my haste, I missed the string and hit the broom which broke in two. But this didn't stop the flag coming up. And good night! It turned out to be the Union Jack that I had slammed away at. Pop and I raced for the wings, he going one way, I the other. The moment we were out of sight we stopped to listen, half expecting to hear the people roaring and hissing. But all we heard was laughter. Pop and I looked at one another across the empty stage where we thought we had just dishonored the British flag. Then we stuck out our heads. The people were still laughing, so we courageously rushed out to take our bow.

My guess is that the audience realized when they saw our horrified faces that we were just as surprised as they were when the flag came up, and that I had swung at it before recognizing it.

We had a speedy revenge on The Three Leightons. The next morning I went down to Ottawa's river-front district and, with the assistance of several small boys, collected eighteen cats. These we brought to the theatre's prop room and put in a trunk that the Leightons used in their act.

Not wishing to be too rough on the cats I drilled airholes in the sides of the trunk. In their act one of the Leightons told another, playing a Negro bellhop, "Boy, open my trunk and get out my parade suit!"

That afternoon when the trunk was opened the cats, snarling with rage and terror, leaped out and streaked in every direction. They ran into the wings, climbed up into the scenery, and disappeared into the flies. Others jumped into the boxes and ran up the orchestra aisles. Pandemonium, needless to say, was the rule for quite a while at that performance.

Now all of this clowning and teasing and horsing around, I repeat, was done utterly without malice. It seems to me that actors, generally speaking, were then far less sensitive to being kidded than today's stars are.

Of course, it was impossible then to make a fortune overnight in show business. Your apprenticeship was arduous and took years to complete. Publicity was in its infancy. Nobody could put you over with the public on your looks, your figure, or your sensational love affairs. There were no TV ratings to arouse the jealousy of other stars.

Performance was the important thing, almost the only thing that counted. The manager who wanted to know if you were any good dropped in at a theatre where you were working and decided for himself. He didn't depend on the calculations of mathematical wizards who had convinced him that they could tell what millions of persons thought of a star after getting opinions from a handful of men and housewives. Instead, he measured your effectiveness by the reception you got from the men and women who paid to see you. As for publicity we felt as George M. Cohan did when he told a reporter, "I don't care what you write about me, kid, as long as you spell my name right."

In vaudeville, of course, we had no publicity problem except when some adventurous spirit like Joe Keaton foolishly tried to snatch some free space. Most of the time local newspapers, who ran the vaudeville theatre's advertising each week, published a few biographical notes about the acts appearing on the next bill, and also flattering reviews. But these appeared in the entertainment section and occupied little space. Those early years of the century were a time of widespread racial and religious prejudice in America, but the last place to look for either then as now was show business. This reminds me of a little incident which may have humiliated Bill (Bojangles) Robinson at the time, but which he recalled with amusement later on.

I was about seven years old when we first worked on a bill with Bojangles. By Tuesday of that week Robinson was broke and had borrowed money from all of the grownups on the bill.

His face lighted up on hearing that, small though I was, I always had money in my pocket. On Wednesday he borrowed two dollars from me. He promised to pay it back but neglected to mention I'd have to wait until Saturday when he got his week's pay.

Nobody else had ever borrowed money from me, and I was very impressed by the transaction. But at every performance after that I asked Robinson, "Mr. Bill, where is my two dollars?"

This depressed him more and more, but he managed to take it until Friday. Then, unable to stand any more dunning, he approached Pop and said, "Mr. Joe, I don't know whether you will approve of this, but I borrowed two dollars from Buster. He has been asking me for it every minute since. Mr. Joe, could you let me have two dollars until tomorrow night so I can pay Buster and not have him asking me for his money any more?" Pop gave Bill the two dollars, and he gave it to me and paid back my father next day.

About thirty years later when Bill was playing with Shirley Temple at Twentieth Century-Fox he encountered me on the lot. He was walking with Darryl Zanuck, then the studio's production chief. We stopped to chat. Suddenly Bill turned to Zanuck and said, "Mr. Zanuck, don't ever borrow any money from *that* man!"

You will notice that I quote Bill Robinson addressing my father as "Mr. Joe," something no Negro performer need say these days.

Although the theatrical profession was the first to break through the color line, throughout my boyhood and youth you never saw whites and Negroes on a stage at the same time. There were very few Negro women performers in vaudeville or on Broadway. The first I recall seeing was Ada Walker, the wife of George Walker, the partner of Bert Williams, when she appeared with Williams and Walker in an all-Negro revue and incidentally sang "Shine," which is still a perennial favorite.

When Negroes were allowed in white saloons at all they were restricted to the end of the bar farthest from the door. Pop ignored this the night he walked into the Adams Hotel bar in Boston, which was conveniently situated, being directly behind Keith's Theatre. Bert Williams, who was again on the bill with us, was standing, as required, far down at the other end.

"Bert," said Pop, "come up here and have a drink with me."

Bert looked nervously from one white face at the bar to another, and replied, "Think I better stay down here, Mr. Joe."

"All right," said Pop, picking up his glass, "then I'll have to come down there to you."

I am not making the point that Pop had no race prejudice. He didn't know what race prejudice was. Nobody had told him that there was such a thing. Like most people in those days if he resented bitterly something a man did and that man was a Jew he called him a "damned sheeny." If the offensive one was Italian, Pop denounced him as a "dirty dago." If he was Irish he called him a "rotten, dumb mick." But this was more a matter of identifying the rascal than denouncing him because of his race. One of Pop's rare barroom battles illustrates the point, I think. At the time at least three of Pop's best enemies were Jews. Two of them, E. F. Albee and Martin Beck, were vaudeville tycoons with whom he had quarreled for years. The third one was Bert Levy, the vaudeville cartoonist, whom Pop had never forgiven because Levy had taken a telegram for him once and failed to pass it on promptly, causing us to lose a booking.

What Pop could not endure was seeing another human being mistreated or unfairly dealt with. If you were being victimized your race didn't count. He was automatically on your side.

I think I have mentioned that my father was one of the country's best rough-and-tumble fighters. I doubt though that I have emphasized what extraordinary weapons he could turn his feet and legs into. His feet were as fast as his hands, and the flexibility of his legs gave him a big edge over any other stand-up fighter. He demonstrated their amazing flexibility one day when he was helping Mr. Pasco serve a fresh fish dinner. One crabby guest brought his plate back to the counter and complained that it wasn't fresh.

Pop was on the other side of the counter. When all verbal arguments failed, Pop swung his leg over the counter, snagged the back of the man's neck with his foot, pulled his head forward until it was only two inches from his own, and said, "It's fresh perch, and you'll eat it."

And the man did.

As a result of throwing me around the stage for so many years

Pop's right arm became twice the size of his left. He demonstrated its punching power to the whole family one morning in Los Angeles. This was at the time when vaccination became compulsory. A great many people, including my parents, were rebelling against it. Some children died after being inoculated, and the number of these deaths was not underestimated, I imagine, for they were talked about all over the country.

We were in a Los Angeles hotel when the medical profession attempted to vaccinate us. Someone knocked on our hotel-room door, Pop answered and found three men there—a county health officer, the hotel physician, and a house detective. When they announced their purpose, he belted the county health officer in the nose so hard that he knocked down both him and the other men behind him. They went down like ninepins; Pop slammed the door. We packed within the hour, moved to another hotel, and were never bothered again about being vaccinated.

For some reason Pop was at his best when fighting more than one man at a time. I have a suspicion he considered it both more fun and fairer to the opposition. He certainly was helped by his talent for fighting with his feet one Saturday night when he entered Considine's Metropole, then the most popular gathering place for sporting men in New York.

Pop went there alone. Mom was playing pinochle at the Ehric House, and I was kibitzing the game. As Pop ordered a beer three college boys came swaggering in. They exploded into jeering laughter on seeing a small man with a beard at the bar.

"Come here, little Jew," one of them said, "help us celebrate, have a drink on us."

Then they began teasing and tormenting him, climaxing their sport by pulling his derby down over his eyes.

"Let him alone," said my father.

"I suppose you're a Jew too," said one college boy.

"I told you to let him alone," yelled my father when the other two youngsters jostled the stranger. The third boy said to my father:

"I asked you something. Are you a Jew?"

"I certainly am," announced Pop, astonishing the bartender, who had known him for years as an Irishman.

The collegiates began to close in on him. One threw a punch. Pop ducked the blow, took out two of the three boys with his feet, and with a right uppercut belted the third one clean through Considine's window.

The bartender and the little Jewish gentleman both stared at the shattered glass, then at the two unconscious young athletes on the floor.

"Well, what will you have, Mr. Keaton?" said the bartender.

Joe rubbed the knuckles of his right hand as he reflected, then he said, "I think I'll have a beer." He said he was going to ask the little Jewish fellow to have a drink but decided he'd done enough for him already.

Meanwhile, as he sipped his beer, one of Considine's waiters slipped out of the Metropole and summoned the fat cop on the beat.

On the way to the police station with Pop, the policeman asked, "Why didn't you run?"

Joe's face broke into a happy smile, "Is it too late?"

"Yes," said the cop sadly, " 'tis too late now. The desk sergeant knows about it."

The first Mom and I knew about it was when George Howard, of the Howard Brothers, a great banjo-strumming team, came bursting in on the pinochle game. His timing was bad—Mom had just bid 350 in spades, which pays double.

"Myra," George exclaimed, "Joe's locked up in the West 47th Street station house. He knocked three guys cold in Considine's. They're holding him in $250 bail."

Little Mom, who had to sit on a couple of pillows to be on the same level with the other players, just glared at the other two players.

"I bid three fifty!" she said belligerently.

George seemed to think Mom had not heard him. "Myra, I said Joe is locked up and . . ."

Mom waved to him to be quiet. When no one outbid her, she laid down her spade flush and other meld, played out the hand, and won easily. Only when she had collected her winnings did she turn to George, and ask:

"How much bail money did you say Joe needs?"

"Two fifty. Two hundred and fifty dollars, that is."

Mom dug down, got the money out of her grouch bag, handed it to George Howard, waved him away, and said, "All right, deal the cards."

Like most vaudeville performers Pop disliked Martin Beck, who ran the Orpheum Circuit, which was the big-time circuit in Chicago and all points west. As a member of the White Rats, the vaudevillians' first union, which Beck fought bitterly, Pop and he had had words as early as 1901. The antagonism between the two increased a half dozen years later when Klaw and Erlanger in partnership with the Shuberts started an "advanced vaudeville" circuit, to compete with both the Keith Circuit and Beck's Orpheum string of theatres. We were among the many acts signed by the new group despite black-listing threats from the United Booking Office, the agents controlled by Keith, his partner Albee, and Beck.

Unfortunately the new venture lasted only three months. Unable to ban all of the deserters, many well-known acts, including ours, were forgiven—for the time being. With the outbreak of war in Europe in 1914 all foreign acts who could reach the United States rushed here. They were promptly put to work, replacing as many of the "disloyal" American acts as possible.

To teach those once rebellious acts that they were using who was boss, the vaudeville magnates' UBO agency harassed them in every way they could think of. They laid out routes so these acts could not make the trip from one city to another overnight. This forced the performers to lay off a whole week between bookings which cut down their income considerably. There would be endless arguments about material used. The worst insult to a well-known act like ours was making it open a show. This meant going on before the audience was warmed up and while some of the people out front were still being seated.

This is what Martin Beck did to The Three Keatons in 1916 when we played the New York Palace which by then had replaced Hammerstein's Victoria as vaudeville's most important showcase.

Pop could not stop talking about this outrage. He called Beck every name in the book. Then, one matinee, when we were on,

Pop looked out into the wings and saw his enemy, arms folded, glaring at him.

"Okay, Keaton," said Martin Beck, "make *me* laugh!"

Pop's face turned purple. The next thing I knew he was streaking toward Beck who turned and ran out the stage door. But Pop wasn't satisfied with chasing the two-a-day tycoon out of his own theatre. He followed the panting Mr. Beck—who was about five feet eight and chunky—up Forty-seventh Street and down Sixth Avenue, only stopping when he lost his man in the crowds.

Meanwhile, left alone on the stage, I didn't know what to do. I sang a song, recited, jigged until Pop came back and we were able to go into our regular routine. At the finish we got our usual applause. But that was the last week The Three Keatons ever played big time vaudeville in New York—or anywhere else.

ONE WAY TO GET INTO THE MOVIES

The next day Martin Beck gave orders that the running time of our act must be cut from seventeen minutes to twelve. Nobody, of course, knew better than he did how difficult it is for a knock-about, harum-scarum act like ours to eliminate five minutes overnight from its running time.

We did not try.

Instead, Pop brought a dollar alarm clock out on the Palace stage as we began our turn. While winding it up and setting the alarm he explained to the audience that, to our regret, the management would not allow us to do our full act. Nevertheless we would do everything we could in the short time we were permitted to remain on the stage. He put the clock down in front of the footlights. The instant the alarm rang we stopped what we were doing. It did not matter whether we were fighting, chasing one another, or dancing. We just stopped dead in the middle of it, Pop picked up the clock, and we walked off.

It was a wonderful way to express our resentment. The audiences were with us one hundred per cent. The trouble was that audiences did not book the acts. We ended the season playing two weeks in the Loew Theatres. That was the small time even though Loew paid us $750 a week, the same salary we got from Keith.

The small time meant three shows a day instead of two. For a standard act like ours which had never played anything but the big time it also meant great loss of prestige. The entire profession assumed you were on your way down—and maybe out—if you accepted smalltime booking.

Right then and there it would have meant everything if we had established ourselves in England and could have gone back there to work.

Rather than play the small time, other big-time acts preferred not to work at all. We were not that stubborn or foolish. We had seen some of them sit and wait for years until something they considered worthy of them came along. For most this chance never came, and after a while they were forgotten.

We agreed among ourselves not to let that happen to us. When the next season came and we could get no big-time bookings we signed a contract to play the Pantages Circuit on the West Coast. But we soon found out that playing our roughhouse, neck-breaking act three times a day was too punishing and bruising.

We begged Alexander Pantages to let us do only two shows. Pantages was a tough old Greek who had started his money-making career as a saloon porter in the Klondike gold rush. His experiences in the Frozen North had not made him benevolent. "You signed to do three shows a day," he told us, "and that's what you'll do."

Adding to the difficulties of playing three shows a day was the fact that Pop had recently switched from drinking beer to hard liquor. Being forced to play the small time gave him an additional excuse for boozing it up.

In an act like ours precise timing, of course, was all-important. Being a half second off in throwing a kick or ducking a punch meant broken bones sooner or later. Pop never did become one of those falling-down drunks. But he didn't need to be to endanger the health of both of us.

"Oh, I am all right," he would say when I mentioned this. "And don't forget, I'm *your* father, so don't lecture me." I tried roughing him up during the act, punishing him a little, but that didn't work either. He laughed at me when I threatened to go it alone unless he got off the sauce.

It was in San Francisco that he got tipsy once too often. We were scheduled to open at the Pantages Theatre in Los Angeles on the following Monday. But during the week in San Francisco I told Mom, "I'm going to break up the act."

Mom made no objection. She herself had tried to talk Pop out of drinking before shows. Anyway, the act had never meant to her what it did to us.

But neither of us could figure out an easy way to tell Pop the bad news. He would break down and cry like a baby, plead for another chance. I was not prepared to watch my father go to pieces. I was not sure I could go through with it. Not that I wasn't damn mad at him.

So Mom and I just did not tell him.

While he was out at some saloon on the night we were scheduled to move on to Los Angeles, we packed our things and took a train East. We didn't even leave him a note.

I went to New York to see if I could get work there on my own. As a single act. That's what vaudeville people called it. Mom went to Detroit to visit some friends for a while.

When Pop got back to our hotel and found us gone, he was not worried. Always the optimist, he assumed that we had gone on to Los Angles without him. It was only when he walked into the Pantages Theatre in L.A. that he learned I had cancelled the rest of our tour.

No one could tell him where we were. Not knowing what else to do he went to Muskegon, hoping to find us there. And that's where he spent the rest of that winter. Our place was a summer cottage and had no furnace or plumbing. But aside from the physical discomfort it wasn't a bad place for Pop. Some of his old vaudeville pals had retired and were living there the year round.

The kids were still in private school nearby which meant he had half of his family close by.

There was enough money in the bank account. Pop wasn't going to die in Muskegon of either hunger or loneliness. Knowing him, I was sure he wouldn't die of remorse either.

Meanwhile I had gone into the movies in New York. After staying a month in Detroit, Mom took pity on Pop and rejoined him in Muskegon. It would have been something to have seen his face when Mom explained to him what I was doing. Pop had always sneered at the movies. He considered them a passing fad, no more important than the peekaboo waist, let us say, and far less interesting.

Not too long before, William Randolph Hearst, already dabbling in the business of picturemaking, suggested to Pop that we make a two-reeler comedy for him.

"What are you *saying?*" thundered Pop. "You want to show *The Three Keatons* on a bed sheet for ten cents?"

Later on, Hearst offered us a contract to make a whole series of two-reel comedies based on "Bringing up Father," the comic strip which his newspapers ran. Pop, Hearst said, could play Jiggs, the main character. Pop again refused.

Like most middle-aged vaudeville actors he would have laughed if anyone had predicted that "the flickers," as they were still called, would soon replace vaudeville as the country's favorite form of entertainment.

On finally hearing the terrible news about me from Mom he groaned, *"Our Buster in the movies?* I can hardly believe it."

Though no more considerate of Pop's feelings than most other long-suffering wives, Mom delayed telling him that I'd passed up a spot in a big Broadway show to take the picture job.

"I didn't want to make the poor fellow froth at the mouth," she explained later on.

On reaching New York in February 1917, I had gone straight to the office of Max Hart, New York's most influential theatrical agent. I told him I had broken up the family act and wanted to work on my own for a while.

"I'll get you all the work you want," Hart told me. He immediately put on his hat and took me to the Shubert Brothers' office which was just down the street. They were casting the new edition of their annual revue, *The Passing Show,* which was then one of the best showcases for actors on Broadway.

Mr. Hart, an agent of few words, took me straight into the private office of J. J. Shubert. As always J.J. was doing the casting with the assistance of a flabby, lisping gentleman everybody called "Mother" Simmons.

"This is Buster Keaton," Max Hart told them. "Put him in your show."

J. J. Shubert looked me over, and asked, "Can you sing?"

"Sure I can sing," I said, even though it was a pretty foolish question. If Mr. Shubert hired me it would be for my comedy. And he did hire me without asking me to sing, or a second question.

The Passing Show usually played in New York for six months, then went on the road for the remainder of the year. My salary was set at $250 a week for New York and $300 on tour. A few days later I got a script of the revue.

But just a day or two before rehearsals were to start, I ran into Lou Anger, a Dutch comedian, who had worked on vaudeville bills with us many times. Anger was with Roscoe (Fatty) Arbuckle, the screen comedian. As he introduced us, he explained that Arbuckle had just broken away from Mack Sennett to make two-reel comedies of his own. Joe Schenck was producing them, and Anger had quit vaudeville to be Joe's studio manager.

I had seen some of Arbuckle's work in Sennett comedies and greatly admired him. He said he'd caught our act many times and always liked it.

"Have you ever been in a movie, Buster?" he asked.

When I told him I hadn't, Roscoe said, "Why don't you come over to the Colony Studios tomorrow morning? I'm starting a new picture there. You could try doing a bit in it. You might enjoy working in pictures."

"I'd like to try it," I told him.

The Colony Studios were housed in a big loft building on East 48th Street. When I got there the whole place was humming with activity. Besides the Arbuckle company, Norma Talmadge's own company, her sister Constance's and a couple of others were making romantic dramas in other parts of the studio. This seemed wonderful to me. It was like being in a great entertainment factory where different shows were being manufactured at the same time.

The two-reeler Roscoe was starting that day was *The Butcher Boy*. The scene was a country store, and my role was that of an innocent stranger who comes wandering in just as he and Al St. John start to heave bags of flour at one another. Like Arbuckle, St. John had been one of Sennett's Keystone Cops.

Roscoe had brown paper bags filled with flour, tied up and ready for use. He lost no time in putting me to work. "As you come in the store," he explained, "I will be throwing some of these bags at St. John. He will duck, and you will get one right in the face." It seemed like nothing at all after the punishment I'd been taking from Pop all of these years.

"Now," Arbuckle said, "it is awfully hard not to flinch when you are expecting to get hit with something like that. So as you come in the door, look back. When I say 'Turn!' you turn, and it will be there."

It was.

Arbuckle, who weighed 280 pounds, had established himself as a master custard-pie thrower while with Mack Sennett. I found out that day that he also could put his whole heart and every ounce of his weight into throwing a flour bag with devastating accuracy. There was enough force in that thing to upend me completely. It put my feet where my head had been, and with no co-operation from me whatever. Enough flour went up my nostrils and into my mouth to make one of mother's old-fashioned cakes. Because I was new to the business, I was politely picked up and dusted off. But it was fifteen minutes before I could breathe freely again.

The plot called for me to buy a quarter's worth of molasses. I had brought along a tin pail for the molasses. But after it was ladled out I discovered that I had dropped the quarter into the molasses. Roscoe, Al St. John, and myself all took turns at trying to get the quarter. The three of us were smeared with molasses from head to foot before we were finished. That same day I was also called upon to be bitten by a dog. Between one thing and another, I would say that my long career as a human mop proved most useful from the start of my work as a movie actor. And everything about the new business I found exciting and fascinating.

Incidentally, I've been told that my first scene in *The Butcher Boy* is still the only movie-comedy scene ever made with a newcomer that was photographed only once. In other words my film debut was made without a single retake.

Roscoe—none of us who knew him personally ever called him Fatty—took the camera apart for me so I would understand how it worked and what it could do. He showed me how film was developed, cut, and then spliced together. But the greatest thing to me about picturemaking was the way it automatically did away with the physical limitations of the theatre. On the stage, even one as immense as the New York Hippodrome stage, one could show only so much.

The camera had no such limitations. The whole world was its stage. If you wanted cities, deserts, the Atlantic Ocean, Persia, or the Rocky Mountains for your scenery and background, you merely took your camera to them.

In the theatre you had to create an illusion of being on a ship, a railroad train, or an airplane. The camera allowed you to show your audience the real thing: real trains, horses and wagons, snowstorms, floods. Nothing you could stand on, feel, or see was beyond the range of the camera.

The same was true of the movie makers' use of light. They had not yet learned how to use mechanical light as effectively as they did a little later. Even so, they were making the *sun* work for them on their open stages on the roofs and in their studios which had large skylights. The sun gave them their back-lighting and cross-lights, and they increased this with reflectors. In the theatre only artificial lights could be used. These produced only effects, could only create and increase an illusion or highlight a particular spot on the stage. And this, everybody in pictures agreed, was merely the beginning!

From the first day on I hadn't a doubt that I was going to love working in the movies. I did not even ask what I'd be paid to work in Arbuckle's slapstick comedies.

I didn't much care.

Men who know a good deal about financial matters have often told me I am stupid in my handling of money. I would not say they are wrong. But even though I've spent my whole life in the most insecure of professions, money somehow has never seemed important to me.

I am not unaware that one can be extremely uncomfortable without money enough for good food, shelter, and decent clothing. But from my babyhood on The Three Keatons always had enough—and a little more—for whatever they wanted. We even managed to stash away quite a bit in the bank against the proverbial rainy day.

It seems to me that if you are a good craftsman your principal concern should be to keep working. If you manage to do that your employers will have to pay you sooner or later exactly what you are worth. How can they avoid it?

I say all of this, but I must admit being quite surprised to find just forty dollars in my pay envelope at the end of my first week as a movie actor. When I asked Lou Anger about it, he said that was all his budget permitted him to pay me. Six weeks later I was increased to $75 and not long after that to $125 a week.

Max Hart, like any other theatrical agent, was not a man to underestimate the importance of a big pay check. But when I told him I wanted to withdraw from my $250 a week job in *The Passing Show* to act in the movies for forty dollars he said I was doing a very wise thing.

"Learn everything you can about that business, Buster," he said, "the hell with the money. Movies are the coming thing, believe me."

On the same day that I entered the business in which I was to enjoy my greatest success, I also met the girl who became my first wife. She had tried bit parts in pictures but without much success. At the moment she was working with the Arbuckle unit as combination secretary and script girl. I was attracted to her at once. She seemed a meek, mild girl who had much warmth and great feminine sweetness. Shortly after our first date I met her mother and the rest of her family. I thought they were all wonderful. They were gay and vital and full of good humor. Incidentally, having grown up backstage, I have never been timid or shy with women. I do not claim I understand them, but neither, I am told, did Socrates, Schopenhauer, or Einstein.

Roscoe and I made only five or six two-reelers in New York. Then the whole unit moved to Hollywood in October 1917. My future wife went along with us. As soon as I got there I sent for my parents. Jingles and Louise, who were still at school in Muskegon, joined us during their summer vacation.

The longer I worked with Roscoe the more I liked him. I respected without reservation his work both as an actor and a comedy director. He took falls no other man of his weight ever attempted, had a wonderful mind for action gags, which he could devise on the spot. Roscoe loved all the world, and the whole world loved him in those days. His popularity as a performer was increasing so rapidly that soon he ranked second only to Charlie Chaplin.

Arbuckle was that rarity, a truly jolly fat man. He had no meanness, malice, or jealousy in him. Everything seemed to amuse and delight him. He was free with his advice and too free in spending and lending money.

I could not have found a better-natured man to teach me the movie business, or a more knowledgeable one. We never had an argument. I can only remember one thing he ever said that I disagreed with.

"You must never forget," he told me that day, "that the average mentality of our movie audience is twelve years."

I thought that over for a long time, for three whole months in fact. Then I said to Roscoe, "I think you'd better forget the idea that the movie audience has a twelve-year-old mind. Anyone who believes that won't be in pictures for very long, in my opinion."

I pointed out how rapidly pictures were improving technically. The studios were also offering better stories all of the time, using superior equipment, getting more intelligent directors. Griffith's *Birth of a Nation* was fascinating people who had never before thought of the movies as anything but an interesting toy. They'd shown Griffith's masterpiece at a two dollar top, which was as much as was charged then for some Broadway plays. "Every time anyone makes another good picture," I said, "people with adult minds will come to see it."

On thinking it over, Arbuckle said I was right. But the low estimate of the audience's mind, I notice, survives to this day in Hollywood. I sometimes wonder if TV, free or not, could have overtaken and overwhelmed the movie industry so quickly if its studio bosses had rejected that myth.

After moving to Hollywood, Pop continued to be snobbish about pictures. But I did get him to work with us in a couple of Arbuckle's. Pop's pratfalls astonished Roscoe and everybody else. The trick of Pop's that truly left the competition speechless was one in which he put one foot on the table, then the other. He'd take the fall, after seeming to be sitting on air for a moment or two.

One day Roscoe was directing a scene in which Pop was supposed to kick me. After the first take, Roscoe said, "The camera is getting this from the wrong side. Would you mind kicking Buster with your left foot?" Pop growled, "I've been kicking Buster's behind now for almost twenty years. I don't need you to tell me how to do it."

Roscoe laughed and called lunch. When we went back he had the camera moved to the other side of the set so Pop could kick me in his traditional manner.

In June 1918 I was drafted into Uncle Sam's World War I Army as a thirty-dollar-a-month private and assigned to the infantry. My salary by that time had been raised to $250 a week, and Joe Schenck generously sent my parents twenty-five dollars a week during all of the time I was in the Army.

My future wife went back to New York. My folks returned to Muskegon where Pop quickly got a job in a munitions plant that was making artillery shells. Ignoring the fact that I was in the infantry Pop wrote in white chalk on every shell he worked on,

"Give 'em hell, Buster."

Our outfit was the Fortieth Division, which was nicknamed the Sunshine Division. I was sent to Camp Kearney, near San Diego, where I had one of the briefest spells of boot training in American military history. After a few days in quarantine I was given shots in double doses. We were to be shipped to France, everyone said, as soon as transportaion could be provided. They weren't kidding. I had only ten days of drilling on the Awkward Squad, or just long enough for me to learn to obey the commands of "Salute!" "Halt!" and "Forward March!" This with arms benumbed by those high-powered injections.

I was then put in with my regular squad. I might have done fine there if some impulsive officer had not given a command I had never heard of. It was: "To the rear, march!" I went forward as everyone else turned and went backward. Immediately I got hit on the chin and knocked down by somebody's gun butt. I wasn't unconscious, but I might as well have been—because I couldn't get up. While I lay there in a dazed condition, my brothers-in-arms, my dear buddies, either had to jump over me or step to one side to avoid kicking me.

Unable to understand what was causing all that jumping and stepping aside several officers came running up along the side of our company. Only after bending down and looking through the legs of the men were they able to see my small crumpled figure.

"Company, halt!" the most alert of the officers shouted. They then ran in, dragged me to my feet, and asked, "Are you hurt?"

Hurt! I was far ahead of them. I imagined I had been wounded and downed in battle with the German Army. "Did we win?" I asked.

I spoke in all seriousness. But nobody knew that, and everyone laughed, which is the sort of thing that often gets a man an undeserved reputation for being a wit.

I was not amused at all to find slapstick flowing over into my new life in the Army. I took being a soldier quite seriously, studied the Morse code regularly, also map reading and semaphore signaling. On mastering these subjects I discovered that I was the best-informed private in my outfit. While in the Service, in fact, I never met an enlisted man, including some who had joined up during the Spanish-American War, who had more than glanced occasionally at an Army training manual.

We were shipped East and quartered at Camp Upton, Long Island. There we were kept up for three days and three nights while being equipped for overseas duty. We also received additional medical shots.

It was not always possible to take that war seriously. In the first place I could not understand why we, the French, and the English were fighting the Germans and the Austrians. Being in vaudeville all of my life had made me international-minded. I had met too many kindly German performers—singers and acrobats and musicians—to believe they could be as evil as they were being portrayed in our newspapers. Having known Germans, Japanese jugglers, Chinese magicians, Italian tenors, Swiss yodelers and bell-ringers, Irish, Jewish, and Dutch comedians, British dancers, and whirling dervishes from India, I believed people from everywhere in the world were about the same. Not as individuals, of course, but taken as a group.

I also resented my uniform which made me look and feel ridiculous. Apparently, the Quartermaster General had never anticipated that anyone five feet five inches tall would be allowed to join the United States Army. My pants were too long, my coat looked like a sack, and wrapping Army puttees around my legs was a trick I never mastered. The size eight shoes handed me were far too big for my size six and one-half feet. The shoes also were hobnailed and made of leather as tough as a rhinoceros's hide. Old-timers in our outfit had long given up hope of ever getting uniforms that fit them. They had theirs altered at civilian tailor shops. They also bought sturdy workmen's shoes, which they managed to disguise well enough to pass inspection.

All of this may explain the few times when I forgot my determination to be a good little soldier. The first of these lapses occurred the day I phoned my girl, and she came to Camp Upton to see me.

She arrived at our Hostess House in her family's oversize Packard at about one that afternoon. The Packard was driven by a liveried chauffeur and had a Victoria top. She looked gorgeous. So did the Packard. The combination gave me ideas. We noncommissioned nothings were restricted to the camp, but our officers were not. However, because it was hot at Camp Upton, those exalted beings were not wearing their jackets, and their khaki shirts and black knitted ties looked exactly like ours.

If I rolled out of camp with my girl in that eye-popping car I might easily get by the sentries, it seemed to me. I would not, after all, be wearing my private's overseas cap or my oversize jacket. Unless one of the sentries looked over the side of the car he would never see my baggy pants and clodhopper hobnailed boots.

I planned to salute the sentries as casually as our officers did. When saluting, the private, particularly if he was a rookie, stiffened up and snapped his left hand to his forehead, holding it there until the officer returned the salute, then snapped it back to his side. The officers (and also veteran professional soldiers) did not snap the hand until they had it almost to their left eyebrow. They did not snap it in taking their hand away, just let it fall to their side.

If I had been able to imitate Houdini, jabbering Chinese, and Pop on the stage, I figured I ought to be able to get away with imitating an officer saluting a sentry.

I asked my girl whether Camp Upton was near any place where we could have some fun. When she said it wasn't far from Long Beach I got into the car, and we started off.

We got out all right. The inner sentry and outer sentry both saluted me smartly as we rolled through the gates. In return I gave them my languid and indulgent officer's salute.

In those days Long Beach was still a fashionable seashore resort. It had a fine eating and dancing place, "Castles in the Air." This was one of the many enterprises started by the late Vernon Castle and his wife, Irene, at the height of their fabulous vogue as a dancing team.

I cannot deny that I felt rather foolish walking into that imposing dine-and-dance palace in my baggy pants and clodhopper boots. But we had a grand time. It was a relief to be eating educated food instead of Army chow, and to drink coffee that tasted like coffee. We had a wonderful eight or ten hours together that day. My girl paid the check as I didn't have enough money on me. Then we drove back to Camp Upton where both the inner sentry and outer sentry saluted me smartly.

A day or two later we left on a transport for France. I must say I have traveled in more comfortable style. We slept in hammocks that were hung three abreast in four tiers, one above the other. The cooties we were to know so intimately later on were already on board.

We got off at an English port—which one is still a World War I secret as far as I am concerned. From there we were walked to something which the British called a rest camp, their greatest case of mistaken identity since Dr. Jekyll turned into Mr. Hyde.

After two days there we were moved to another rest camp. At both camps the English fed us the same stuff three times a day. The trouble was we didn't like it the first time. The meal consisted of a bit of yellow cheese about the size of two dominoes, one hardtack biscuit, and a cup of tea without sugar, milk, or lemon. After a day at the second camp, we boarded a transport that carried us across the English Channel to that beloved France which is always so jolly a place except when a war is going on.

The Channel boat was so crowded that we crossed standing up. There was room on the boat to sit down, but it was being used by other soldiers who were standing up. On debarking we were marched eight miles to another camp. There was one thing I never could figure out about the French terrain in that war. Wherever we marched in France we seemed to be going uphill. This was true whether we were leaving camp or coming back to camp. Walking in oversized hobnailed boots may have a stronger effect on the human brain than psychologists realize.

In the French rest camp we slept in circular tents, our feet in the center and our heads close to the drafts from the great outdoors. We were told not to open our packs except to get out our blankets. This, it was believed, would enable us to get to a shelter more quickly in case of an air raid. This was the beginning of an experience I have never forgotten.

During my seven months in France as a soldier I slept every night but one on the ground or on the floor of mills, barns, and stables. There is always a draft close to the floor of such farm buildings, and I soon developed a cold which imperiled my hearing.

In that war we saw little but rain and mud. But this is not the reason I recall so clearly the first day that the sun shone. I found some blackberries along a road that afternoon, and climbed up on a low stone wall to pick them. While bending over I became aware that someone was behind me. Looking through my legs I could see the leather puttees of an officer and the end of his little swagger stick.

I straightened up, turned around, and came to attention. He was a major.

"As you were!" he said.

I had been taught that "As you were" meant that I should immediately resume whatever I had stopped doing at the command "Attention!" As I had been bending over picking blackberries when interrupted by the major I went back to that. It never occurred to me that this unimaginative major would wait there to be confronted squarely in the face with my rear end. Instead of saying something witty, he hit me over the bottom with his swagger stick. Caught off balance I fell head first into the prickly blackberry bushes.

Before I could get up, the major started down the road. I yelled after him, "I hope your war's a failure!"

His shoulders wiggled. He may have been amused. The important thing is that he didn't turn back, and I was free to continue eating those good wild French blackberries.

No matter how tired and dirty we got, no matter how some of us squawked, there were always doughboys who kept their sense of humor. I remember the day a mob of us tumbled off an overcrowded train. We were filthy and felt the cooties were eating us alive. But one buddy, who was washing and had his face full of soapsuds, yelled, "Childbirth may be painful, but if you get any of this Army soap in your eyes it's hell!"

The Army delayed for quite a while before giving us any part of our thirty-dollar monthly pay. Doubtless, General Pershing did not want us to waste it on riotous living. Until that first payday came we thought of nothing but food, for we'd been given nothing but Army rations—beans, canned corned beef, and hot liquids of mysterious origin. That first payday we jingled the francs in our pockets and hurried to get all of the food possible into our bellies.

The rations had brought out the long-dormant executive side of my character. Weeks before a pal and I had dickered with the keeper of the nearest French tavern for the franchise on two plates of steak and French fried potatoes. We had been dreaming about how that steak would taste every night since.

But that was going to be only part of our big meal. On getting our money we went from one farmhouse to another, buying eggs. They cost a franc apiece and the franc was then worth twenty cents. But we didn't stop until we had twenty-two of them.

We carried the eggs to the tavern and asked the owner to use them for a giant omelet which we ate as a side dish to our steak and potatoes. The steak was about a quarter-inch thick, but it tasted better than all of the chateaubriands I've had since.

After the Armistice we were shipped from Amiens to a little town near Bordeaux. Along with our infantry division, two others —engineers and machine gunners—were quartered in that town whose population was about 12,000. That meant 45,000 American soldiers. We waited there for months to go home and again had to sleep on the ground or on the floors of barns, mills, and cellars.

We organized a few entertainments built around our regimental band. I did a burlesque snake dance and other routines in these hastily thrown together shows. One day an officer read me a Headquarters directive instructing me to do my snake dance at a dinner being given for a brigadier general at his Headquarters about ten miles away.

I had to walk there. When I finished the show a lieutenant asked how I was going to get back to town. On hearing I'd have to walk, he managed to borrow the general's official car for me.

I might point out here that all of that sleeping on the ground had done nothing to improve my appearance. My trousers were still too long, sagged in the seat, and my puttees were full of knots. My once jaunty overseas cap had shrunk in the rain. Unfortunately, the size eight shoes on my size six and one-half feet had not shrunk at all. And they now had horseshoe plates over the hobnails.

The general's insignia was, of course, on the door of the car, and an American flag flew bravely above it. All of this gave me an idea. If the general's orderly, who was driving, would co-operate, I could surprise any buddies of mine who happened to be in the town square that night. They all figured to be there.

Another payday had just rolled around which meant every-one not crippled would be there, singing, drinking that good

French wine straight from the bottle, and kissing any French girls within kissing distance.

The orderly agreed to co-operate. So I got into the back seat, pulled down the car's side blinds, and suggested he head for the town's Hotel Grand. Except for the town hall it was the most prominent building on the square. None of the carousing privates, corporals, sergeants, and young officers there had seen a general for six months, and they all jumped to their feet as the car stopped before the hotel. The orderly got out and hurried around the car to open the back door for me. All over the square I could hear bottles dropping on the ground as the men and officers jumped up and came to attention. "My" orderly also stood at attention as I stepped out of the car in my dusty, wrinkled uniform. Over my shoulder I said, "I won't need you any more this evening."

I was permitted to proceed unmolested for about fifteen feet. Then the whole gang recognized me and let fly with curses, bottles, tomatoes, apples, and eggs.

"You sonofabitch!" went up from hundreds of parched throats. I cut for the nearest alley, and thanks to my arduous stage conditioning got up enough steam to race out of town, where I slept peacefully through the night in a barn. I sneaked back again in the dawn's early light, but a sergeant spotted me.

"Captain wants to see you, corporal."

I didn't know what my captain wanted, though I knew damn well he wasn't summoning me to promote or decorate me. But when I reached the captain's office he said: "Those were two great shows you put on last night. I liked the second one best—I could court-martial you, I suppose, but you sure put life into the old town square last night, not to mention scaring the hell out of a lot of my young officers who thought they were in for a surprise tour of inspection. We must not let them get too smug, corporal, must we?"

I agreed that we mustn't.

Later on I was assigned to a train that was carrying about 900 wounded men to the redistribution center at Le Mans. I was the only noncommissioned man sent on the trip. It proved a complicated job. We had to get the wounded men all of their equipment and rations, then settle more than forty of those poor fellows in each of twenty-two 40-and-8 boxcars.

On our way back from Le Mans we were to make connections at Paris for the train to Bordeaux. We could have made them but preferred to miss them and stay overnight in Paris. As Paris was out of bounds, that meant technically being AWOL, but it also meant we'd sleep in beds for one blessed night and could enjoy a real dinner. I had thirty-five francs for that big feed.

Now I must go back for a moment to an incident that occurred shortly before I was drafted. For some time Roscoe, Al St. John, and myself had been annoyed by the airs and graces of a sissy type Romeo who was paying court to beautiful Anita King, who was making a picture on the next set.

This ninny would hold her coat, skip ahead to open doors for her, kiss her hand, and pick up her glove as though she had done him a favor by dropping it. Needless to say, we found all of this sickening.

One day I observed that this mushhead was watching us start a sequence in which Roscoe was to throw a pie at Al who would duck, letting me, standing right behind him, catch it right in the face. It was a simple matter, of course, to set this up so that Anita's hand-kissing fool would be right behind me. All I had to do was also duck, and the mincing Romeo got the pie right in his obsequious kisser.

The three of us ran up, apologized loudly. While pretending to help clean the mess off his suit we managed to spread it around a little more. He was suspicious, but had to take our word for it being an accident.

On our great night in Paris we were in the middle of our meal when this same little man, now a major, strutted into the restaurant. We stood at attention. I took one look, and the moment he said, "At ease!" I scooted out the back door. If he had recognized and questioned me, he could have had me court-martialed as technically AWOL.

By that time I had become almost stone deaf due to my being exposed to floor drafts each night. Before I was overseas a month my superiors had to shout orders at me. Late one night I had a narrow escape while coming back from a card game. A sentry challenged me, and I didn't hear his demand for the password or the two warnings he gave me after that. Then he pulled back the breech of his gun, prepared to shoot. My life was saved by my sixth sense which enabled me to hear that gun click—and stopped me dead in my tracks. After bawling me out the sentry listened to my explanation and got me past a second guard.

From that day on the fear of losing my hearing drove me half crazy permanently. On getting back to New York I was sent to a receiving hospital which originally had been the Siegel-Cooper Department Store. Specialists told me I would have to remain under observation for a while. But they assured me that with proper treatment my hearing would be restored.

I prayed they were right.

The moment I could get to a telephone I called my girl at her home. Joe Schenck's office was nearer the receiving hospital so she asked him to hurry over. When he saw me Joe looked as though he was going to cry.

"You look terribly peaked, Buster," he said. "You've lost so much weight. I never saw you look so sick and miserable."

"Why shouldn't I look miserable—with my beauty gone forever?" I asked.

But I wasn't fooling Joe Schenck that day with wisecracks. "Of course you haven't any money," he said. He took out his wallet and gave me all of the money in it.

The first things I bought with the money were a decent-looking uniform and shoes that fit me. I wore these the first night I went to dinner with my girl and her mother in their Park Avenue apartment.

Shortly afterward the Army sent me to Johns Hopkins Hospital, in Baltimore, for observation. The doctors there found my hearing and my health generally so improved they kept me there for only three days.

While I was in New York I had found it impossible to believe I was really home. Then one day in Baltimore the doctors let me take a walk. I headed straight for the local Keith Theatre which Pop, Mom, and I had played dozens of times in the old days.

I walked through that stage door, and the house manager, the crew, the orchestra boys, and the acts greeted me like a long lost pal. Then I knew I was indeed safe home at last. On the bill was one of my best friends, Artie Mehlinger, the singer. I stood in the wings and watched his act—Step, Mehlinger, and King—hoping with all my heart that I would never again have to leave show business and its bubbling, joy-filled, gifted people.

When I became strong enough to travel I couldn't wait to get back to California and my job. I had been mustered into the service at Camp Kearney, and I should have been mustered out there. But the discharge clerk made a mistake. He sent me to Camp Custer, Michigan, because I had given Muskegon, Michigan, as my home on joining the Army.

Needless to say, this caused considerable confusion at Camp Custer, but the clerk kindly gave me the fare to go on to Los Angeles. The mistake enabled me to see my folks and our old neighbors, but I was so eager to get back to work that I stayed in Muskegon for only three days.

WHEN THE WORLD WAS OURS

Before I was out of uniform I received two $1,000-a-week offers. One was from Jack Warner, the other from the William Fox Company. But I preferred to resume working for Joe Schenck at my old salary of $250. I couldn't see how I could go wrong stringing along with a square shooter like him who had been so kind to my family. I had never met a finer man in show business. I haven't yet.

I sometimes wonder if the world will ever seem as carefree and exciting a place as it did to us in Hollywood during 1919 and the early twenties. We were all young, the air in southern California was like wine. Our business was also young and growing like nothing ever seen before.

Nobody suspected that the World War just ending would prove to be merely the first one. Had not President Wilson proclaimed it the war to end all wars—if we jumped in and did the dirty job?

There were bad times elsewhere in the country for a while. And there were other troubles: strikes, race riots, a Red scare. But everybody said that was to be expected with millions of men getting out of uniform and trying to find civilian jobs.

In Hollywood you could all but feel prosperity in the sun-bleached air. Actors, directors, and other lucky people were getting salaries unheard of before in show business or, for that matter, any industry. That was what we had become overnight: an industry that was straddling the globe. Combines were forming and re-forming with skullduggery on a scale to make a Ponzi or a George Graham Rice sick with wistfulness.

War industries had put money into the pockets of millions of Americans who never before had money to pay for entertainment. Everywhere magnificent theatres seating thousands of persons were being built. These were designed to make the movie fans feel like kings and queens. Now the stage show, when there was one, was the secondary attraction.

The most important of all the movie groups formed that year was United Artists, which was founded by the world's three most beloved movie stars—Mary Pickford, Douglas Fairbanks, and Charlie Chaplin—and D. W. Griffith, the screen's most distinguished director.

Each of the four, it was announced, would control every detail in the producing of his own pictures, including their financing. United Artists' one function was to be distribution of their films.

I made only two more two-reelers with Roscoe. Then Adolph Zukor, head of Famous Players-Lasky Corporation and an ever-growing chain of movie theatres, bought Arbuckle's contract from Joe Schenck. Zukor had decided to star Roscoe in full-length, five-reel features. *The Roundup*, the first of these, was a box-office triumph.

Shortly afterward, in January 1920, Marcus Loew bought the Metro studio. He wanted to make sure his chain of theatres would have a steady supply of quality pictures. Its stars then included Nazimova, Viola Dana, Bert Lytell, and May Allison, among others. Being a good showman, Loew saw from the beginning the need for better stories. He engaged John Golden, the Broadway playwright, song writer, and producer, as an adviser on theatrical properties. Among other old plays Golden suggested he buy was *The New Henrietta,* in which the famous William H. Crane had starred on Broadway. Douglas Fairbanks had played the juvenile role of "Bertie Van Alstyne" on Broadway, and also portrayed the same character, Bertie, in his first picture, *The Lamb.*

When Doug and Mary Pickford, who were married soon afterward, were asked to suggest someone to play Bertie in the Metro version of *The New Henrietta,* they said, "You have the perfect man for it right here. Fellow named Buster Keaton."

Mr. Crane was brought out to play his original role, but the story was rewritten so that Bertie became the main character. It was called *The Saphead* and ran for seven reels at a time when Metro's biggest dramatic stars were making only five-reelers. This picture, the first I was starred in, was one of the company's big hits that year.

But the golden age of comedy was just beginning. The whole world wanted to laugh as never before, and Hollywood had the clowns to do the job. There were soon to be years when the pictures of Chaplin, Harold Lloyd, and myself would outdraw the pictures of most the screen's romantic stars. Mack Sennett's Keystone Cops and Bathing Beauties were still popular. But that king of comedy makers was soon to be overshadowed.

One reason was that Sennett could not or would not pay the performers who started with him the sort of money other studios offered them. He kept losing them as fast as they became prominent. And what talent he developed! Chaplin and Arbuckle were only two of them. Charlie Murray, Andy Clyde, Chester Conklin, Clyde Cook, Hank Mann, Ford Sterling, Harry Gribbon, Heinie Mann, and Ben Turpin were Keystone Cops at one time or other. Even Harold Lloyd was a Keystone Cop briefly. Gloria Swanson, Carole Lombard, Marie Prevost were among his bathing beauties. W. C. Fields, Mabel Normand, Wallace Beery, Polly Moran, Marie Dressler, Louise Fazenda, and Bing Crosby all made their early movies with him.

However, there is one guy who never worked for Mack Sennett, although practically every screen historian insists he did. That's

me, Buster Keaton. It was an easy enough mistake to make because I appeared in so many of Roscoe Arbuckle's comedies immediately after he quit Sennett.

In those free-and-easy days we all had fun making comedies.
We worked hard. We stayed with the story all of the way. In the
old days all of us—Chaplin, Lloyd, Harry Langdon, and myself—
worked with our writers from the day they started on a story. We
checked on the scenery, the cast, the locations—often going on
trips with the unit manager to pick these out ourselves and make
sure they were suitable. We directed our own pictures, making up
our own gags as we went along, saw the rushes, supervised the
cutting, went to the sneak previews.

Because of the way we worked in those days I am baffled by
the lackadaisical working habits of many modern-comedy stars.
This could be one of the reasons for the deterioration in screen
comedy since the talkies came in. There are other reasons, of
course. In the silent days we could try anything at all, and did.
We were not supervised by business executives who lacked a
sense of humor. We were the ones who decided what should go
into a script to make the audience laugh. All our bosses asked of
us was that our pictures make fortunes, and our pictures did.

In the early twenties we also had a whale of a time for ourselves after working hours playing practical jokes. In this Roscoe
and I were aided by Lew Cody, the screen Romeo, Syd Chaplin,
Charlie's half brother, and other happy-go-lucky confederates.
Some of our practical jokes are still rated as classics. First-rate
practical jokes, by the way, are far easier to dream up than to
execute.

We worked ours only for laughs. We never used cruel gimmicks
that hurt and humiliated people. I mean such things as the hot
foot, the electric goosing cane, the "electric chair," and the bugged
boudoir sofas, wired so that every word and sound a love-making
couple makes can be heard by their fellow guests in the other
rooms of the house.

Our practical jokes were of the sort the victims could laugh at
with us later on. They were quite ingenious. This earthy art, by
the way, is the subject of much misunderstanding. Really clever
practical jokes are impossible to plan and put over on the spur of

the moment. They must be plotted as carefully as a movie scenario, but precautions must be taken to protect the gag in the event something goes wrong.

Soon after Joe Schenck sold Arbuckle's contract to Famous Players-Lasky we read in the newspapers that Roscoe's new boss, Adolph Zukor, was about to make his annual trip to Hollywood. During this visit he would inspect the studios, confer with his executives, and discuss the plans for the lot's stars.

On hearing this earth-shaking news, Roscoe wired Mr. Zukor an invitation to dine with him and a small party of other Zukor admirers at the humble Arbuckle home on his first night there. Mr. Zukor promptly wired back: "Delighted to accept."

I was cast as the butler. We relied on the theory that no one looks at the butler. I had not yet been starred in a picture. It seemed unlikely that anyone in Mr. Zukor's party would recognize me, even though Frank Newman, the well-known Kansas City exhibitor, was in the group. But as an added precaution there would be only shaded lights in the three downstairs rooms where the guests would have a chance to see me—just in case one of them was the odd type that looks at butlers.

All of the Hollywood people we invited were in on the gag. Among them was Sid Grauman, the builder and operator of the Egyptian and Chinese Theatres in Hollywood, who was himself one of Hollywood's outstanding pranksters. For women guests we had four beautiful screen performers: Bebe Daniels, Viola Dana, Anna Q. Nilsson, and Alice Lake. Before the dinner Roscoe briefed them. He explained, "Nothing is quite so humiliating as giving away a practical joke to the person who is supposed to be the fall guy. So if something we do breaks you up, turn quickly to the man at your side, and tell him, 'I was just thinking of something that happened at the studio today. It was the funniest thing——' But you must have a really funny story ready, or else he'll think you are silly to be laughing so uproariously at something that, to him, doesn't sound amusing at all."

On the great night, the guests sat down after enjoying several rounds of cocktails. I brought in a tray of shrimp cocktails. Ignoring Roscoe's glaring eyes, I served these to the men, beginning with Mr. Zukor, our guest of honor. The shrimp were very large and luscious looking. Though somewhat embarrassed at being served ahead of the women, a couple of the men could not resist the shrimps and ate one or two.

When I came in with a second platter of shrimps and placed these before the girls, Roscoe was unable to restrain himself. With an embarrassed smile, he apologized to his guests, rose from the table, and followed me out to the butler's pantry. There he yelled loudly enough for them to hear, "You stupid numbskull, don't you know better than to serve the men first?"

He was hardly back at the table when I was out once more to shift the men's half-eaten shrimps to the women and theirs to the men.

My next appearance was with a stack of soup plates and a silver ladle, which I placed carefully on the table next to Roscoe. But I brought in no soup. Instead, once back in the pantry, I created a terrible din by rattling dozens of knives and forks in a tin washtub, then dropping the whole business on the floor. I also doused myself with water so I'd look as though I'd spilled the consommé all over myself. I went back to the dining room and placidly, explaining nothing, took away the soup plates and ladle.

This put Roscoe into so explosive a rage that Mr. Zukor, from away out in right field (the other end of the long table), leaned forward and said earnestly, "That is perfectly all right, Roscoe. I never eat soup anyway."

Roscoe refused to be placated by this comforting news. He told his chief, sorrowfully, "We have a *terrible* problem here, Mr. Zukor—the servant problem."

Zukor, nodding in agreement, said, "But, Roscoe, in the East we also find it impossible to find intelligent servants."

At this point I reappeared, carrying ice water in a silver pitcher. As I moved around the table I filled each guest's glass. That is until I got to Bebe Daniels, who was sitting next to Roscoe. I passed her by, and as I was about to pour Roscoe's ice water, Bebe held up her glass, and asked, "Won't you give me some, please?"

Seemingly bewitched by her beauty, I stared down into her

great brown eyes as I poured. I missed her glass but splashed the ice water into Roscoe's face.

With a bellow Roscoe jumped up, grabbed me by the back of the neck, and started to drag me back into the pantry.

"Roscoe, control yourself!" wailed Mr. Zukor. An imaginative man, he could see his great new comedy star bursting a blood vessel before his very eyes.

Arbuckle permitted me to escape. After his guests dried him off he sat down with a hopeless and defeated air in his drenched tuxedo. He resumed the discussion about the terrible servant problem, gradually working himself up into another rage. And nobody could fake anger better than goodhearted Roscoe.

"I am going to give up this house and move into a hotel," he roared, banging on the table.

Willing to say anything to calm him, the flustered Mr. Zukor went the limit. He said he would give up *his* house in the East and move to a hotel.

"I think I have the explanation of this man's inept behavior," then said Sid Grauman. "A while ago I went to telephone, Roscoe, and I saw him take a manhattan."

Before Roscoe could comment, Zukor purred, "You see, Roscoe, your butler has entered into the spirit of the occasion."

But now came the *pièce de résistance* of the evening. For this, we had obtained the help of Roscoe's physical trainer.

The *pièce de résistance* was a twenty-four-pound turkey, browned to a turn, and surrounded by artfully arranged sprigs of parsley, potatoes, and sculptured cranberry sauce. I brought it in on a beautiful silver platter.

I showed the turkey to Roscoe, who nodded and smiled. "Carve it in the pantry," he said.

At the pantry door I dropped my service napkin. As I bent over to retrieve it, Roscoe's trainer pushed the pantry door, hitting me on the backside and propelling me astride the turkey. I was covered with turkey gravy when I got to my feet. But feeding the guests being the first thing on my mind I lost no time in trying to brush off the crushed and battered turkey with my napkin.

Gurgling with maniacal fury, Roscoe again grabbed me by the neck and hauled me into the pantry. The last view the guests had of me I was still trying to clean off the turkey enough to make it presentable.

Once the door shut Roscoe made an ungodly racket by throwing around dishpans, pots, and knives and forks. Above the din, Roscoe could be heard shouting, "I'll kill you, you damned dumb bastard."

Meanwhile back in the dining room the agitated Mr. Zukor was pleading with Bebe Daniels to go into the pantry and try to calm down the raging fat man.

Then something happened that was not in the script. As Bebe got to the door it was pushed open by Roscoe who wanted the guests to see him brandishing a brandy bottle over my head. It was, of course, a breakaway bottle. We had filled it with tea. When Roscoe smashed this over my head some of the pieces and a good deal of the tea fell on poor Bebe's bosom.

Not knowing what hit her, she screamed. Without waiting to investigate, Roscoe chased me through the back door. There he permitted the guests to catch up with him and stop him from murdering me.

While they were all jabbering and milling around out there, I raced around the house to the front door. I slipped in and tiptoed upstairs where I cleaned up, got into a natty sack suit, and brushed my hair flat. I'd fluffed it up for the butler bit.

Downstairs, Roscoe, having allowed his guests to calm him down once again, was having his real butler (whom he introduced as his chef) serve a second turkey. Luckily, he told his guests, he had had two birds roasted just in case one proved not to be enough. As his servant, wearing a chef's hat and apron, was serving this the phone at Arbuckle's side rang. It was I, phoning from upstairs. He listened to me for a moment, then replied, "Why yes, Buster. I'm glad you could make it. We have almost finished dinner, but if you come right now you can at least have dessert and coffee with us."

On hanging up, he said, "That was the little fellow who has been working with me in my pictures. You gentlemen must have seen him. I'm sure you will want to meet him."

Zukor said I was a wonderful performer. Grauman chimed in with, "He's the rarest kind of actor: the unforgettable type."

I crept down the stairs and out of the house. Once safely on the porch I rang the bell. On joining the party I was introduced to the guests from the East and seated next to Frank Newman, the Kansas City exhibitor, who said, "You should have been here earlier, Keaton. We had the damnedest waiter you ever saw." Then he hesitated and gave me an appraising look. "The odd part is that he looks very much like you." That caused Mr. Zukor to scrutinize me more closely. Then he got it but took it dead pan. His eyes moved from me to Roscoe, then back to me. Sid Grauman was the first to laugh. Pointing his finger at Zukor, he said derisively, "Then came the dawn."

Zukor didn't smile, just said in an even tone, "Very clever boys, *very* clever!"

But he loosened up later when Roscoe took everybody to the Ship Café, at Venice, for some drinks. At midnight we all went back to his house for a few snacks.

Next day Zukor surprised us all by telling reporters about the hilarious dinner Roscoe had given him, and the story was printed all over the country. When Zukor got back to New York, his old friend, Marcus Loew, kidded him about being taken in.

"What did you expect to happen, you stupid man?" demanded Loew. "You knew whose house you were going to. You should have expected just such shenanigans from a man like Fatty Arbuckle."

When word of this reached us, we decided that such disrespect for our practical jokes must not go unpunished. When Loew made his annual visit to the Coast to inspect his new studio, Roscoe contrived to be on the Metro lot, visiting a friend.

Running into Loew just as he was leaving, Roscoe asked, "Where are you going from here?"

"To the Alexandria Hotel," replied Mr. Loew. "I'm stopping there."

"What a coincidence!" exclaimed Roscoe. "I am going there right now. Can't I drive you there? My chauffeur is waiting outside."

I, of course, was the chauffeur. I wore livery, a mustache, and goggles. The Alexandria, then *the* hotel in Los Angeles, was downtown. I drove my passengers straight down to Alvarado

Street, where I turned up a street so steep that you could only make it to the top in low gear. And the top—when you got there—was shaped like a whale's back, from which one looked straight down into Silver Lake directly below.

I had raced cars so much in our comedy movie chases that I had become quite an expert at wild crazy driving. But that day I delivered my most masterful exhibition. As we started up the hill in low gear, I raced the motor. The racket this produced convinced Mr. Loew that we were achieving rocketlike speed, though we couldn't have been making more than fifteen or sixteen miles an hour. And I did not brake the car until we were straddling the street's whaleback top, the eminence from which my passengers and I could look down straight into Silver Lake.

Instead of plunging down, I braked and reversed the car, coming down the hill by another route. Next I gave Mr. Loew a rough ride by taking a short cut through a recently plowed orange grove.

Close by this grove was a street on which there were six trolley-car tracks. The outer tracks on each side were used by the local trolleys, those in the middle by the express interurban cars. The center tracks were reserved for use in rare emergencies.

Needless to say, Roscoe and I had made a careful study of the line's schedule. We had also measured our car and found to our delight that it would just straddle the emergency tracks. This meant that the express cars would narrowly miss our auto's front and rear if I could stall the car in precisely the right position.

About a block from the spot we had selected for our exhilarating little adventure, I started to make the engine cough. This gave Mr. Loew fair warning (even though our harassed guest could not take advantage of it) that our motor might stop dead. This happened just as we got across the middle tracks.

With a disgusted shrug, I got out, lifted the hood. After staring at the motor for some time, I walked to the toolbox and got a whole armful of monkey wrenches, hammers, and other tools. I started to work on the rebellious motor, and Roscoe stepped out to help me.

We noticed with satisfaction that the trolleys were right on schedule. First an express car whizzed by at about sixty-five miles an hour, narrowly missing our front end. Next, one headed the other way missed our rear end just as narrowly. Meanwhile on the outer tracks the local trolleys were racing past in both directions at no mean speed. Between one speed-mad trolley and another, Marcus Loew was too nerve-wracked to jump out and run for his life.

Only when we decided he was thoroughly cowed did we get the car started. And en route to the Alexandria I was lucky enough to come across a street which had recently been washed. This enabled me to demonstrate my skill at skidding and turning corners on two wheels.

As we approached the hotel I managed to put the fender and the two left wheels up on the sidewalk. At this Marcus Loew got out of the car so damn fast we missed the chance to ask him how he had enjoyed the ride. Marcus went through the Alexandria's revolving door like a whirling dervish.

Roscoe went up to Loew's suite first. That frightened millionaire, though never much of a drinking man, was putting away his second straight slug of whiskey. When I walked into the suite a few moments later, I took off the chauffeur's cap, goggles, and false mustache. Mr. Loew lashed around for something heavy enough to throw at me.

But after that first tense moment, Marcus Loew started laughing and kept on until he almost became sick.

Some of the great movie queens of that day also were good sports, Pauline Frederick for one. Polly was one of the first of the truly talented Broadway beauties to make her fortune and increase her fame in pictures, playing to great success in such screen melodramas as "Zaza," "La Tosca," and "Madame X."

Miss Frederick was also the first screen star to build a luxurious home in the Beverly Hills section of Sunset Boulevard. Her mansion stood on an immense lot with a 150-foot front. But Polly's gardeners had endless difficulty in growing the imposing lawn she had set her heart on. The experts she called in blamed it on the heavy amount of alkali and adobe mud in the soil. But after spending many thousands of dollars Polly finally got the velvety lawn she wanted.

Every time Roscoe and I drove past her mansion he called my attention to the progress her landscape gardeners were making.

Soon after their work was completed he called me and Lew Cody to the studio early one Sunday morning and had us put on dirty, old workmen's clothes that we dug out of the studio's wardrobe department. We dumped surveyors' instruments, picks, shovels, and other tools in the back of a beat-up old Model-T Ford that we'd been using in our chase sequences, and drove it to Beverly Hills. We parked the Ford in front of Polly's magnificent estate. Before getting out, we pulled our hats down over our foreheads and our bandannas up over our chins. We dumped our equipment in the middle of Miss Frederick's beautiful lawn and prepared to go to work.

We set up a tripod, and Lew measured the ground through the telescope. Meanwhile, Roscoe and I got ready to assault the expensive green scenery with our picks and shovels.

In no time at all Miss Frederick's butler came running out of the house in a panic. "What are you men doing?" he demanded.

"We are from the Beverly Hills Gas and Electricity Department," I explained politely. "There is a leak in our gas main somewhere along here. We'll have to dig up this lawn to find it." He was joined first by Polly's chauffeur and then by her horrified head gardener. The gardener protested that a great fortune had been spent on the lawn we were trying to dig up.

"Oh, we can see that," said Lew Cody, placidly, "but duty is duty. If there was an explosion and that big house of yours was blown up, what would we say to our superintendent?"

The argument was getting heated and noisy when two windows on the mansion's second floor popped open. In another moment Pauline and her uncle, in dressing gowns, were out on the lawn, pleading with us not to wreck it. Then Polly recognized us. When she stopped laughing she invited us in and served us a breakfast fit for a king.

We enjoyed our little joke so much that we planned to repeat it at Pickfair, the estate of Douglas Fairbanks and Mary Pickford, which had an even bigger and more expensive lawn. But we were the victims of our own success. The story went all over Hollywood too quickly for us to work it on anyone else.

Our most elaborate practical joke though was played on Vic Levy, a Belgian dress manufacturer who lived in Los Angeles. Vic doted on movie people and had entertained crowds of us at big parties in his home at which he served the best imported wines.

But that was only until Prohibition arrived. Against that evil day Vic had stored an immense stock of vintage wines. But he got very stingy with these. He let you look admiringly at the stuff in his cellar but served only bootleg booze and near beer at his parties. Roscoe and I almost developed a persecution complex over this as we had been Vic's most appreciative guests.

We decided to teach him a lesson that would bring him back to his senses—and his hospitable habits.

But we could think of no way to show him his error in becoming so tight with his vintage wine until we read that the King and Queen of his native land were in America and would visit Los Angeles while here. During the war Vic had devoted much time to organizing benefits for the Belgian War Charities, a circumstance that inspired us.

We called in Syd Chaplin as our practical joke consultant. He suggested that stationery from the local Belgian consul's office would prove useful, and got it for us. We wrote a letter to Vic on this stationery, saying that Their Royal Highnesses had expressed a desire to dine incognito in Los Angeles at some prominent Belgian's home.

Because of Mr. Levy's selfless services in raising money for Belgian war sufferers, the consulate had selected him for this unique honor. The letter went on to explain that, though it was not generally known, the King and the Queen had long been great movie fans. If Mr. Levy wished to surprise his Monarch and the Queen he would invite their favorites.

Among those we listed as favorites of the King and Queen were the three of us, Tom Mix, Hoot Gibson, Lew Cody, Marshall Neilan, Jack Pickford, Norman Kerry. These all were to come with their wives or sweethearts.

The letter went on to say that the King and Queen would fly down from San Francisco and would arrive at a local airport two hours before the time announced in the newspapers. Glowing with pride on getting the letter, Levy did not doubt its authenticity for an instant. Our next task was to produce a fake King and Queen. Going through the casting book we found a man and woman who were dead ringers for the Belgian rulers. We rented costumes for them from the Western Costume Company. For our phony King we got a duplicate of the Army uniform which he wore on all public appearances. For the fake Queen we got the Sunday-go-to-meeting clothes and fantastic hats the Belgian Queen, like all European Queens, then wore—apparently to outdo Queen Mary of Great Britain.

For many days Vic abandoned his business affairs to take personal charge of the preparations for the gala party. He decided that his own cook would not do and borrowed a chef from the Jonathan Club for that one evening. He hired a Russian string orchestra to play during dinner, a maid, and a couple of extra butlers. He also chartered a limousine, attended by a chauffeur and footman, to carry our impostors from the airfield to his home. Our impostors took off in a plane from Burbank and landed at the Chaplin Field in Los Angeles, which is only a few minutes away. We had a dozen motorcycle cops on hand and four "Los Angeles police detectives" (really movie extras) to pose as bodyguards.

On arriving we found that Vic had decorated his house with acres of flowers and crossed Belgian and American flags.

It was a most elegant dinner and beautifully served, with a different wine with each course. Rare old 100-year-old Napoleon brandy and liqueurs almost as ancient were brought in with the coffee.

We cutups and cute kids only had one bad moment during that unforgettable meal. This came when the host leaned toward His Highness and said something in French. But the extra man who was playing king for a night saved the gag. He had the presence of mind to say that while he was in a foreign land he preferred to speak the language of the country.

The whole thing was so beautifully done that no one told Vic the real story. And when he heard three months later how he had been hoaxed he refused to believe it. It was months more before he accepted the true story. On finding out who the main conspirators were and why he had been deceived, he laughed, and from then on, each time we were his guests, we were served only the very best stuff in his cellar.

BOFFOS BY MAN AND BEAST

While I was making *The Saphead* Joe Schenck bought the Charlie Chaplin lot and renamed it the Keaton Studio. When I finished that picture he turned over Arbuckle's unit to me and handed me a new contract, which gave me $1,000 a week, plus 25 per cent of the profits my pictures made. I suggested that I make only features in the future, but he wouldn't agree. Schenck insisted I return to the two-reel field. I couldn't convince him that comedy features were the coming thing. If I'd won that argument it could have made a big difference in my career. Neither Chaplin nor Lloyd were making features at that time, and I would have had a headstart on both of them.

In saying this, I am not trying to belittle the achievements of either of them. But who could? Their popularity is even more impressive today than in the twenties when they were active.

No comedian ever has been so worshipped around the world as Chaplin was in those years. Kids in the streets of cities and towns on the five continents imitated Charlie's quarter-to-nine walk, his smile, gestures. They wore derbies like his, smudged shoeblack on their upper lip for a Chaplin mustache. They skittered around corners and tipped their derbies as his little tramp did, tried to do the tricks Charlie did with his bamboo cane. Theatres all over the world kept holding endless Charlie Chaplin contests. Their customers insisted on it. It is not too hard to understand. At his best, and Chaplin remained at his best for a long time, he was the greatest comedian that ever lived.

Like everyone else, I'd been aware of Charlie Chaplin's talent from the first time I saw him in the vaudeville sketch "A Night in an English Hall." But I must confess that it never occurred to me that he would one day be acclaimed as the greatest comedian of all time. One reason I underestimated Charlie, I think, was because there were so many other first-rate comics on the stage in those days. I had seen all of them, worked in vaudeville with all of them. At that time Charlie did not seem to me funnier than Will Rogers, Willie Collier, Bert Williams, Frank Tinney, and some of the others.

I was always puzzled later on when people spoke of the similarities in the characters Charlie and I played in movies. There was, to me, a basic difference from the start: Charlie's tramp was a bum with a bum's philosophy. Lovable as he was he would steal if he got the chance. My little fellow was a workingman and honest.

For an example, let us say that each wanted a suit he saw in a shop window. Charlie's tramp would admire it, search his pockets, come up with a dime, shrug, and move on, hoping he'd be lucky next day and have the money to buy it. He would steal the money if he couldn't find it any other way. If not, he would forget all about the suit.

Though my little man also stopped, admired the suit, and had not the money to buy it, he would never steal to get it. Instead he would start trying to figure out how he could earn extra money to pay for it.

Lloyd's screen character was quite different from both Chap-

lin's and mine. He played a mama's boy who continually surprised everyone, including himself, by triumphing over an impossible situation and displaying, in fits and starts, the fighting
heart of a lion. Often Lloyd seemed more acrobat than comedian.
But whatever he was on the screen he always did a lot better than
all right.

During the years the three of us were going good we had no
failures. That's right. There were no flops for any of us all through
the Golden Twenties. Nothing but smash hits all over the world.
Chaplin's features earned an average of $3,000,000 each in theatre
rental fees. Lloyd's $2,000,000; mine between $1,500,000 and
$2,000,000. That was in a day when theatres charged only a frac-
tion of what they charge now for their attractions. As I have said,
often our silent comedies out-grossed the feature films made by
the most popular romantic performers in Hollywood.

When we were making two-reelers theatre owners would bill
them above the full-length films they were showing.

That was one reason I was eager to make features like those
Roscoe Arbuckle was successfully turning out at Paramount. It
seemed obvious that rental fees for full-length pictures would continue increasing. But I also believed that Joe Schenck, being a
shrewd businessman, must know what he was talking about.

Charlie Chaplin and Harold Lloyd from the start were smarter
businessmen than I. They became millionaires early in the game
by producing their own pictures and retaining control of their film
properties. They still own these properties. This means they are
in a position to earn fresh fortunes for themselves any time they
feel like leasing or selling the TV rights to their old silent movies.
(As this was written Chaplin's old movies, in fact, were being revived successfully.)

No one knows exactly how much money Chaplin made out of
his pictures, possibly not even Charlie himself. The reason is that
there is no way of figuring out how much they cost. There is no
secret though about how much Lloyd's features earned for him.
These each cost from $300,000 to $350,000 to make. The distribution costs were about 35 per cent of the $2,000,000 in the rentals
paid for them, or $700,000. That puts Lloyd's earnings at almost
one million dollars per full-length feature! Or about $30,000,000

in all for the thirty features Lloyd made. The bankers got none of this loot because Harold, as soon as he was able to finance his own pictures, stopped borrowing from them. My own features cost from $200,000 to $220,000 to make. Add to that 35 per cent of the rental fees, and you can compute the profits. I refuse to do it on the grounds that it will degrade and depress me.

As long as we're on the subject I will break down and admit that I, like everyone else, would like to be a millionaire. Yet it also seems to me that I am a far happier man today than either Lloyd, who retired years ago, or Chaplin, who is in virtual exile.

I never knew a real actor who was happy when he wasn't working. And working is something I manage to do a lot of these days, between appearing in night clubs, in summer theatres and European circuses, an occasional movie job, TV guest appearances and doing commercials for Alka-Seltzer, Northwest Orient Airlines, and other companies.

I like to think that I'm a man so devoted to acting that having a million bucks would not stop me. At the same time I wonder if I could have as much fun and satisfaction. Could I really work as hard as I do if I had more money than I could spend during the rest of my life?

It has been my observation that being a millionaire alters almost everybody's attitude, and can be as distracting as inheriting a zoo or a harem. The only millionaires I ever saw working in a circus were the folks who owned it. Millionaires, willingly or not, take on a certain dignity. Some of this may be due, of course, to the wistful way other people look at them. Getting very rich, shall we say, eliminates some of the incentive for taking pratfalls and clowning it up generally as I do every time I work.

In this also may lie a clue to why certain of today's comedians don't work any harder than they do. Some of them became millionaires awfully fast.

After writing all of this it occurs to me that I might be far less philosophical on this subject if I were broke. But if I'm no millionaire, I'm not poor either. I drive a Cadillac, have a beautiful home deep in the San Fernando Valley and a pretty wife, and there is nothing I want that I cannot buy. The fact is that I'm rapidly approaching the point where I'm making almost as much as when I was a $3,000-a-week silent-movie star.

I'm still, thanks to our income tax laws, in no danger of becoming a millionaire. As George Gobel would say, they just don't hardly make those kind no more.

I loved having my own studio. Schenck and Anger very seldom interfered with me. Neither did Metro which released my first two-reelers. I was able to supervise each phase of my pictures. Movie-making was a very informal business in those days, of course. When the boss walked into a studio the carpenter and the electrician could call him by his first name.

The greatest thing about working in a small studio like ours was having the same bunch of men going with me as a team on each new movie. The director, two or three writers, and myself would figure out the story. But the others—the prop man, the unit manager who found our locations, the two cameramen, and the cutter —all sat in with us.

Because we worked this way each man in the crew knew what would be required of his department, thereby eliminating much of the fantastic waste of time, energy, and money that later went on in the big studios.

Two cameramen, by the way, were necessary in those days because we shot everything with two cameras placed side by side. One made the negative for the American market, the other the negative for the market abroad. After the first American print had been cut, edited, previewed, furnished with subtitles, and was ready for release, the European negative was matched to it and shipped abroad where title and subtitles were translated into the various foreign languages.

Even when making my two-reelers I worked on the theory that the story was always of first importance. But one thing we never did when making our silent comedies was put the story down on paper. On the other hand I never would agree to start shooting until I had in my mind a satisfactory ending for a story. The beginning was easy, the midddle took care of itself, and I knew I could depend on my writers and myself to come up with any gags we might need as we went along.

The daily story conferences at the studio usually lasted from ten to six. We worked the six-day week then, but I never was such a bear cat for work that I couldn't take time off on a Saturday afternoon to see any big football games.

What I never could understand was why I got so few good ideas during those long story conferences. My best notions would invariably occur to me at home, more often than not in the least inspiring room in the house, the bathroom. But I also never went fishing without coming back with a brand-new story idea.

The cast for our two-reelers was always small. There were usually but three principals—the villain, myself, and the girl, and she was never important. She was there so the villian and I would have something to fight about.

The leading lady had to be fairly good-looking, and it helped some if she had a little acting ability. As far as I was concerned I didn't insist that she have a sense of humor. There was always the danger that such a girl would laugh at a gag in the middle of a scene, which meant ruining it and having to remake it.

By now, of course, all sorts of laurels have been handed the slapstick comedies that Chaplin, Lloyd, Harry Langdon, and I made. They have been acclaimed as screen classics, masterpieces of the comic art.

This is most flattering, but it came as a complete surprise to me. I never realized I was doing anything but trying to make people laugh when I threw my custard pies and took pratfalls. Like anyone else I enjoy being called a genius. But I cannot take it seriously. Neither does Harold Lloyd, as far as I know. The only one of us who listened and accepted the role of genius intellectual critics thrust upon him was Chaplin. Sometimes I suspect that much of the trouble he's been in started the first time he read that he was a "sublime satirist" and a first-rate artist. He believed every word of it and tried to live and think accordingly.

One reason I never took extravagant praise seriously was because neither I, my director, nor my gagmen were writers in any literary sense. The writers most often on my staff were Clyde Bruckman, Joe Mitchell, and Jean Havez. They never wrote anything but gags, vaudeville sketches, and songs. I don't think any of them ever had his name on a book, a short story, or even an article in a fan magazine, entitled, "How to Write Gags for the Movies."

They were not word guys, at all.

They didn't have to be. The only words we had to write were for the title and subtitles. The fewer subtitles we used the better it was for the picture. What made audiences laugh at our silent comedies was what they watched happening on the screen. The sight gags we used served to bring out the absurdity of things, people's actions, the preposterous situations the movie characters got into and had to escape.

From time to time we brought famous and talented writers from New York. I do not recall a single one of these novelists, magazine writers, and Broadway playwrights who was able to write the sort of material we needed. An example is Al Boasberg. When the talkies came in Al Boasberg became the best-paid gag writer in Hollywood, a walking marvel of verbal firecrackers and yak-getting wows. But he had been a terrible flop when he tried to do sight gags for us. So were a hundred other writers we imported from New York. It is possible, of course, that we kept sending for the wrong ones.

I always thought that Otto Soglow, the cartoonist who draws "The Little King," would have made a great success dreaming up sight gags for us. But I never was able to complete the arrangements to bring him to the Coast.

Bugs Baer is another one who could not have missed. I think he would have made the same sensation writing sight gags as he scored with the daily humorous columns he is still doing for the Hearst newspapers.

I actually did manage in 1922 to hire Bugs Baer to write gags for me. I had gone to New York to attend the World Series that fall and ran into Bugs at the Friars Club. He told me he was very sore at Hearst at the moment. When I offered him a job he accepted it immediately.

Though eager to work with me, Bugs explained that he was getting married and would be away for two or three weeks on his honeymoon.

When he arrived at the studio I asked him where he and his bride had gone on their honeymoon. "Oh," he said, "we went to that place they call 'the bride's second disappointment,' you know, Niagara Falls."

Bugs had hardly picked out his desk when long-distance calls started flooding the studio switchboard. A procession of Western Union boys also began streaming in. It turned out that Bugs had told nobody in the Hearst organization that he was quitting. They had just found out about that and that he was working for me. Bugs's editors informed him that they had him sewed up under an iron-clad contract. The messages reminding him of this, ranged in tone and spirit from, "Come home, dear Bugs, come home to us now" to "Our lawyers will call on you tomorrow!"

As the day wore on the wires became more urgent. Any stranger reading them or listening in on the frantic incoming phone calls would have thought I had kidnaped Bugs Baer and was holding him for ransom. The Hearst executives had gone to my boss, Joe Schenck, for he wired me from New York, "Release Bugs Baer at once."

They also appealed to Will Hays, newly appointed czar of the Motion Picture Industry, and his wire read: "Bugs Baer is the exclusive property of William Randolph Hearst. He is to take the first train back to New York."

Bugs took the first train back to New York and kept right on going until he reached Europe, where he remained for two years, only returning to work for Hearst on being given a big raise.

Two years later, in 1924, I hired Robert E. Sherwood, then the movie critic of *Life*, the old humorous weekly, to write an original story for me. This was some years before Sherwood wrote *The Road to Rome*, his first Broadway comedy hit. One could tell, however, from the perceptive and amusing reviews he wrote that he had a true comedy mind. Bob had just been made managing editor of *Life* when I hired him. But he said he would come out to Hollywood and try to write a story for me during his two weeks' summer vacation. Bob was six feet four inches tall, but I'll leave it to the psychologists to decide if that was the reason the story he wrote centered around a skyscraper.

In Sherwood's story the skyscraper is only half-finished. I was operating the elevator that carried the masons and bricklayers and steelworkers up and down to their jobs. One day the pretty daughter of the architect comes to look over the building. She accepts my shy invitation to let me take her to the top of the structure where she can enjoy the beautiful view. While we are up there a strike is called. Every worker in the place walks out. One of the men shuts off the power that operates the workmen's elevator.

But I discover that the elevator is not working only when we try to start down. Nothing I can do will make it move. And so there we are, trapped, isolated, high above ground, in the heart of the world's largest city. It is the middle of winter, and no one knows we are up there.

As it gets dark we wave frantically at people in nearby buildings. They think we are very friendly characters and wave back.

It is the perfect situation for a Buster Keaton feature, with the indomitable little man facing what seem impossible odds. And Bob Sherwood had thought up some clever devices. He had me building a shelter for the girl and myself with pieces of sheet metal and some loose nuts and bolts I found lying around on top of a girder. I make a receptacle to catch rain water in. Also a crude trap for pigeons and sea gulls, using some crumbs I find at the bottom of my lunch pail for bait.

I write a note with the girl's lip rouge, and with beating hearts we watch this flutter down, almost into an open window, then into the hands of a man on the street who reads it. Thinking it a joke, he doesn't even look up, just shrugs and throws it away.

There was only one thing wrong with Sherwood's story. He couldn't think of a believable way to get us down from the top of the building, a place where we could not survive once snow fell. I told him that the finish couldn't be any simple thing like having me slide down the steel beams to the ground. Having a dirigible take us off the skyscraper would not do either. After all that build-up the audience would expect me to rescue the girl.

Sherwood went home without delivering the finish. His vacation was over, and he had to get back to his job in New York. Bob never did think of a finish. Neither could we.

I did not see Bob until sixteen years later. By that time he had written a whole sheaf of wonderful Broadway stage successes, including *The Road to Rome, Waterloo Bridge, Idiot's Delight, The Petrified Forest,* and *Abe Lincoln in Illinois.*

That day in 1940 I was sitting in the lobby of the Dorchester Hotel in London. Suddenly lanky Bob Sherwood came in through the street door. He saw me out of the corner of his eye, but didn't stop. However, as he passed he whispered, "Stop worrying, Buster, I'll get you down off that building yet!"

Even in those early days we pretested pictures by sneak previewing them before an audience. It was important that the audience not know they were seeing a picture never shown before. Otherwise they became self-conscious, and their reaction was correspondingly untrustworthy. After such a sneak preview I have cut out scenes that we had thought sidesplitting when we looked at them in the projection room. I have also left in scenes which I had considered weak, but which the audience greeted with hilarity.

A preview audience sometimes also told me when something might be added to help a picture. That proved to be the case with *The High Sign.* In that two-reeler I played the owner of a shooting gallery who is a brilliant shot. In it I hit bulls'-eyes, firing over my shoulder, standing on my head, and from a variety of other difficult positions. A man whose life is threatened by the Mafia finds out about this and hires me to protect him.

But the Mafia, also admiring my marksmanship, force me to join their secret organization against my will. As my first assignment they order me to kill the man who has just hired me to protect him from them.

One scene in *The High Sign* showed a man dropping a banana peel. When the audience saw me approaching they expected me to slip on it. But I didn't, and then passed right before the camera. I tried to get my laugh by using the Mafia's secret sign, thumbs held crossed under the nose with the hands spread out on both sides of the face. But this was like thumbing my nose at the audience, and saying, "Fooled you that time, didn't I?"

In the end, I decided that I had made the mistake of outsmarting the audience a little too much. But instead of cutting this scene out I added a shot. In this, after passing the camera and giving the sign, I slipped on a second banana peel somebody had dropped. That worked fine.

Fans earlier had taught me another thing about my work I had not known. A few fan letters to Roscoe asked why the little man in his pictures never smiled. We had been unaware of it. We looked at three two-reelers we'd done together and found it to be true. Later just for fun I tried smiling at the end of one picture. The preview audience hated it and hooted the scene. After that I never smiled again on stage, screen, or TV.

Like everyone else in the slapstick industry, the gagmen's favorite sport was playing practical jokes. They enjoyed best, of course, those they worked on other gagmen. They never tired of discussing the more successful ones like the ordeal Lex Neal, my old drinking pal from Muskegon, was put through when he bought a house. Some time before I had added Lex, who had been working in vaudeville as a song-and-dance man, to my writing staff. He worked out fine with us as a combination gagman, story constructionist, and title writer.

Though a bachelor Lex had the yearning of most hard-traveled vaudevillians for a home of his own. After extensive searching Lex found a $10,000 house he liked on the outskirts of Beverly Hills. He had saved up little money of his own, but I advancéd him some, and a Los Angeles bank loaned him the rest.

As the deal was being closed, Lex could talk of little else but the haven he had found for himself and what it would mean to him to putter around in his garden of a Sunday morning and be able to say to himself, "This is mine, by God! *Mine!*" He brought his friends out to see the house and was hurt if all of them didn't rave about it.

The day he moved in Lex gave a housewarming for his friends. The following morning Lex could talk of nothing but his home and his plans for changing and improving it. The houses on his street were similar, though not identical, and Lex thought a few little touches here and there would give it a quite different look. Little did he dream that Johnny Gray, a gag writer at Harold Lloyd's studio, was even then changing the look of his house by planting trees and bushes in front of it.

Lex could hardly wait until quitting time to start for home. He was quite irritated when he got a last minute invitation to a cocktail party. When he tried to beg off, the caller insisted and acted as though he would be insulted and deeply hurt if Lex didn't show up. I heard later that Lex was restless at the party and left after having only two or three drinks.

But when he finally got to his street he could not find his house. It was as though somebody had whisked it away during the night. He was unable to remember the exact address and searched his pockets hoping to find a scrap of paper on which he had written it down—but in vain.

Driving slowly up and down the street, over and over again, Lex stopped before each house and studied it carefully. But before very long he became aware that women and children in each home were watching every move he made.

It was obvious that his mysterious behavior was alarming them. He became apprehensive that they might telephone the police.

Not knowing what else to do he drove to my house and in some embarrassment told me the story. "Now what am I to do?" he asked. "My clothes are all in the house. I haven't even got a place to sleep tonight."

I suggested he stay over with me. "In the morning," I said, "you can call up the bank and get the address from them."

Lex didn't sleep much. Neither did I. All night I could hear him restlessly prowling up and down in the guest room. And how he hated to call up Mr. Frost at the bank the next day! But he finally did.

"Mr. Frost," he said, "do you remember that house you loaned me a few thousand dollars on last week?" He paused while Mr. Frost replied, then, "I've lost the address, Mr. Frost. Could you give it to me?"

After another pause, Lex scribbled something on a piece of paper. "Thanks, Mr. Frost," he said. But on hanging up and turning to me, he murmured, "Cheerful guy, that Mr. Frost. Wasn't even surprised. You'd think the people he lends money to mislaid their houses every day. I would never put much money in *that* institution. The people who run it are too frivolous."

I went with him to the address he had been given. It was easy to see why Lex had been unable to identify it. Someone had planted bushes and trees about ten feet tall all over the front yard. Six trees lined the little stone walk leading to the door, three on each side. There were two big bushes in front of the house and two more along the curb.

By then poor Lex was so rattled that he could not quite believe it was his house until he unlocked the door and saw his own furniture inside. I told him to relax, if he could, for a few hours before coming down to the studio.

Later when Lex reproached Johnny Gray he got no satisfaction at all. Johnny pretended to be deeply offended.

"That's the thanks I get from *you*," he said. "You are as ungrateful as all of my poor relatives put together. I spend a small fortune improving your property. And all I get for it is abuse."

When I said that everybody in the slapstick movie business played jokes on everybody else I was being conservative. I should have included props which never acted the same way twice when the camera's eye was on them.

Animals were even worse, being both temperamental and unpredictable. Even the more tranquil and seemingly well-adjusted mammoth beasts got capricious and flighty the minute you pointed a camera at one of them. Of course, you never could be quite sure the trainer who rented beasts to you on a daily basis was not responsible. After all, the longer it took to shoot the scenes his animals were in the more money he made.

The director of one of the Tarzan films once told me the sad story of what happened when he rented three hippos from a local zoo and had the trainer swim them into a lake. The monstrous beasts promptly disappeared.

The director asked, "Are they trying to commit suicide?"

"Oh," said the trainer, "I forgot to warn you that sometimes they dive to the bottom of a body of water like this. They love the mud at the bottom, you know, and bury themselves in it."

"For how long?" asked the director.

"Oh, just for a few days. They have to come up finally to breathe, you know."

Holding his head, the director asked, "Is there anything we can do to make them come up?"

"Well, if you disturb the mud enough they become irritated and rise to the surface."

The director thereupon sent several jittery members of his crew out with long poles to stir up the mud at the lake's bottom. The boys didn't seem too energetic. One of them said later, "The last thing in my life I want to do is irritate a herd of hippos."

In any event, nothing happened, and the whole company and crew sat at the lakeside for four days until the hippos finished their mud bath and came to the surface.

Birds can be completely unco-operative. In 1928, when Twentieth Century-Fox was making one of its first sound pictures, a rebellious rooster cost the company $50,000.

All Hobart Henley, the director of that picture, wanted this rooster to do was crow at daybreak, exactly as he did every morning. With sound itself still a novelty on the screen, any sort of familiar noise, bellow, squeak, bark, or scream was considered exciting. Henley thought it would be sensational if he could show his lovers' final clinch just as a rooster was crowing and dawn broke over the horizon. It would symbolize perfectly the wonderful future awaiting the boy and girl after all the hellish trouble they had been through in the picture.

Arrangements were made for the use of a poultry farm out in the San Fernando Valley. The farmer's best-looking rooster was selected to do the crowing. Shooting at daybreak meant that the two romantic leads, the director, his assistants, and other crew members had to be out at the farm several hours before the sun came up to make their preparations.

The rooster proved amiable enough about sitting on the fence. The sun also came up on schedule. But when Henley yelled, "Camera!" the bird became frightened and flew off the fence. By the time they got him back on the fence the sun was too high to make the scene.

With a sigh, Henley instructed everybody to return next morning at three again. "This time," he vowed, "we'll make sure that damn rooster can't fly away on us. We'll tie his feet to the fence with wire."

But on this second morning when the sun came up the rooster was so intent on freeing his feet of the wire that he did not crow.

"There is only one way to make that rooster crow," announced the cameraman, a know-it-all who now suddenly claimed he was born on a Kansas farm whose roosters for years had won all prizes at the County Fair. "You get a second rooster to crow. On hearing this, our rooster will get jealous and will try to outcrow him."

It was possibly a sound theory, but neither rooster uttered a sound on the following morning. "I forgot to tell you one thing, Hobart," the cameraman whispered to the director, "that was to have a lot of hens around so the roosters will have something to crow for." This resulted only in another failure. Either the hens placed on display were less alluring than anticipated or possibly the rooster was too fussy. The important thing was that once more he failed to crow.

At this stage of the crisis somebody in the crew recalled that there was an amateur performer in South Gate who might solve the whole situation. His specialty was imitating the birds and beasts of forest and farmyard. When a representative of the movie company went all the way out to South Gate, a remote Los Angeles suburb, to call on him this chap thought his fortune was made.

He told his wife, "My big movie break has come at last."

On arriving at the farm he kept asking for the make-up man. He was crushed when told he would need no make-up as they weren't going to photograph him crowing, as that would destroy the illusion they were seeking. He was just to imitate the rooster off stage.

The human rooster was a whiz, it turned out. The real rooster may have been too impressed to attempt to compete with him. Anyway once more he didn't crow, meaning the loss of another morning's work.

Though the farmer was enjoying all of these profitable delays and his wife was making pin money each morning providing breakfasts for the whole troupe, he was an honest man and explained at this point: "My rooster can see that it's a man crowing at him," he said. "That's why he refuses to crow back."

Henley decided to try just once more. This time he instructed the animal imitator to hide behind a corner of the farmhouse until the sun peeped over the horizon. He handed the fellow a big branch of sagebrush. "Just as the sun rises," he said, "stick out your head and crow like mad. But hold that branch in front of your face so the rooster won't know it's you."

That next morning, while preparing the breakfast for the crew, the farmer's wife looked out of the window and discovered a man she had never seen before crouching under her window. She took it for granted he was crazy because he was holding up a sagebrush before his face.

She telephoned the sheriff who hustled over, took in the scene with his own eyes, and demanded of the loiterer, "What do you think *you're* doing here?"

The bird and beast imitator assumed that the sheriff was one of Henley's aides. "Oh, I'm the rooster," he explained.

"Well, I'll take you to a place where you'll find some lovely hens," said the sheriff. Without further ado, he rushed off the man from South Gate to the lockup to await a sanity hearing.

When Henley discovered that his rooster imitator had vanished, he gave up the whole idea. He let his lovers kiss for the fade-out without the aid of a cock saluting the dawn.

My own experiences with animal movie actors were at times just as exasperating. The first of these occurred while I was making a two-reeler with Roscoe Arbuckle called *The Bellhop.* In this story we were running a hotel, assisted by Alice Lake.

The climactic scene was a bank robbery. After pulling off this job the robbers, making their getaway, jumped on a horsecar that was going up hill on a cobblestone street. They forced the driver to whip up his steed. The big moment was supposed to come near the top of the hill when the traces broke, jerking the driver through the air so that he landed squarely on the horse's back. Meanwhile the horsecar with the bandits still aboard rolled downhill right into the bank they'd just held up. But the driver missed the horse's back the first time he tried it.

When the driver proved a bit shy about repeating the jump, I offered to double for him. It was a tough jump to make because the horse had to be kept four and a half feet ahead of the car. This prevented his kicking the front of it with his hind hoofs.

I had the prop man put a box in the car for me to stand on.

This enabled me to make a better take-off. I also wound the reins tightly around my wrists so they couldn't slip.

Not being horsy people we didn't know that horses can see backward or that this one may have resented being jumped at by the first driver. Otherwise we would have put blinders on him. If we had he couldn't have seen me coming and neatly stepped to one side, causing me to miss him completely.

He was a mean critter, pardners, that innocent-looking horse. The moment I jumped he bolted like mad up the street, dragging me bumpety-bump on my chest over the cobbles for almost a block before anybody could stop him.

Even after that experience, I expected no trouble from a sway-backed old mare we bought for *Cops*, one of my two-reelers. By that time, incidentally, the studios were buying the livestock they needed. It was cheaper than renting them, they had found, and they could sell the animals when the picture was finished.

In *Cops* I was a New York junkman, and we bought a spiritless, broken-down horse to pull my wagon. In the picture the nag was supposed to be deaf. We put earphones on her, connected by wire with an old-fashioned telephone box on the side of the wagon. When I wanted the horse to stop or move, I picked up the phone, cranked it, then said, "Whoa!" or "Giddap!", and she immediately obeyed these orders.

The plot had me picking up unknowingly a homemade bomb. This explodes just as I am crossing Fifth Avenue during a police parade. In the chase the entire New York police force pursues me. One of the last scenes was supposed to show the horse riding in the wagon with me between the shafts pulling it.

The horse was the soul of co-operation until we tried to get her to walk up the ramp into the wagon for that scene. Then she balked. I had a crane brought to the studio, planning to hoist her up by putting a veterinarian's saddle under the horse.

We got the vet's saddle under her all right, but the moment we tried to lift her off the ground Old Dobbin started kicking away viciously at everything and everybody.

We were on location. It was Saturday, and we took her back to the studio. I decided we would have to find another horse that resembled her to double for her on Monday. But when we returned to work on Monday we found a new-born colt standing beside her. As has happened in many another case, mother knew best in this instance.

Somebody, we figured, ought to tell us about the birds and bees. The foal was perfectly healthy and friendly. And his mother now walked up the ramp like a real trouper, and we finished the picture in jig time.

We called the little fellow "Onyx," short for unexpected, and he became the pet of the lot. He would walk into my dressing room, or on the set to see what was going on, or into Lou Anger's office to find out if the bookkeepers were on the job.

Old Mother Nature made a shambles of my shooting schedule later on when I made *Go West!* In this I played a tenderfoot whose life is saved by a cow.

Weather is only one of the hazards of working outdoors. Anything at all can happen from the moment you take your camera out of the studio. When you worked outdoors with a cow as your leading lady you were really asking for trouble. But I always preferred working on location because more good gags suggested themselves in new and unfamiliar surroundings.

The cow we bought for this great honor was a Holstein. She was a beautiful creature, and I named her "Brown Eyes." But as she did not appear to be any more intelligent than other Holsteins I took great pains in training her for her new work. It was summer, and the location was on the desert near Kingdon, Arizona, a place so hot at midday that you have to pack ice around your camera to prevent the emulsion on the film from melting.

I began my training of Brown Eyes by leading her around the studio on a rope. I continually fed her carrots and other culinary delights for bovines. When she became convinced that following me about paid off big, I substituted a string for rope and finally a thread for the string.

I never had a more affectionate pet or a more obedient one. After a while I was able to walk her through doors, in and out of sets, even past bright lights. The only difficulty we had was when I sat down and she tried to climb into my lap. I didn't take her on location until I had her perfectly trained to obey my orders.

Everything went fine until we got Brown Eyes out there on the

When only nine months old, as you can see, I had my heart set on keeping my face in a deep freeze. "Smile at *what* birdie?" is what I was trying to ask the photographer.

I was six when another photographer tried to distract me with a toy and a painted seashore backdrop. He too said "Smile, Buster!" but the most I would give him was my Mona Lisa look.

"The Three Keatons" when it was the roughest, rowdiest act in vaudeville and featured your Buster and mine as "the human mop."

All of us five Keatons — Louise, Mom, Jingles, me, and Pop — at the start of my happy and golden years in Hollywood.

A still from *The Butcher Boy,* the two-reeler starring Roscoe "Fatty" Arbuckle, in which I made my screen debut in 1917. That's me on the extreme right, trying to pull Arbuckle away from the menacing pitchfork wielded by Al St. John.

A cliff-hanging scene with Fatty made for another of his two-reelers, this one on location in California. Arbuckle, the best friend I ever had, taught me everything I ever knew about making movies.

We had the New York subway going to Alaska in my own two-reeler *The Frozen North*. This was a travesty on the enormously popular William S. Hart Westerns. Bill Hart did not speak to me for two years after he saw it.

Henry Ford did not speak to me for ten years after he saw what I did on the screen to this Model-T job of his. As he had never spoken to me before that anyway — I didn't care. The shot is from my 1923 feature *The Three Ages*.

These two scenes are from one of the last two-reelers I ever made, *The Balloonatic*.

Big families and seagoing cars got belly laughs in the early twenties. I was a pint-sized caveman with a gigantic wife and eleven kids in *Three Ages* (1923). The still below is from *Sherlock, Jr.*, made the following year.

Kathryn McGuire, my leading lady in *Sherlock, Jr.*, who took that wild car ride through the lake with me, gives me back my engagement ring. This was the feature in which I broke my neck but was too busy to notice it until some years later.

In *The Navigator* (1924) I boil an egg. This and *The General* were the most popular pictures I ever made.

Another shot from *The Navigator*. Though moviegoers laughed at this audacious defiance of the laws of gravity they disliked another gag in this movie so much that we had to take it out. In my opinion it was the funniest one I ever dreamed up.

If I had known how long this cow's personal love life would delay the production of *Go West* (1925) I would have shown her less affection.

I also made a mistake about that snake shown here crawling around my neck in *Go West*. I assumed it was my leading lady's ever-loving arm.

In *The General* (1927) I was a wistful and lovelorn Confederate soldier.

My curiosity about why this big Civil War cannon was not working properly got me a big laugh in *The General*. Another shot from
the same comedy is shown below.

With Florence Turner, playing my mother, in *College* (1927). Below, I am shown with Ernest Torrence in *Steamboat Bill, Jr.*, which was made the following year. We had decided to finish *Steamboat Bill, Jr.* with a flood, but at the last minute my producer decided that would be too harrowing on the audience and we settled for a hurricane as a more restful type of calamity to watch.

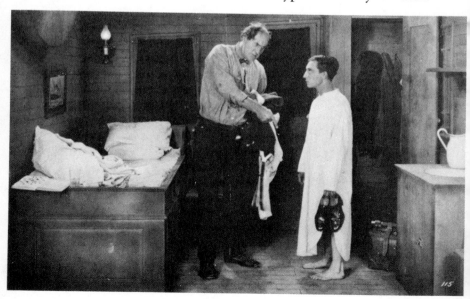

I played a tintype photographer who cherished dreams of becoming a crack newsreel man in *The Cameraman* (1928) and winning the love and admiration of beautiful Marceline Day, who is shown with me here both above and below. I also had the delusion that New York had given me a ticker-tape parade, but it turned out to be for an obscure stunt flier, fellow named Lindbergh, who had just flown solo across the Atlantic.

In 1939 they needed a custard pie thrower in *Hollywood Caval-cade*, a picture about the old silent Mack Sennett era, and they called in the champ — shown here. My most perilous assignment on that job turned out to be giving beautiful Alice Faye the full treatment when she didn't expect it.

A recent photograph, showing Mr. and Mrs. Buster Keaton arriving in New York for four months of dates on Ed Sullivan's and other television shows.

This was taken of me with Zsa Zsa Gabor in Paris, in front of the Moulin Rouge, just before this book was published. If Toulouse-Lautrec ever had it so good, he never mentioned it in *his* memoirs.

steaming hot desert. There I couldn't do a thing with her, not one thing. We were mystified until a rancher told us, "That cow's in heat. She won't be a bit of use to you until she's over that."

"How long does that take?" I asked.

"Oh," he said, "about ten days or so."

We had thirty people in the unit on location. The idea of how daily expenses would mount while we waited for that cow to get her mind off sex was dismaying.

We had selected Brown Eyes because of her unusual beauty and striking markings. She had been in too many scenes already to start looking for another Holstein to double for her. I did the only sensible thing. I ordered her let out of the corral so she could find an affectionate and empathy-loaded bull for herself. She picked a bull, but he was not affectionate. In fact he snubbed her by walking away.

The cattle on that ranch were Baldfaced beef cattle, and had not been dehorned like our dear little Brown Eyes. However, I never suspected bulls were so clannish and choosy.

We turned our lovelorn bossy out again. This time, not only did she fail to attract the Baldfaced bulls, but she aroused the jealous wrath of the Baldfaced cows who started to charge her. They would have gored Brown Eyes, too, except for the interference of some ranch cowboys who rode up just in time to save her.

There was nothing to do after that but wait for our cow to get out of heat. We spent our time taking shots of the lovely country all around us but later never figured out how to use that film. When Brown Eyes finally was ready to turn her attention to movie-making again we did fine with her.

Joe Schenck heard about our wait and said the sort of things bosses usually say after budget-busting incidents. In this case: "That's Keaton for you! If there is a costly way to make a movie he'll find it."

143

THE DAY
THE LAUGHTER
STOPPED

Though Mack Sennett made his stage debut as the rear end of a horse, he considered his judgment of comedy infallible. "I have my fingers on the public pulse," he was fond of saying. "If I laugh at a gag on the screen I know the public will laugh."

Mack always enjoyed playing a role in each picture he made, but he got no encouragement from his comedians who told him that he was the unfunniest man ever to walk in front of a camera. But it took them years to convince him.

The mystery is how this seemingly humorless man managed to find and develop more first-rate comic talent than anyone else in the history of show business.

Some students of Sennett's career try to explain his unique gift by saying he was in the market when great screen comics were available in quantity.

That's true enough. But it is difficult to remember one performer comparable to Arbuckle and Chaplin and the other great comics who came out of the Keystone fun factory who was developed by the other screen comedy producers who were also around then. Not to be overlooked, too, are the great directors—Frank Capra, Leo McCarey, Malcolm St. Clair and Roy del Ruth—who first learned their business while working with Sennett.

I have mentioned that Sennett's refusal to pay high salaries invariably lost him his great stars as they became prominent. His Keystone Cops, even after he had been coining money with them for years, remained the worst-paid performers in Hollywood. At first they got only three dollars a day for risking their necks. After Sennett made a fortune with *Tillie's Punctured Romance* he raised them to five dollars a day.

The Cops were dreamers. All of them lived on the hope of becoming a star or a featured player one day. Every time I saw them on the screen I howled with delight which, of course, broke my rule against being caught laughing in public. Even so, I couldn't understand how they could ever expect to attract attention as individuals, to stand out in the crowd. They were wonderful, in my opinion, but only as a group. In the same way, say, as the Radio City Rockettes in New York are. It turned out, of course, that I couldn't have been more wrong, for a great many of them did become stars or featured players.

Even more astonishing to me was discovering how few of them knew the first thing about taking a fall. The ex-Keystone Cop, Al St. John, for example, worked side by side with Roscoe for five years without learning one damn thing about protecting himself in a fall. As an old trip-and-tumble expert myself I advised St. John to use elbow pads, something he had never heard of until then. He had been using his hands and elbows each time to break his falls. The result was that he was continually suffering from water on the elbow which, of course, was bound to have serious consequences sooner or later.

Hank Mann, one of Sennett's best comics, was dragged by a horse across a just-plowed field and a couple of city blocks when he tried something new. The horse was supposed to jerk him off his wagon, causing Mann to fly through the air. Without telling anyone of his inspiration Hank decided to turn over while in the air. If he had succeeded he probably would have broken his back. He escaped this only because his trick failed, although he got plenty bruised and bumped before the horse was stopped. Hank also had tightly wrapped the reins around his wrists to make sure he wouldn't let go of them while astonishing everyone with his new trick.

There are few bigger hams, by the way, than these horses. Their ears go up and they are off to the races when they hear the cry, "Camera!" If the leading lady happens to be sitting sidesaddle for the moment it makes no difference; they will prance, bolt, and throw her off like a limp dishrag. That could mean so limp a leading lady that you'd have to get yourself a brand-new one.

One reason Sennett did not hire trained acrobats for his Keystone force was because a trained acrobat seldom can get laughs in pictures when taking a comedy fall. He looks what he is, a trained acrobat doing his stuff, instead of a character in the picture taking a tumble accidentally. The only trained acrobat I ever saw who could take a fall and make it look funny was Poodles Hanneford, the great circus clown.

Though I have been called an acrobat I would say I am only a half acrobat, at most. I did learn to fall as a kid, just as Chaplin, Lloyd, and Fairbanks did. And I taught myself a few acrobatic tricks, including the round-off back somersault and other simple stunts. I could do butterflies, a series of cartwheels in a circle, without touching hands to the floor. But anyone who ever saw me throw a flip-flap realized I wasn't a professional acrobat. Audiences think a back somersault, in which you regain your feet without touching the floor, is difficult. But much more difficult to do is the flip-flap, a back somersault in which your hands do touch the floor. The back somersault only looks harder. What I do know about is body control. When you start to go through the air your head is your rudder—it steers you. If Steve Brodie had mastered body control he could have jumped off Brooklyn Bridge and had a good chance of surviving, instead of just pretending to have made that jump. The man who jumps or dives has control of his body but, of course, if he is pushed, thrown, or falls accidentally he has none at all. That is why a man falling off a ladder can be terribly hurt.

In my opinion, even Doug Fairbanks was merely a superior YMCA acrobat. His leaps and other acrobatics made him look better than he was, because Fairbanks thoroughly understood camera angles and used them most effectively.

The Cops, though, knew nothing whatever about falling. Seemingly no one had told them that *both* ends of the spine have to be protected when taking a fall. Or that for one kind of fall you must relax your whole body, for another you tighten up the muscles of both your back and backside.

Jimmy Bryant, who had been the anchor man for the Cops, was another doughty fellow who did not know how to take a fall. The fact is that Bryant did not even know how to turn a cartwheel, a trick most nine-year-old American boys learn quickly after they first turn a somersault. Jimmy, a heavy-set man with a bull neck, was the only Keystone Cop who looked like a real policeman. Along with Al St. John, Jimmy left Sennett to work with Roscoe when Arbuckle started making his own two-reelers.

I discovered just how much punishment Bryant was willing to absorb to stay in pictures in one of the earliest Arbuckle two-reelers I was in. I think it was called *His Wedding Night.*

This picture opened in a room above a general store where the girl is fitting her wedding dress on me, using me as a clothing form. The villain's roughnecks rush into the room to kidnap her. But she has just gone to the next room to get some pins. They mistake me for the bride-to-be because I have on the wedding dress, and carry me out the window and roll me down a slanting roof. On the street below Jimmy Bryant is waiting with a seagoing hack. As he waits to catch "the girl" in his arms he braces himself with one foot on the ground, the other on the step of the hack. I was supposed to fall on him headfirst. He was supposed to try to catch me, and miss. We seldom rehearsed bone-breaking scenes like that one. It was too easy for someone in the scene to be hurt or badly injured. Even if not put out of action the bruised man might dog his work the second time. For the same reason we tried to avoid retakes.

But Roscoe, who was directing, didn't like the way we did this scene. As we were getting ready for the repeat shot, Jimmy Bryant came over to me and whispered, "I don't know how to take off on this one or how to take this fall. So really *hit* me so it will look all right."

"I'll hit you all right," I said. "But be sure and get a good hold."

As I fell on him I shoved him with both feet as hard as I could. Jimmy hit the ground, going backward, head over heels. He kept on going for about twenty feet, far out of camera range. Meanwhile, I had landed on the hack's two facing seats. One of the roughnecks, Joe Bordeaux, to make sure that the "bride-to-be" would not escape jumped off the slanting roof and landed on top of me.

Typically, it did not occur to anyone there to ask Jimmy if he was hurt. But if someone had, he would not have complained. Later on, when I had my own company, Jimmy worked with me in many of my pictures. I was able eventually to put him on the regular payroll as a $125-a-week cameraman. Jimmy was a puzzler. He was intelligent enough to learn all about the intricate film camera. But somehow he just never learned to fall properly and kept taking the punishment like some battered old club fighter right to the end of his acting days.

The Keystone Cop who seemed to me the most courageous and lionhearted of them all was little Bobby Dunn, a professional diving champion who was only five feet four inches tall. Bobby joined the Cops one season when the demand for carnival high divers was slack, and Sennett kept him on because of his agility and fearlessness. He placed Bobby next to Slim Summerville, his tallest Keystone Cop, because they looked so funny standing together.

The bravest stunt Bobby ever did, though, was not in a Sennett picture. It was in one of the Sunshine Comedies Henry (Pathé) Lehrman was making just then for Fox.

On hearing that Bobby was a professional high diver, Lehrman offered him five dollars to jump off the Hotel Bryson roof into a mortar box full of water. The Bryson, in downtown Los Angeles, was eight stories, and from its roof eighty feet above the street the mortar box, which was nine feet long, five feet wide, and five feet deep, looked about the size of a domino.

When Bobby accepted the offer Lehrman asked him if he could make the jump on that Friday afternoon. "I'm making a picture for Sennett all this week," he said thoughtfully. "They'll be shooting on Friday, but I doubt that they'll be using the Cops that afternoon. I'll be able to sneak out all right."

Bobby made the dive headfirst. Diving eighty feet into water five feet deep meant he must hit just right with his chest, then immediately cut upward in an arc. He came up without a scratch, collected his five dollars, dressed, and hurried back to the Sennett lot before he could be missed.

Those two, Bobby Dunn and Slim Summerville, the tiniest and the tallest of the Keystone Cops, were inseparable. They shared a dressing room and never tired of playing all sorts of tricks on one another. The dressing room faced an open shooting stage. On the other side of this was a roofed passageway.

One day, while they were sitting in their dressing room, Summerville remarked, "Did you get a load of that Palm Beach suit and new straw hat that Ben Turpin is wearing today?"

Bobby Dunn nodded his head and said, "He'll be coming to work in a dress suit next thing you know."

"Let's fix him," suggested Slim with a giggle. "I just saw him go through that arch. He'll be coming back in a couple of minutes. Why don't we get a pail of water, then you can get on the roof over there and dump the water on him as he walks through?"

"Well, how will I know he's coming?"

"I'll sit in the doorway here, Bobby, where you can see me. When I take out my handkerchief, give it to him good. Okay?"

"Okay!" said Bobby, and in a jiffy he was on the roof with his pail of water. On getting the signal from Slim, he dumped the water. But Mack Sennett, not Ben Turpin, happened to be the man who was passing through and got the dousing. Later Slim swore to Bobby it was a case of mistaken identity. Sennett was twice as big as the cross-eyed Mr. Turpin, but Bobby did not argue with his best friend.

A few nights later Slim and Bobby were enjoying a few drinks in the Vernon Country Club, a favorite drinking spot for Keystone Cops and other local characters who enjoyed staying out late. Los Angeles had an early closing hour, but Vernon, just beyond the city limits, had none. Bobby that evening bribed the club's bartender to put double shots of whiskey into Slim Summerville's highballs. The supercharged drinks soon made Slim so drowsy he fell asleep at the table.

Bobby got out pencil and paper and wrote a note which he asked the waiter to give to a girl at a nearby table. She was with a man who had the shoulders of a gorilla. She read the note, then passed it on to him. It said:

"Why don't you get rid of that big bum you're with? Don't look around now, but I'm at a table right behind you, pretending to be asleep. I'll meet you out at the back door in ten minutes."

"Who is this wise guy?" he asked. She looked around, saw the sleeping Summerville, and shrugged. "I never saw that funny-looking string bean before in my whole life."

Her boy friend got up, walked back to the sleeping Slim, and grabbed him by the throat. The next thing Slim knew he was out the back door and flying through the air. On hitting the hard, hard cement he looked up to find Bobby Dunn's smiling face peering down at him.

"What in heaven's name happened?" he asked.

"Don't give it a thought," Bobby told him. "It's just one of them California earthquakes."

(Later I got a big laugh in my feature picture *Three Ages* by using this note-writing incident. I had Wallace Beery, the villain of that movie, write the note while I slept at the table.)

When Bobby Dunn died his tall, skinny pal was inconsolable. Slim cried like a baby, and he paid more money than he could afford for a funeral wreath. On the way to the church for the funeral ceremonies Slim picked up his mail and during the services kept nervously opening the letters and glancing at them. He lined up with the other mourners to bid a last good-by to the deceased before the casket was closed. As he passed the body he waved over the dead man's face the bill he'd just got from the florist for the flowers.

"See this?" he sobbed brokenly. "Even when you are dead you cost me money, you little sonofabitch."

Then his knees buckled, and he would have fallen if the man next to him hadn't held him up. With tears streaming down Slim

Summerville's long face, he was half-carried to one of the waiting funeral cars.

As far back as I can remember baseball has been my favorite sport. I started playing the game as soon as I was old enough to handle a glove. A sand lot where baseball was being played was the first thing I looked for whenever The Three Keatons played a new town. We always had a team in Muskegon, and later I organized baseball teams at my own studio and at M-G-M. I also played in the annual Comedians-Leading Men games that amused Hollywood for years. Each September I did my best to finish my fall picture in time to go to New York for the World Series.

I took Marcus Loew to one crucial World Series game back in the twenties. In the eighth inning, with the Yankees one run behind, they got two men on base and had Babe Ruth at bat. Nobody in the crowd of 68,000 tense fans seemed to be breathing when Marcus turned, looked over the packed stands, shook his head, and said, "You know, Buster, this raises hell with our matinees!"

I loved the yearly Comedians-Leading Men benefit games played in Hollywood each year, because they gave me a chance to combine baseball and comedy, the two great loves of my life. But I suppose none of these could compare with the mad routines Roscoe, Al St. John, and myself put on during a "one ol' cat" game at the Vernon Baseball Park.

Vernon then held the franchise in the Pacific Coast League which was later transferred to Hollywood. A brewer owned the club, and he had talked Roscoe into investing a few thousand dollars in the organization. The brewer also suggested we put on a little show before the opening game of the season.

We started with Roscoe pitching, Al St. John at bat, me catching, and Rube Miller, a one-time Keystone Cop, umpiring behind the plate. After Roscoe threw two perfect strikes, which Umpire Rube Miller called balls, I signaled to Roscoe for a high one. When it came I let it go right through my hands. It hit Miller square on the mask. He did a typical Keystone Cop leap into the air and fell backward. His mask rolled off, and he lay as though dead.

Though we ignored him and let him lie there, he came to life in time to join us in the next play. In this Al St. John kept creeping up a little closer to the pitcher's box each time Roscoe started to wind up. Arbuckle would get discouraged, would stop, look, then start winding up again. Each time the batter took another little step forward both Rube Miller and I would follow close behind him, maintaining the traditional crouch. By the time Al St. John was almost halfway to the pitcher's box Roscoe decided he better take a few steps back himself. When he finally threw the ball he was pitching almost from second base. The ball (made of plaster of Paris at our studio) exploded into dust and vanished the moment St. John whacked it. Pitcher Arbuckle, Catcher Keaton, and Umpire Miller looked everywhere for the vanished ball, in the air, in our pockets, in the pants of Roscoe's capacious uniform and under Umpire Miller's chest protector. Meanwhile Al St. John had streaked for first base, stopping there to bow and tip his hat to the spectators. Going to second, to third, and home he stopped at each bag to acknowledge the plaudits of the crowd.

On Al getting to bat again, Arbuckle wound up. But before he could throw the pitch, a ball dropped from the sky at his feet. It came down five to ten minutes after the ball was hit. It was, of course, a regular Coast League baseball thrown by an unseen outfielder from back of the grandstand. And now I tried to tag out St. John and a general melee and hubbub followed.

There were other surprise features, including a bat loaded with gunpowder which exploded when Arbuckle hit the ball and sent it spinning out into the wild blue yonder, farther than any ball hit by Ruth, Gehrig, or Mickey Mantle. And a little ceremony in which Umpire Miller was dumped into a grave we had prepared for him back of third base. After that, the season's opening game began.

The ballplayers enjoyed all of this clowning, but not the umpires. They got hold of the four of us after the League game was over and gave us hell. One said, "You have given the players murderous ideas with that pitch you let go into the umpire's mask. They will all be trying that within a month in every ball park in the league. We will have to bench every catcher in the Pacific Coast before the season is over."

Few of us in that whole Hollywood gang had had time to acquire an education. I suppose we were doing the things in our twenties that we would have done earlier if we'd gone to high school and college. We also drank a lot just as young people all over the country were doing as the Riproaring Twenties rolled in on endless barrels of bootleg booze.

There was a period when our whole gang, meaning Roscoe Arbuckle, Norman Kerry, Buster Collier, Lew Cody, and a few others, were barred from half of the movie lots in Hollywood. One of the studios was Samuel Goldwyn's.

The bars went up there the morning after a party at Goldwyn's house that Kerry, Buster Collier, and I attended. Collier started to tell about his grappling match with a professional wrestler in the picture he was making. In telling a story, Buster could be almost as spellbinding as Willie Collier, his father. When he mentioned a hammer lock Frances Goldwyn, Sam's wife, kept asking so many questions about it that Buster finally said, "It will save time if I demonstrate it."

Frances laughingly suggested he demonstrate it on her. While showing Mrs. Goldwyn the hammer lock, she resisted, and the next thing anyone knew they were scuffling and rolling around on the floor. Everyone was laughing and enjoying this when Goldwyn, who had been playing cards in another room, walked in. He stared at them, said, "Oh, my!" and walked out. Norman Kerry, who was standing next to me, said, "Well, that's one more lot we are barred from, Buster."

But one day in September 1921, all of the laughter in Hollywood stopped. Overnight what had been innocent fun was suddenly being denounced as "another Hollywood drunken orgy" or "one more shocking example of sex depravity." The day our laughter stopped was the day Roscoe Arbuckle was accused of having caused the death of Virginia Rappe, a Hollywood bit player and girl about town, in his suite at the St. Francis Hotel, in San Francisco. They'd had several weekend dates together, but there had been no arrangements made for this one. She just happened to be up in San Francisco at the time.

The full poignancy of what followed can be grasped only when one considers how touched with magic Arbuckle's life had been during the years he had been a movie actor. Roscoe was born in Smith Corners, Kansas, on March 24, 1887, which meant he was only thirty-four when catastrophe overwhelmed him. He was a small child when his family moved to California and at eight made his stage debut in San Jose with the stock company of Frank Bacon. If he ever went back to school after that it was not for long. He did anything he could to stay in show business: was a ticket taker at one theatre, sang sentimental ballads in a nickelodeon, worked as a smalltime vaudeville blackface monologuist up and down the West Coast.

Roscoe got his first movie job by dancing up the steps to a porch where Sennett was standing with Mabel Normand and casually doing some back flips. Sennett, thinking a policeman that fat might be very funny, put him on as a Keystone Cop at three dollars a day. His fame started shortly afterward when he appeared with Mabel Normand in a series of shorts called *Fatty and Mabel*. Roscoe had been with Sennett for four years when Schenck gave him his own unit. Yet it was only when he started doing features for Famous Players-Lasky that Roscoe Arbuckle got into the big money. Then it became very big money indeed, $7,000 a week.

Jesse Lasky was in charge of that studio which later became Paramount. In his autobiography, *I Blow My Own Horn*, he calls Arbuckle "conscientious, hard-working, intelligent, always agreeable and anxious to please," and adds, "He would invent priceless routines and also had a well-developed directorial sense."

Once Lasky handed Roscoe the tough assignment of doing three feature pictures in a row without a day's rest in between.

"I don't know of another star," said Lasky, "who would have submitted to such exorbitant demands on his energy. But Fatty Arbuckle wasn't one to grumble. There were no temperamental displays in his repertoire. He went through the triple assignment like a whirling dervish, in his top form. They were the funniest pictures he ever made. We were sure they would reap a fortune. . . ."

It was on finishing that backbreaking triple assignment that Roscoe drove up to San Francisco in his $25,000 Rolls Royce for the Labor Day weekend. With him were the actor Lowell Sherman and Fred Fischbach, a comedy director. San Francisco always has been a high-rolling good-time town but never more so than in the early twenties when flouting Prohibition became the new competitive sport. Roscoe checked into a large suite at the St. Francis. Friends and free-loaders, including several of San Francisco's most important officials flocked there the moment news got around that Arbuckle, that prince of a fat man, was in town. Roscoe liked nothing better than playing host to all comers. He ordered three cases of the best whiskey and gin obtainable and all sorts of food sent up to his suite.

The day was hot, and he had put on pajamas with a dressing gown over them. Among his guests that weekend was Virginia Rappe, the twenty-five-year-old Hollywood bit player. She had a reputation for getting hysterical and tearing off her clothes after taking a few drinks.

On hearing Roscoe was in town, Virginia joined Arbuckle's party with an older woman and her own manager, Al Seminacher. After her death, everyone in Hollywood who knew Virginia was surprised to read newspaper descriptions of her as a frail little flower, a starlet whom death had robbed of the chance to achieve the heights on the silver screen. The truth is that Virginia was a big-boned, husky young woman, five feet seven inches tall, who weighed 135 pounds. She was about as virtuous as most of the other untalented young women who had been knocking around Hollywood for years, picking up small parts any way they could.

After taking a couple of orange blossoms, a cocktail made of orange juice and gin, Virginia got sick. Most of the persons present testified later that she had started to tear off her clothes. She also complained of feeling ill. Roscoe had a couple of girls—one was the woman Virginia had arrived with—take her into the bedroom. He joined the three of them a little later and found Virginia in bed. Suspecting she might be faking he placed a bit of ice against her thigh. She failed to react, and he asked the women in the room to undress her and put her in the tub. When Virginia continued ill, Roscoe sent for the St. Francis's house physician.

Virginia was removed to a hospital where she died a few days later. According to her woman friend, she had kept moaning just before she died, "He hurt me. Roscoe hurt me." It was largely on the basis of this statement that Roscoe was requested to come back to San Francisco for questioning by District Attorney Matthew Brady. He returned immediately, accompanied by Lou Anger and Frank Dominguez, an associate of Earl Rogers, California's most famous criminal attorney.

On September 12, a Coroner's Jury returned a true bill against Arbuckle charging manslaughter. He was jailed, held without bail until he was arraigned in a police court. Then the district attorney demanded that the charge be changed to murder. On the plea of Dominguez this was refused. The official charge became "involuntary manslaughter," and Roscoe was released in $5,000 bail.

Realizing the seriousness of Roscoe's situation, Joe Schenck tried to get the fabulous courtroom spellbinder Rogers to take over the case himself. But Rogers, old and sick and near death, begged off. He told Schenck, "Arbuckle's weight will damn him. He will become a monster. They'll never convict him. But this will ruin him, and maybe motion pictures also for some time. I cannot take the case but prepare Hollywood for tornadoes."

The tornadoes were already exploding all around us by then. Along with other friends of Roscoe's, I offered to go to San Francisco to testify. Among the nasty rumors circulated was one that Arbuckle had pushed the piece of ice into the girl's private parts, thus contributing to her death. As Roscoe's intimate friend I knew that any such obscene act would have been beyond him. I was eager to tell the jury this and also to explain that it was I who had first told Roscoe that ice held against a person's thigh was the quickest way to discover whether they were faking illness.

Mr. Dominguez talked us out of going to the trial. He said that there was bitter feeling in San Francisco even against him for taking a case that local people felt should have gone to one of their own lawyers. "They would resent you fellows even more," he said, "and discount your evidence, feeling you were merely Arbuckle's front men."

Meanwhile an unprecedented storm of hatred and bitterness was sweeping the country against Arbuckle. Before he even was tried his films were barred in many communities including New York City. Reform groups everywhere threatened to boycott any theatre which exhibited Roscoe's movies. Churches of many denominations rocked with their preachers' denunciations of the famous funny man. At a meeting of the League of Nations in Geneva, Switzerland, a Danish delegate, Mrs. Forchhammer, dragged Arbuckle's name into a discussion of international white slavery.

Adolph Zukor and other producers of Arbuckle films received such a flood of abusive and condemnatory mail from Roscoe's former fans that they were frightened into promising that none of his pictures would ever be shown again. With all of this came persistent threats of national censorship. The studio heads, hoping to avoid that, decided to ask Will Hays, United States Postmaster General, to become czar of their industry and to censor themselves. They chose Hays, who had also been President Harding's campaign manager, because he was the most influential politician in the United States.

In all, there were three trials of Roscoe Arbuckle in San Francisco for manslaughter. The first two resulted in hung juries. In the third he was acquitted by a jury that said he deserved an apology from those who had wrecked his career with the baseless charge of contributing to the death of Virginia Rappe.

Before his first trial started, he had returned to Los Angeles to await the start of court proceedings. With some other of his close friends I went to meet him at the old Santa Fe Railroad Station in Los Angeles.

So did a hate-frenzied mob of 1500 men and women who seemed to want only to get close enough to tear him to pieces. And they yelled at the fat man they had loved so much a few weeks before, "Murderer!" "Big, fat slob!" "Beast!" and "Degenerate bastard!" Some in the crowd had come to cheer him, but they were drowned out in the din.

Roscoe never got over that experience. He never could forget how those people had looked at him and cursed him, how it had been necessary for the police to rush to protect him from them. People everywhere in the world seemed to feel the same way about him as that mob. By then the letters of abuse and vilification were flooding in from every country in the world.

However, there was one spot on earth where nobody hated Roscoe Arbuckle or thought he was guilty. That was Hollywood, the town so often pictured as turning on its own people whenever they get into trouble. What Hollywood did later on to encourage this bewildered, baby-faced fat man to stand on his feet and face the terrifying outside world might well be remembered, I think, by all of us.

MARRIAGE
AND PROSPERITY
SNEAK UP ON ME

Early in 1921 I broke my leg while making a two-reeler called *The Electric House.* The accident happened on a studio-made escalator when the sole of my slap shoe got caught in the webbing of the moving machine. As I got to the top of the escalator I was tossed for twelve feet, breaking my right leg. I was unable to go back to work for four months.

I had been discharged from the hospital but was still using a cane when I received a letter from my girl in New York: "I am alone now, the only one left living with mother. If you still care all you have to do is send for me."

We had had a sort of understanding for more than a year, but I hadn't seen her during all of that time and wished to think the whole thing over carefully. In the end I wired her that my leg was not yet strong enough for me to go to New York. However,

I added that Lou Anger and his wife were going to New York in about two weeks, and I'd travel with them.

That telegram started fireworks. All of the Louellas and Heddas of the day wrote that I was coming East to marry the girl. They weren't sure she would accept me or another ardent suitor. He was an enormously wealthy Chicago dairyman. "So which shall it be?" they wrote. "Will she choose Buster's custard pies or her Chicago beau's butter and eggs?"

Riding across the country, reading this kind of stuff in the papers we bought at the various stops, I understood for the first time the power of the press. When I saw my bride-to-be, the big butter-and-egg man was hardly mentioned. She had only one objection to marrying me. She hated to leave New York, something that was not hard to understand. New York then, at the beginning of the Riproaring Twenties, was the most exciting town on earth.

"Well, we gotta bring this thing to a head," I said.

She smiled and told me, "Oh, Buster, you know where I'm going."

"Okay, where and when will we be married?" I asked in a brisk, businesslike tone.

"Let's make it a week from Saturday at my sister's home." Though I didn't say, "But this is so sudden," I certainly thought of it. But all joking aside, I was very happy about the whole thing.

Shortly after getting out of the Army, by the way, I had brought my family back to California, and I'd been living with them ever since. Pop visited my studio each day for lunch, spent his evenings in the backstages of Los Angeles vaudeville houses, finishing up each night in the speak-easies with old vaudeville pals.

As newlyweds my wife and I at first lived in a modest house in Hollywood. Her family moved to the Coast shortly before our first son, James, was born on June 2, 1922. Our second boy, Robert, was also born in June two years later.

In my entire life I never knew a family so devoted to one another as my in-laws were. They all worked and thought together as a team without conflict or jealousy. They all liked me, I think, and I certainly liked and admired them. But there were times when I had the disquieting feeling that I had married not one girl but a whole family.

I discovered that this had also occurred to other people. My wife, two of her sisters, and I attended a rather formal party Mack Sennett was giving. The guest of honor was an aristocratic woman in her late twenties. Mack was so smitten with this society girl that he was using the broad "a," saying things like, "May I get you a drink, my dear?" and generally flouncing around like some ridiculous old French roué.

Being a humanitarian at heart, I took it upon myself to bring the grandfather of movie slapstick back to his senses. I did this by getting his goat. This was never difficult, I might add. That night I simply asked the lady to dance and kept whirling her past him, cheek to cheek.

When the dance was over, Mack came over to me. He was such a violent-tempered man that I did not know exactly what to expect. Putting his hand on my shoulder, he waited until he had my attention. Then he looked at the couch where my wife, her two sisters, and mother were sitting side by side. I watched his eyes move slowly from the face of one to another. Then he said, "Buster, if I wanted to, I could keep you busy for years just explaining!"

Usually I try not to interfere in other people's affairs. But that evening, inspired by a few highballs and righteous anger, I was provoked by the behavior of a famous woman star. She had been a Broadway show girl and resented the attentions being paid Mack's high-toned woman friend. Her husband, one of Hollywood's more dignified directors, was sitting, drink in hand, minding his own business. Childishly she walked up to him and accused him of flirting.

When he denied this, she pulled back her hand and slammed him on the cheek as hard as she could. Then she asked for her wraps and left. I was standing at the door and observed all of this. In going out, the star didn't give me a chance to get out of her way. She just shoved me to one side. Being no respecter of ladies who didn't act like ladies, I stepped through the door behind her and kicked her little behind so hard that I lifted her about a foot in the air.

She neither cried out nor looked back, just kept on going to her car. And she never told her husband about the incident. I know because I asked him about it years later, after they'd been divorced.

Breaking my leg, needless to say, had come as a shock to me. I took it almost as a personal insult. Yet I'd had a pretty bad scare while making *One Week*, the first two-reeler I'd been starred in. Except for the opening scene (which showed me getting married) the whole picture was built around my efforts to put together the portable home I'd bought for our love nest. The villain, enraged at losing the girl to me, revenged himself by changing the number of my lot, which tricked me into putting up the house on someone else's property. He also switched the numbers on the crates containing the various sections of the house. So I built my house on the wrong lot and also ended up with the craziest-looking house you ever saw. Every part of it was in the wrong place. The front door, for example, was on the second floor. There were no steps, and anyone walking through it would fall straight down into the garden. This gave me the chance to make a sensational fall. To lessen the impact we dug a deep, very wide hole in the garden, filled this with straw, and replaced the squares of sod on top of the straw. The lawn looked solid but collapsed like paper when I fell on it. I only felt a jar at the time. It was about two hours before quitting time, and I finished out the day.

But as I was getting dressed I discovered that my left elbow had swelled to double its normal size. I could not even get my jacket on. My other elbow, my back, and both arms were also swelling up fast.

Al Gilmore, my unit's physical trainer, put me under a shower with the water as hot as I could stand. He kept me there for fifteen minutes, then got me under an ice-cold shower for almost as long. When I was dry he rubbed me down with olive oil. That was to prevent the horse liniment, which he applied next, from taking my skin off. Under this treatment the swelling went down little by little. When I was dressed for home, Al told me, "Get a good night's sleep. You will not need any extra blankets. That horse liniment will keep you warm." Al was right.

A few years later I broke my neck while making *Sherlock, Jr.* But I did not even know about it until long afterward. One day when my doctor was giving me a physical checkup, he asked me when I'd sustained the fracture which, of course, had completely healed by then.

I had to think for quite a while before figuring out that it must have happened during a sequence of *Sherlock, Jr.* In this I ran along the top of a train and grabbed a rope dangling from a water tower to swing off to the ground. This set up the gag for the spout to open.

But we underestimated the volume of water that would fall on me from that ten-inch spout. The stream struck me so hard it tore loose my grip on the rope. I fell back on the track with my neck snapped down square across the steel rail.

Conditioning is the one thing, I suppose, that can enable a man to walk around unaware that he has a broken neck. While making another feature comedy, *The Navigator,* I was almost strangled while experimenting with a new deep-sea diver's suit. Conditioning couldn't help me out of that jam, of course, but an alert co-worker did.

The gag called for me to be smoking a cigarette when the girl tried to put my helmet on. I left the cigarette in my mouth while I reached up to help her get it on. Accidentally, she gave it a half twist, locking it. The smoke from the cigarette threw me into a frenzy of coughing. Fortunately, Ernie Orsatti, the St. Louis Cardinals' ballplayer who was working with our crew, noticed the trouble I was in and twisted off the helmet in the nick of time.

My acting career continued to prosper after I was married. When I completed eight two-reelers for Metro release, Joe Schenck set up a deal for me to make a dozen more to be distributed by First National, a company organized by independent theatre owners. They were trying to make sure that Zukor, Loew, and the other theatre chain operators would not control all of Hollywood's movies.

I still enjoyed doing burlesques and travesties more than anything else. In the first of the First National two-reelers, *The Playhouse,* I kidded the habit of Tom Ince, an outstanding director, of giving himself every sort of screen credit possible on his pictures. I did this by having the photographer make shots of Buster Keaton on the stage and also playing the various instruments in the orchestra. I was also the conductor. There were additional Buster Keatons in the audience. In 1921, this required trick photography of a sort that had never before been attempted. Until then a double exposure that showed a star (usually one playing twins) on the screen twice at one time made audiences gasp. It was considered a scientific miracle. But my cameraman managed to get nine different Buster Keatons on the screen at once.

In *The Frozen North*, which I made the following year, I did a burlesque of William S. Hart, the great Western star. At one time Hart's popularity was exceeded by only three other performers, Chaplin, Fairbanks, and Mary Pickford. In 1922 he was still a great drawing card. Bill, though, was not one of your handsome movie cowboys, and he took himself and his art quite seriously. In his pictures he did not sing, whistle, or yodel. Nor did he dress like some Dapper Dan of the Great Plains. As a boy he had lived on the Frontier, and he tried hard in his pictures to show the Old West as he remembered it. The saloons in Hart's pictures looked like the ramshackle bars he had seen there. The people who sat drinking, playing poker, and had gun fights in them behaved like human beings, equally capable of good and evil. Bill himself played what came to be known as a good bad man.

But Bill, in his youth, had left the West to become an actor. He had played Shakespeare, toured with Modjeska, appeared in the original 1899 production of *Ben Hur* as Messala, the villain. All this had given him some taste for ham flavoring. If Bill didn't romanticize the Old West he sure gimmicked up his good bad man with plenty of imaginative touches. He rolled Bull Durham cigarettes with one hand. He kept his Stetson on with a leather string tied under his chin. On his gaunt eagle face this looked good. But no real cowboy ever wore one, to my knowledge. Real cowboys also didn't blaze away at human varmints with guns in both hands as Bill did on the screen. But the main thing he did in his pictures that they didn't do in real life was cry. After about 1918 there was at least one scene in every Hart movie in which Bill broke down and unashamedly let glycerin tears roll down his thin, leathery he-man cheeks.

In my burlesque of Bill Hart I got a good laugh by opening

with a scene showing me coming up out of a New York subway-exit kiosk situated in the middle of frozen Donner Lake. Like Bill, I kept my hat on with a leather string tied under my chin and I carried a six-shooter on each thigh. I made futile attempts to roll a cigarette with one hand.

But it was an action gag in this picture that burned up Bill Hart when he saw it. This showed me coming home and discovering a couple hugging. Though I cannot see their faces I am convinced it is my wife and a lover. I turn pale, then amazed, and finally am crushed. Huge glycerin tears roll down my face. It is as if I am saying to myself, "The better man won." I shrug hopelessly as I turn away.

Yes, I turn to go. But just as I reach the door I look back and discover them kissing. This is too much even for me, the human worm, to endure. I pull out both guns and shoot them down like dogs. But they don't fall like dogs. They stand up, whirl around, and then kerplop dead on the floor.

Full of power, I walk back masterfully to look at them. I gaze in indifference at the stranger who has wrecked my home, savagely kick his lifeless form to one side. I am about to kick my wife's dead body aside also when I get my first look at her face. It isn't my wife at all. It is some other woman I've never seen before.

A subtitle flashes on the screen. It reads, "My God! I'm in the wrong house."

Bill's fans knew, of course, when they saw this picture that I was burlesquing their idol. As an old-time trouper Bill should have known that you can only burlesque successes, never flops. Also that if I imitated him it was only because I admired him so much that I wanted to be Bill Hart for a little while on the screen.

Ballet dancers, along with tenors, are supposed to be the most temperamental of performers. I've done imitations of both without hurting their feelings. Once when I was a kid we played on a vaudeville bill with Pavlova, the world's greatest ballerina. I imitated her doing her classic, "The Dying Swan," and Anna Pavlova loved it.

But Bill Hart, the Western sheriff with the heart of oak, couldn't take it. Mutual friends told me that he didn't mind too much the leather string under my chin, the two guns blazing away, or my messing up his one-handed cigarette-rolling trick. What really got him, they said, was my kidding his crying. My guess is that he knew in his heart how fake that was. Perhaps he did it just to prove that his fans would accept anything he did on the screen. Bill did not speak to me for two years after he saw that picture.

I very much liked another two-reeler that I made for First National. This told the story of a man with a wife and two kids who built a 20-foot boat in his cellar and then found it was too big to get out of the house and had to knock out a wall. But after all that, it sank when he finally got it into the water. The end of this picture drew a lot of favorable comment. It showed my porkpie hat valiantly floating along on the surface of the water as though I were walking underwater just beneath it.

I had made eleven of the twelve pictures for First National and was starting the last one when Joe Schenck got this telegram from John D. Williams, president of the company:

WE DO NOT WISH TO RENEW KEATON CONTRACT STOP WE CANNOT BE BOTHERED WITH HIS SHORT SUBJECTS

Schenck showed this to me. "Okay," I told him, "I will do them an additional favor! I won't make the last picture for them."

"Buster," said Joe, "your contract calls for you to make twelve pictures. I can handle this situation—but not if you refuse to make the final picture for them."

"But if they say they can't be bothered," I said, "my answer is 'Fine, then I'm doing you a favor in not bothering you with a twelfth picture.'"

I explained that Mr. Williams was putting me in the same ridiculous position as Martin Beck had when he stood in the wings and said to Pop, "Make me laugh!" "How can I make a man laugh," I asked, "who tells me that he can't be bothered with my comedies? Why should I want to?"

When Schenck saw Mr. Williams later Williams admitted the wire was a bluff, sent to counter the demand for more money they expected us to make.

That being the case, Mr. Williams outsmarted himself, for I never did make that twelfth little movie for First National. Just about that time Loew sent word that he wanted me to make full-length features for his company, Metro, to release.

Working with my own unit on my own lot I made several successful ones. The first of these Metro releases was *Three Ages*, the second, *Our Hospitality*. As I mentioned, most of my features cost from $200,000 to $220,000 to produce and grossed in rentals $1,000,000 upward. The enormous profits justified our spending that much on production, 20 to 30 per cent more than the average dramatic feature then cost to make.

The new deal enabled me to do two features a year, one for spring release, the other for the fall. These took about eight weeks to shoot against three for a two-reeler. This new schedule allowed me much more time for building up the story and the other preparatory work. Cutting required from two to three weeks. This allowed me three weeks off between the end of one picture and the start of the next.

In one or two of my later two-reelers I had tried putting in a story line. But this had not always proved feasible, and the faster the gags came in most short comedies, the better. In the features I soon found out that one had to present believable characters in situations that the audience accepted. The best format I found was to start out with a normal situation, maybe injecting a little trouble but not enough to prevent us from getting laughs. That permitted us to introduce the characters getting in and out of situations that were not too difficult. It was when we approached the final third of the picture that we had the characters in serious trouble which permitted bigger laughs, the biggest of all coming when catastrophe threatens. I never repeated a gag or used the same plot twice unless these could be so heavily camouflaged as to be unrecognizable. Often the plot was based on a melodramatic situation as in *The Navigator,* where one nation's agents set adrift a steamship just bought by its enemy. But the situation need not always be a serious one. A good example of a lighthearted plot is *College,* in which I played an honor student who finds out he is unpopular with his girl and everyone else after he denounces college athletics. To win back his girl he decides to go in for sports.

When we turned to the making of features we found a whole set of new problems facing us. One of the first decisions I made was to cut out custard-pie throwing. It seemed to me that the public by that time—it was 1923—had had enough of that. The pies looked messy on the screen anyway. So no pie was ever thrown in a Buster Keaton feature.

We also discontinued using what we called impossible gags or cartoon gags. These can be very funny in a cartoon short, and sometimes in a two-reeler. I'll illustrate with one I had used in *Hard Luck,* one of my own two-reelers. At the end of this I go swimming at a fashionable country club. There are many elegant society people and beautiful girls around the pool.

To impress the girls I climb to the high-diving board and spend whole minutes testing it, flexing my muscles, measuring carefully the thirty-six feet between me and the water. After all that, I do a swan dive but miss the swimming pool completely and crash through the adjoining cement walk, making a big hole as I disappear.

After the fade-out a subtitle reading "Years later" is flashed on the screen. Again the pool at the country club is seen, but the whole place is now a deserted ruin. There is no water in the swimming pool. In a moment I clamber up out of the hole in the cement walk. I am in Chinese costume, complete with pigtail, and help my Chinese wife and kids up out of the hole. In pantomime I point to the high-diving board, then to the hole I made, and we all laugh.

The people in the audience also were laughing as they went out. But that sort of gag I would never use in a full-length picture —because it could not happen in real life, it was an impossible gag. If we had done what we were trying to do in a feature the audience would go along with us, believing in the characters they were watching. So in pulling an impossible gag on them in a feature, we were saying, "April fool!" or "Sucker!" to them for believing in our story.

Another interesting thing I learned later was that once you got the audience interested in what the hero was doing they deeply resented anything that interrupted him. It didn't matter what terrific gag you gave them.

I had this demonstrated to me some years later when we were previewing *The Navigator,* my biggest money-maker. I consider

The Navigator and *The General* the two best movies I ever made. In one scene in *The Navigator* I was alone with the girl on a beached ship close to a cannibal-infested island.

To save her and myself, I went underwater in a diver's outfit in a heroic effort to dislodge the ship. While working mightily, I used many gags the audience loved. I set up a sawhorse labeled "men at work" in the sand at the bottom of the sea; I caught a swordfish, and, when another swordfish attacked me, I used the first fish to duel with him. I got my hands dirty while at the bottom of the sea and washed them in a bucket of water. Finding I'd forgotten my pliers, I picked up a lobster which bit a wire in two with one of its claws.

The gag that failed was my favorite, and it cost a lot of money. After we figured it out, I had the property department construct 1,200 rubber fish each fourteen to fifteen inches long. These were suspended on thin strings the audience couldn't see. We used a big machine that looked like a newspaper printing press to revolve them in front of the camera. The effect we got was that of a large school of fish passing by in a steady stream. One big fish came up but could not get through the school. To solve his problem I pick up a starfish that is clinging to a rock, attach it to my chest, and start directing the piscatorial traffic like a submarine traffic cop. Holding up my hand so the big fish could get through did the trick. The stream of fish passing by stop, the big fellow crosses, then I wave to the school to go on.

In my opinion this was as good a sight gag as I ever had, and it still is my favorite. When we put it in the trailer, announcing *The Navigator* as a coming attraction, the audience howled. But when we previewed the whole picture at Long Beach it brought not a titter. The same thing happened when we tried *The Navigator* out in theatres in Riverside and a couple of other nearby towns.

It took us a long time to figure out why that wonderful gag laid an egg. One of my gagmen, Clyde Bruckman, was so stunned he almost took the pledge. It is always an interesting problem to me when an audience rejects any such sure-fire laugh-getter. I wonder whether it is because the customers were too concerned in figuring out the mechanics of the gag, how it was done, to be amused. Or it might be something else. In this case we showed it again in the trailer, and everybody once more liked it. That gave me an answer that satisfied me. The other gags were accepted by audiences who saw the whole picture, because they did not interfere with my job of saving the girl. But when I directed the submarine traffic I was interrupting the rescue to do something else that couldn't help us out of the jam.

I threw the gag out. There was nothing else to do. Some of my co-workers thought the gag flopped because it was too intricate. But I still believe it fell dead because it showed the hero interrupting the job of saving himself and the girl.

From that day on, I realized that my feature comedies would succeed best when the audience took the plot seriously enough to root for me as I indomitably worked my way out of mounting perils.

There was also the matter of timing. Just as in vaudeville, you lost the laugh when you threw a gag at them too quickly, or for that matter too slowly. The difference was that on the stage you had the chance to test and retest your comedy material before live audiences. The customers only saw a gag or comedy scene in a movie after it was made, cut, and in the can. Often it was expensive remaking scenes with brand new gags in them. And that's how the protection or alternate gag was born.

During the years we were trying to figure out what made movie fans laugh, and why, there was an extraordinary silent-pictures comic who made many successful one-reel and two-reel pictures. His name was Larry Semon, and he was so weird looking that he could have posed either as a pinhead or a Man from Outer Space. His movies were combinations of cartoon gags, fantastic gags, and farcical plots.

Chaplin, Lloyd, and myself just couldn't make two-reelers as packed with laughs as Larry's. But when an audience got half a block from the theatre, after being convulsed by Semon's whammios, they couldn't have told you what they had laughed at. I would say this was because they were impossible gags. Only things that one could imagine happening to real people, I guess, remain in a person's memory.

The same thing is true, for some reason, with most word gags. Bob Hope is one of the funniest men alive. He can double you up with bright quips and dazzling sallies. But how many of his jokes can you recall five minutes after the Bob Hope show goes off the air? People talked about the sight gags in our silent comedies for weeks and months. Some of them are still remembered by certain of our fans, now middle-aged. I was talking to one of these fellows just the other day. I happened to mention that *The Butcher Shop* was the first movie I appeared in.

"Just a minute," he said, "wasn't that the one in which Fatty Arbuckle had a raccoon coat hanging on a hook that he put on to go into the store's big refrigerator, and he took off again when he came out?"

He was right to the point in that he had seen that picture just once, in 1917, forty-two years before.

So much has been written down through the years of that fabulous 1924 merger in which Loew's company, Metro, bought the Samuel Goldwyn lot in Culver City that I am astonished that one detail of the deal has never been described in the public prints: namely, how the greatest of all film studios acquired its name.

Marcus Loew's first decision was to call it Metro-Goldwyn. But Louis B. Mayer, then an independent producer, was eager to get into the big deal. In the dickering he had three aces to play, or so he thought. They were his exclusive contracts with two stars, Anita Stewart and Mildred Harris Chaplin, the estranged wife of Charlie, and with a youthful genius named Irvin Thalberg. Mayer had recently hired Thalberg, then twenty-three, away from Universal where he had started his career as an office boy.

Mayer got a bad shock when it turned out that Loew wanted neither of his stars for the new company. What he wanted more than any star in pictures was the brilliant young Thalberg. By then Loew had become more convinced than ever that superior stories were the key to box-office success. And his friends at Universal had told him that Thalberg had a great story mind, could select screen material and work without discord with the most temperamental of writers.

During the dickering in New York between Mayer on one side and Loew and Nick Schenck on the other, it was agreed that Mayer was to be vice-president and general manager of the new concern, Thalberg second vice-president and supervisor of production.

When that was settled Louis B. Mayer said, "Why don't you use my name as part of the firm's name?"

"Why should we?" asked Nick Schenck. "Marcus and I are not putting our names in the firm's title."

"But that would give me so much more incentive to work hard out there," argued Mayer. "And anyway three names sound more impressive than two. Listen!" As they did, he said, "Metro-Goldwyn," paused, and after a moment, "Metro-Goldwyn-Mayer!" Then he demanded, "Can't you hear what *class* the three names give it, what solidity and distinction? It's the same way with Hart Schaffner and Marx. Hart Schaffner sounds like nothing at all. Neither does Schaffner Marx. But Hart Schaffner and Marx! With that they had something. And look what a firm that has become just because they use three names instead of two."

And, sure enough, when the announcement of the merger came it included the news that the new studio would be known not as Metro-Goldwyn, but as Metro-Goldwyn-Mayer!

In time, Louis B. Mayer became the highest paid executive in the world with over a million-dollar annual income. If it is true that you can't laugh at a million dollars you can laugh even less at a million a year. But, besides his gifts as an executive, Mayer was also the industry's greatest salesman, and he proved it that day when he elbowed his name into "Metro-Goldwyn-Mayer," which became the trade-mark for elegance in movies the world over.

MY $300,000 HOME AND SOME OTHER SEMI-TRIUMPHS

Like many movie people I made considerable money during the early twenties in real-estate deals. After living in our modest Hollywood house a short while, I borrowed $50,000 from Joe Schenck to buy a home of my own. After living in it for six months, I resold it for $85,000. Then I bought another house for $55,000, lived in that one for six months, and sold it for $85,000. I used some of my profits to help Mom buy a large home for the family.

In 1924 I built a beautiful three-bedroom home in Beverly Hills for my own family. It cost only $33,000, but it was on a large lot, had a swimming pool, and was ideal for the four of us. I was so sure of this that I wouldn't let my wife see it until it was ready to move into. I wanted to surprise her.

When the great day came for her to look it over we brought

along Mrs. Berenice Mannix, whose husband Eddie was then Joe Schenck's studio manager.

My wife took one look at the house and announced that it was too small. "In the first place," she said, "it has no room for the governess. Where would she sleep?"

Our Jim was then three years old, Bob—a year-old baby. Until then I had not been told they required a governess who would sleep in.

"Can't you see, Buster?" she said. "We will need one bedroom for ourselves, the boys another, the butler and cook another. So we better have a place with another bedroom for her."

Meanwhile Mrs. Mannix had been ohing and ahing very audibly about the new house. "Oh, what wouldn't I give for this house!" she kept exclaiming. "It's perfect."

I looked at my wife, then at her. "If you really want it, Berenice," I said, "it's yours. Have Eddie look at it, and if he likes it I will sell it to you."

Eddie liked it almost as much as his wife did. His only doubt about buying it was due to the possibility that Schenck might decide to return to New York and make his headquarters there. If that happened Mannix would have to go back with him. In view of this, I would buy the house back at that same price if he had to return East at any time. Not long afterward Eddie became one of the Big Three at the Metro-Goldwyn-Mayer Studios. He has outlasted everybody there but still lives in the home that was too small for my first wife.

I was risking nothing, of course, in making that offer. In the mid-twenties real estate was booming all over southern California, and the choicest lots and houses were right there in Beverly Hills.

The house I finally built in Beverly for the four of us was large enough to satisfy anyone. It was a two-story mansion with five bedrooms, two additional bedrooms for the servants and a three-room apartment over the garage for the gardener and his wife, who worked as our upstairs maid. This made six servants with a cook, butler, chauffeur, and governess. It stood on three and a half acres of beautiful lawn.

The land and house together cost me $200,000, and we spent another $100,000 furnishing it. I designed some of the furniture myself—the king-sized bed that my wife wanted for her room, the fancy bed I put in mine, and a wonderful pair of high bedroom bureaus of dark oak, with a full-length mirror set between them. I had these pieces built by the carpenters at the studio.

I still remember the thrill of pride that went through me the day that Nick Schenck saw that house for the first time. That multi-millionaire whistled, and whispered, "I hope, Buster, you aren't going over your head on this place."

I told him "No," and I sincerely believed that. By that time I was getting $2,000 a week, plus 25 per cent of my pictures' profits which brought me an additional $100,000 a year.

The $300,000 investment in that house seemed to me the safest I could make. The last thing that occurred to me, of course, was the possibility that my wife might one day take away that wonderful property from me. Which reminds me that after we moved into that house my wife's personal expenses for clothes and other knickknacks averaged $900 a week. I put no rein on her spending at any time.

I realize now that one thing wrong with our marriage was that the one way that my wife, a frustrated actress, could compete with the famous women stars we associated with was in spending and entertaining and living as luxuriously as they did. This was quite a job, for it was an era of wild spending, and few of the silent women stars were frugal, and their earnings were enormous.

But it would be unfair and ridiculous for me to pretend that I myself was the frugal type. I bought myself everything I wanted, including the finest clothes, cars, hunting and fishing equipment. I spared no expense on our huge swimming pool or on the patio I had built behind the house. I spent $14,000 moving to the rear of the house forty-two towering palm trees that had lined the drive in front.

I also enjoyed as much as my wife did throwing big parties. During the winter we had costume balls at the house. Excepting only the invitations to the fabulous shindigs given by Hearst and Marion Davies, invitations to our parties were the most eagerly sought in Hollywood. Best of all I liked the barbecue parties we gave each Sunday from May to October except when we went out of town over the weekend. I'd draft Buster Collier and Ed Brophy to help me serve the eighty, or so, guests we had invited. Many others came uninvited. They had heard about our wonderful barbecued chickens, steaks, and English lamb chops.

Wilson Mizner, the country's greatest wit, had a standing invitation. He boasted that he could smell my cooking even in Santa Barbara, ninety miles away. Among other guests who seldom failed to appear were most of the M-G-M big shots and directors and their wives; the Mayers, the Mannixes, and the Thalbergs, the Clarence Browns, Jack Conways, Bob Leonards, also Sam Goldwyn, Howard Hughes, Hearst, Marion Davies, Joe Schenck, and, of course, each and every in-law.

When the boys were little I worried about the way they were being spoiled by my in-laws with the wholehearted assistance of my own mother and sister. Whatever my boys wanted they were given immediately. It was for their own sakes that I did not want Bob and Jim to be spoiled. Like everyone else I have noticed how difficult and disagreeable life can become for the spoiled child when he grows up.

Being Buster Keaton's kids, the boys were wild Katzenjammer types whose imaginations did not incline them to constructive projects. On one occasion they became fed up with being told to wash their hands and face before each meal. They managed to turn off the house's water supply. All of it. Unable to get a drop of water from any faucet, upstairs or down, my wife called the Beverly Hills Water Department which dispatched some experts. The Department's men dug up 150 feet of lawn, seeking a break in the main, before someone discovered that the whole trouble was due to the water being shut off under every sink in the house.

On another occasion the boys decided they didn't care for the food they were being served. Informed by the governess they must eat it anyway they waited until her back was turned. Then they dumped the food on their plates into the heating grate built into the floor. The heat had been turned on so their misdemeanor was quickly discovered when the food started burning in the grate.

A Rabelaisian side of those two kids was aroused the day a very social Beverly Hills woman called on my wife to ask her to work on some charity drive. The matron had her golden-haired little daughter with her. She was about four and romped off merrily to play with Bob and Jim. A half hour or so later my wife invited her visitor to have tea on the porch.

On walking out there they found the little girl doing a spring dance on the lawn, with my boys laughing their heads off and applauding. Jim and Bob had taken off all her clothes.

The lads developed another little trick I did not care for at all. Whenever a picture of mine was showing at a local theatre my sons would storm inside without tickets. When the ticket taker or an usher tried to stop them they became abusive.

"What have *you* to say about it?" they'd demand. "After all, it is *our* father's movie you're showing here. So why should we buy tickets?"

The governess meanwhile was at the box office buying the tickets. Each time she warned them to wait for her, but they'd just run in anyway, stopping only to browbeat the man at the door.

My wife also was strong minded in certain ways. She had wanted a girl for her first child and put pink ribbons on the baby clothes. When the baby turned out to be a boy she refused to change them to blue.

"Pink is for girls," I told her. "Blue is for boys."

"No, pink is for boys," she insisted.

I didn't argue, figuring she preferred pink.

What did hurt me a little was when she insisted on naming our first boy Jimmy. I thought he should have been named Joseph like the four first sons of first sons who preceded him. But James was the name she preferred, and James he was christened.

Though bridge was always Hollywood's favorite indoor sport—well, with one exception—I had no interest in playing it until I went on a trip to New York and found myself on the same train as Nick Schenck and Mr. and Mrs. Hiram Abrams. Abrams, who was president of United Artists, and his wife were excellent bridge players. On learning that neither Nick nor I played they offered to teach us the game. I drew Mr. Abrams as a partner.

Like so many old pinochle players trying bridge for the first time I was reluctant to sacrifice my hand for the sake of my partner. Mr. Abrams kept telling me that I was stupid and became more abusive as the day wore on. Finally I said, "We better play some other kind of game, because if you bawl me out once more I'll slap the taste right out of your mouth."

With that I rushed out of their drawing room. Nick Schenck followed me to the observation car and tried to calm me down. But I was past calming and refused to have anything more to do with Abrams on that trip.

That man had me so sore that I spent hundreds of my spare hours during the next six months studying up on the game. I read everything about bridge I could find. Only then did I begin to play, starting with games at a quarter of a cent a point. As my game gradually improved I went to a one cent a point game, next jumped to ten cents a point and finally to games at twenty-five cents a point, which is big-league bridge and big-league money anywhere.

A little over two years after that train trip I was invited to Joe Schenck's New York apartment for dinner. Sam Goldwyn and Abrams also were there. After dinner Abrams said, "I guess we'll not be able to have our usual game tonight. We haven't got a fourth, have we?"

"Oh, yes we have," said Schenck.

"Who?"

"Buster plays," said Joe.

When we cut for partners, Abrams and I drew each other as partners. Mr. Abrams shuddered and suggested a re-cut. Neither Schenck nor Goldwyn objected to this, for they had both played with me recently in games on the Coast. That night I drew Goldwyn as my partner in the re-cut.

I was in New York two weeks on that trip and played a lot of bridge at twenty-five cents a point, with Mr. Abrams in on many of the sessions. I made a point of asking for a re-cut each time I drew him as my partner. The day I started home I had the pleasure of accepting his check for $3,400. This covered his losses to me during the two weeks.

"Next time," he said as he forked over the check, "you will please take me as your partner."

"What for?" I replied. "It's more fun for me this way—and also more profitable."

Smiling Sam Goldwyn was another movie bigwig who could get

very testy at a bridge table. But then Goldwyn, the greatest of all independent Hollywood producers, has always had a mind that seems childlike at times.

One evening when he, his wife, and the Joe Schencks were dining at my house, Goldwyn announced, "I have just bought the book of the year."

"You mean *All Quiet on the Western Front?*" asked Schenck.

Goldwyn nodded, and Schenck told him, "I was interested in bidding for it but after thinking it over decided I did not want to buy it. I felt it had a sort of gruesome story to tell and, worst of all, was the sad ending. The hero, after all, is a German, and his side loses the war."

"I got that all figured out," said Goldwyn with a happy grin. "I am going to have the Germans win the war."

We both looked at him in astonishment. Schenck said, "You are kidding, Sam."

"No, I'm not," said Goldwyn.

"If you ever tried to change the ending of the World War," Schenck said earnestly, "you'd make yourself the laughingstock of the world."

The following week when the three of us were again together, Goldwyn announced, "I sold *All Quiet on the Western Front* to Universal for $10,000 more than I paid for it, and was I glad to get rid of it!"

The footnote to the story was that the picture, in which the Germans did *not* win the war, grossed a whopping $8,000,000 and saved Universal Pictures from bankruptcy.

Sam and I had a run-in one evening when we were partners in a bridge game. My cards were bad, and he became quite abusive.

When I'd taken all I cared to, I pointed out that when he was playing with Schenck, Louis B. Mayer, and other big shots he managed to control his temper quite well. I told him he could control it now.

My cards continued to be bad and so did his abuse. "Do you want me to force the cards?" I asked. "Or do you want me to break this bridge table over your head?"

"Oh, now you are a table-thrower?" he said. The game ended

when Frances, his wife, fearing we would come to blows, came to the door of the room with Sam's hat and coat in her hands.

This was soon after the breakup of my first marriage. I never played bridge with Sam Goldwyn again. I do not think I saw him again until a day when I was down and out and needed work badly. This was no secret in Hollywood, and I was grateful when Sam's secretary phoned me to say that her boss wanted to see me about a part in a picture he was making about John L. Sullivan, the old bare-knuckle champion. When I got to his office at the appointed time the secretary told me, "Oh yes, Mr. Goldwyn is waiting to see you. I walked in, Goldwyn looked up. After staring at me for quite a while, he shook his head.

"I had this part in a picture that I thought you could do, Buster," he said, "but now I see you I realize I was wrong. You'd never be able to do it."

I do not know what Sam expected me to do, leap at his throat or get down on my knees and beg for the part. But he did not expect me to do what I did: laugh and walk out.

I suppose Sam felt as foolish that day as I did on a certain Sunday in 1926. I was sitting alone on the porch of Bebe Daniels's beach home when I noticed that a girl out in the rough surf seemed to be having trouble. The breakers kept rolling in, knocking her down. Every time she managed to get to her feet another big wave would come in and bowl her over.

Just to be on the safe side I went out there to help her get safely to shore. As it turned out, she got in all right on her own. As we came out of the water Bebe ran down to us and asked, "Have you two met?"

When I said no, she said to the girl, "This is Buster Keaton," and to me "Buster, this is Gertrude Ederle. You've read about her. She swam the English Channel a couple of weeks ago."

Throughout the twenties one of the great social events each year was the New Year's Eve party given by Joe Schenck at the Casino at Tijuana. James J. Coffroth, the old-time boxing promoter, and Baron Long, the man who ran the Casino, tried to make it the Western Hemisphere's first complete playground for adults.

But its main lure to people in our part of the Prohibition-harried United States was its accessibility as a legal drinking place.

I had one of my goofiest adventures there because of a beautiful woman whom I was eager to stay as far away from as possible. What happened to men who didn't was depressing even to think about.

The woman was Mary Nolan, the blonde, slim, and gorgeous M-G-M movie star who had been Imogene (Bubbles) Wilson in the days when she was a Ziegfeld show girl and universally acclaimed the most beautiful girl on Broadway.

Frank Tinney, the stage comedian, was the first of her ill-starred admirers, and he didn't even fall in love with her. She fell in love with him. Before she fell out of love with mild little Frank he had lost his wife, his home, his life savings, his job, and his reputation. All he acquired in exchange was the police record he got when she had him arrested for beating her up. There were several such beatings, one so severe that the hospital doctor who examined Imogene said, "This woman looks as though she'd been hit by an automobile." Imogene sued Tinney for $100,000, then pursued him to London where he was trying to start a new career for himself. There was a reconciliation and more beatings. It all ended when Frank returned to America and went into one mental hospital after another.

It was the end of his career but only the beginning of hers, for Imogene went on to Berlin where she became a screen star under the name of Imogene Robertson. She also continued getting into the newspapers, first as the companion of King Alfonso of Spain, who gave her a bejeweled brooch and a weekend in the royal palace, and later of a German baron who carried her off to a castle on the Rhine.

As Mary Nolan she became an M-G-M star and the sweetheart of one of its top executives. He also beat her up so badly that she was again taken to a hospital. From her room there she phoned him and got him into such a rage that he went down to the hospital and beat her up all over again. Subsequently she sued this lover for half a million dollars.

However this double assault on Mary occurred some years after the New Year's party at Tijuana. Among the other guests present were Tom Mix, Gary Cooper, John Barrymore, Richard Dix, Buster Collier, Louis Wolheim, David Wark Griffith, and several younger performers, including one who was just becoming famous. He was there with the girl he later married. As they are still prominent, let's call them Walter and Evelyn.

Griffith, the greatest of the early movie directors, had not made a film in years, but his camera eye and romantic story sense never stopped working. They were both at their liveliest on an evening such as this one when, with the rest of us, he was imbibing very select strong waters.

It so happened that Mary Nolan and Walter were sitting opposite him, side by side. And in that young couple he saw beauty and glamour enough to strike the whole world with awe and wonder: the girl, a blonde with a crown of lovely hair, diaphanous skin, the face of an angel with the bluest eyes in Christendom; the boy, handsome with black, curly hair, powerful shoulders, and as unworldly as any youth from the backwoods.

Griffith's wrinkled, eaglelike face lighted up as he studied them. He seemed enraptured.

"Are you two engaged?" he asked.

"No," said Walter, shyly smiling at Miss Nolan. Apparently he had forgotten for the moment that his girl was sitting at his other elbow.

"What a pity," said Griffith in that benevolent old Southerner's voice he had used to charm great performances out of Dick Barthelmess, the Gish girls, and so many others. He added softly, "Why don't you think of it?" Swept away, the screen's first master storyteller began weaving a real-life romance. "Why shouldn't you two beautiful young people marry here in these picturesque surroundings of romantic old Mexico? What a union! This young woman who even now is wearing the lovely white evening dress that might well be her wedding gown! And for her groom, this man, one of the most handsome youths in all the world."

Both of them modestly cast down their eyes. But Evelyn looked as though she were turning to stone.

"Why *don't* you think of it?" repeated the old man in that throbbing and persuasive voice of his. "An enchanting idea, isn't it? To be married as the bells of Old Mexico toll in the New Year."

Everybody at the table by this time had stopped chattering, and even drinking, as he continued: "Soft music. The ceremony performed in an old monastery. And the church bells. Think of the bells of this quaint, picturesque old country. Each year for centuries they have brought new hope of happiness and freedom to a warmhearted, valiant people. And those old church bells tolling would bring the hope of happiness to you also, my dear children."

"I'm willing," said Mary, who had never had time enough between romances to be married.

"I guess it would be all right," said Walter.

The first opportunity I had after dinner I got hold of Buster Collier and Louis Wolheim and said, "Let's promote this thing."

Being as mischief-loving as I, they were eager to help. We discussed what important local resident should be asked to tie the knot. The archbishop? The mayor?

Then Wolheim, who'd been a college professor although he didn't look it, pointed out that in a Catholic country like Mexico there might be certain formalities that would delay the ceremony. We decided then that it would have to be a fake wedding. There was a New York lawyer at the party who looked like a Mexican. Someone suggested he might do if he could be persuaded to officiate. It also occurred to us that before long Walter might appreciate the favor we'd done for him in making it merely a fake wedding.

All our wedding plans, though, were canceled quickly by Evelyn, our prospective groom's fiancée. "Walter," she asked in a honeyed voice, "have you seen how beautiful the moonlight is in the patio?"

"No," he admitted.

"Well, come with me," she told him. He went along obediently, after excusing himself to Mary Nolan.

"Look, darling," exclaimed Evelyn when she had him out there in the clearing. "Did you ever see anything so lovely?"

Walter inspected the moonlight but not for very long. He had no more than turned his eyes heavenward than Evelyn reached back to left field. She hit him only with her open hand, but it was such a haymaker that it split his lip and also knocked him into a cactus bush. It took Walter fifteen minutes to tidy himself up enough to be presentable; half of that time, the bootblack there said later, was spent pulling the thorns out of his rear.

When he returned to public view he hurried to Evelyn's side and stayed there. Meanwhile Mary Nolan had disappeared—and everybody hoped she'd remain out of sight.

At one o'clock that evening I was at the bar minding my own business, which was for the moment the pleasant business of drinking. Suddenly Mary rushed up to me, seized my hand, and pulled me away. Her breath was coming in little puffs which made her bosom rise and fall in a very attractive manner. While thus distracted, I was led through various rooms, past the gambling tables and another large bar. Pointing to a muscular stranger, she half sobbed, "*There* he is!"

"Who?" I asked, staring at the man.

"The man who insulted me."

They say nothing can interrupt gamblers at a craps table, but that fluttering voice did. There seemed to be, in a moment, 1,000 faces watching and waiting to see what I would do.

All I could think of were the many husky guys in Schenck's party, romantic, gallant types like John Barrymore and Richard Dix, cowboy stars like Tom Mix. Why had she picked on me to defend her honor, if any?

But I patted her hand and went over to the stranger who by now was glowering. "I don't suppose you did anything," I said in my lowest and most refined voice, "but she's had a few drinks. Why don't you apologize just to shut her up?"

By way of reply, the stranger explained what I could do to Mary, using the filthiest of the four-letter Anglo-Saxon words.

Now Keaton was really on the spot, and everybody seemed entranced. At least none of the men watching us tried to interfere. While I was pondering the problem, and getting pretty damn mad at this clown for compounding Mary's nonsense, he settled matters by saying, "That goes for you, too."

"You've put me on a fine spot," I told him, "but we're not doing this one for an audience. Let's get down to the back patio where we can settle the whole thing very quickly."

"No," he said.

"What do you mean, no?" I demanded, going up and taking his arm, trying to lead him away. But to the horror of the gamblers, he grabbed and clung to the edge of the nearest craps table, pulling it about three feet. I tried to drag him away, but his grip on the table was tenacious. Meanwhile the chips on the craps table were skittering in all directions with the deeply distressed gamblers trying to restore them to their various positions on and back of the "Come" line, on the "Don't come" line, in the "Field," and the other spots on the green table.

I kept jerking on the big coward's free arm, but I was unable to tear him loose. Finally, not knowing what else to do I walked away, heading toward the bar where I'd been before all the nonsense started. On the way I met Buster Collier and Louis Wolheim and told them what had happened.

On seeing that I was still steamed up, they lured me to a patio where there was a wishing well. They lifted me up and hung me head downward in this.

"This is a party. Why let a little thing like this upset you?" said Wolheim. Like everyone else Louis was usually philosophical about his friends' troubles.

Needless to say, I was in no position to argue with him. They set me on my feet only after I calmed down. Then we went back into the Casino where Buster Collier got me a drink.

In a little while Mary Nolan came fluttering back. "Here we go again," I said to Wolheim.

"Forgive me," said she. "Forgive me, Buster, for involving you. I'll explain to your wife so she won't think . . ."

"Don't bother," I said. "But what did that guy do to you?"

"He put his hand *on my breast*."

I looked at her very low-cut gown. One of her breasts had tumbled out. "It probably fell out," I told her, "as it has now. That big coward is also a gentleman. He politely stuffed it out of sight for you. But I'm no gentleman, and this time you'll have to put it back yourself."

The features I started making in 1923 for M-G-M's release had a gratifying reception. *Three Ages,* the first of these, was in three episodes that showed me living in the Stone Age, the Roman Era, and Modern Times. The point of this comedy was that love and the relations of man and woman had not changed since the dawn of time.

Three Ages did well, and my next feature, *Hospitality*, did even better. In its first week at the Capitol, Loew's big Broadway presentation house, it equaled the box-office record, and in Loew's Circuit's hundreds of theatres it nearly tied the box-office record for the chain. I made five more features on my own lot for M-G-M release. *Sherlock, Jr., Seven Chances, Go West,* and *Battling Butler,* and the second of my two favorites, *The Navigator.*

We were about to start *Sherlock, Jr.* in 1924 when I decided that I must do something for my pal, Roscoe. More than three years had passed since his acquittal by a jury that said an apology was due him—but he was still barred from acting in pictures.

Roscoe was down in the dumps and broke. He had been unable to pay the staggering legal fees demanded of him after the three trials. Quietly, Joe Schenck had picked up the tab of more than $100,000 for him.

Roscoe had taken a trip around the world, then tried vaudeville. Finally he made appearances at the Cotton Club, a Culver City night club.

Nobody but friends of his and curiosity seekers went to see him. And it was a dismal experience to watch him. Roscoe just was not funny any more, was like some washed-up old performer who knew he was through and was just going through the motions because he had no alternative.

When he finished his engagement at the Cotton Club I suggested to Lou Anger that we give Roscoe a job directing *Sherlock, Jr.*

Lou said it could be arranged, but that we better get him to use some other name. I suggested "Will B. Good," but this was considered too facetious, so we changed it to "Will B. Goodrich."

The experiment was a failure. Roscoe was irritable, impatient, and snapped at everyone in the company. He had my leading lady; Kathryn McGuire, in tears a dozen times each day.

One day, after Roscoe went home, the gang of us sat around trying to figure out what to do next. It was obvious that we couldn't make the picture with a man directing whose self-confidence was gone, whose nerves were all shot. The question was which of us would have the heart to tell Arbuckle he was through?

It was Lou Anger, bless him, who thought of a way out. He said that Hearst, who was producing Marion Davies's pictures, was looking for a director for her new one, a film version of the old Victor Herbert musical, *The Red Mill.*

"Hearst," he said, "has already interviewed two well-known directors but doubts that either can do the job. He and Marion have always admired Roscoe's directing. They've told me so. They also feel sorry for him now." It seemed to us quite possible that Roscoe, with a new gang to work with and on another sort of picture, might turn in a good job.

I happened to know that Marion was having a few friends to dinner that evening at her beach house. I was eager to talk to her about taking Roscoe as a director before approaching Hearst. I counted on Marion's good heart, and I knew that she could get the publisher to do almost anything she wanted. That evening I drove out to Santa Monica to see her. She invited me to join her dinner party.

"No thanks," I said, "I would like a few minutes with you alone."

Marion led me to another room, and there I told her of the terrible state Roscoe was in. "One directing job," I said, "even if he had to do it under another name, might make all the difference in the world to him, might get him started all over again."

It was typical of Marion that she did not ask me why, if I felt so badly, I didn't let Roscoe direct one of my pictures. I was relieved that she didn't. The last thing I wanted to tell her was that we'd had no luck trying to work with him.

I said, "I am just about to start my new picture with him directing. But I'd be tickled to death if you would let him do yours instead. Yours is so much bigger a production. Also he would realize he was getting the chance because you and W.R. always liked his work. Roscoe and I were such close pals that getting a job from me would mean little. He might misinterpret it as merely an act of friendship."

Marion sold the idea to Hearst. I think it helped that Hearst had never believed what his newspapers printed about Roscoe during his trouble. Once I heard him say he had sold more newspapers when that story was running than he had on the sinking of the SS *Lusitania*.

Over the weekend Roscoe called up Lou Anger in great excitement. He was in a dilemma. To his amazement Hearst wanted him to direct Marion's new picture—and the Davies pictures were all lavish productions costing over a million in a day when million-dollar pictures were rare.

"What am I going to do, Lou?" he said. "I can't let Buster down."

"Don't worry about Buster," Lou said. "Grab this big chance, Roscoe. Buster will finish it himself." Roscoe used the name William Goodrich in the credits. And *The Red Mill*, oddly enough, was a pretty good picture. Roscoe had somehow managed to do a first-rate directing job on that period show.

The lift directing it gave to his spirits did not last long unfortunately. In 1927 he made a road tour in *Baby Mine*, the stage farce, but with little success. The next year he was hooted in Paris when he appeared there. Not because of the scandal. The French just didn't find the once-great comic funny any more. Yet only a few years before he had been worshipped so in Paris that the Government allowed him to place a wreath on the tomb of its Unknown Soldier.

When Roscoe died in 1933 he was making two-reel comedies for Warner Brothers at their Flatbush studio. But these also lacked the quality and inspired comic flavor of his old pictures.

The day I heard Roscoe was dead I recalled a little incident which reveals just how much of a monster my old friend was. It happened when we were making our last two-reeler in New York. We were going down to Coney Island that day to make some scenes on the beach. Roscoe told Lou Anger we needed a pretty girl who would look good in a bathing suit.

A casting call was sent out, and Roscoe selected from the crowd a sixteen-year-old blonde. On the day we were going to Coney Island, she walked into Roscoe's dressing room and turned around so he could admire her in her bathing suit.

"That's fine," he told her and turned away.

"Wait a moment, Mr. Arbuckle," she said. "I brought another one along with me. Maybe you'll like this one better." She unwrapped the second suit, shut the door, and started to take off the suit and put on the other. Before she got very far with her strip-tease act, Roscoe left her on the run. He busted into the dressing room I shared with Al St. John and told us what was going on. At his insistence Lou Anger got another girl for the role.

Yes, this was what the man denounced as a sex fiend by press, public, and pulpit was really like. The story also illustrates pretty well, I think, to what length certain teen-age girls were ready to go to get into the movies even in pre-World War I days.

Yet even in this tragedy of the funny fat man there is one heartwarming note. Hollywood, the "town where love is unknown," "the town which can keep no secret," never let the outside world know who "William B. Goodrich" was until it could not hurt Roscoe Arbuckle.

THE WORST MISTAKE OF MY LIFE

In 1926 Joe Schenck became one of the chief executives of United Artists. As part of the deal, he brought to that company the releasing rights of the pictures made by Norma Talmadge, Constance Talmadge, and myself. We continued to produce our own pictures, independently, however. But I made only three for United Artists: *The General, College,* and *Steamboat Bill, Jr.*

Then, in 1928, I made the worst mistake of my career. Against my better judgment I let Joe Schenck talk me into giving up my own studio to make pictures at the booming Metro-Goldwyn-Mayer lot in Culver City. Even then it was the Studio of Stars and had under contract John Gilbert, Marion Davies, Wallace Beery, Lon Chaney, Lionel Barrymore, William Haines, and Greta Garbo. Marie Dressler, the greatest comedienne I ever saw (until Lucille Ball appeared) was also under contract there but only as a featured player.

From the very start I was against making the switch to M-G-M. It seemed to me I would be lost making pictures in such a big studio. When Joe continued to argue for it, I asked Charlie Chaplin what he thought.

"Don't let them do it to you, Buster," he said. "It's not that they haven't smart showmen there. They have some of the country's best. But there are too many of them, and they'll all try to tell you how to make your comedies. It will simply be one more case of too many cooks."

Harold Lloyd was of the same opinion. Both Charlie and he had retained their own units. Their pictures were first-rate and were coining money.

I was so impressed by what they said that I asked Adolph Zukor, head of Paramount, if he would be interested in releasing my pictures. I explained that I wanted to make them in my own studio. Zukor just shook his head. He explained that he had just completed arrangements to release Lloyd's pictures and that having two comedians on Paramount's list made no sense. But he wasn't fooling me. Zukor was interested, all right. But on his desk, as we talked, lay a directive from Will Hays, the movie czar, which said, "Buster Keaton is the exclusive property of Metro-Goldwyn-Mayer."

Joe Schenck kept saying that I would be happy at M-G-M. "I'm just turning you over to my brother Nick," he told me. "He'll take care of anything you want. And as you know, Buster, my brother and I have been partners in every deal either of us ever made. It will be the same as though you were still working for me."

"You mean I have no choice?" I asked. Joe smiled and shrugged.

In the end I gave in. Joe Schenck had never steered me wrong in his life until then. I do not think he meant to that time either. But letting him override my own instinctive judgment was stupid. As I have said, it turned out to be the worst mistake I ever made.

I found out what I was up against when we started talking story for the first picture I was to do at M-G-M. I can best explain this, I think, by going back for a moment to *Steamboat*

Bill, Jr., my last independently made picture. The idea of that story was brought to me by Charles (Chuck) Reisner, a burly, brawny actor who had turned director. Some old-time movie fans may remember Chuck Reisner's performance as the father of the tough kid who fought angel-faced Jackie Coogan in Chaplin's *The Kid*. There have been few funnier scenes on the screen than the one in which the huge Reisner terrifies Chaplin by telling him "If your kid licks mine, I'll lick you." That made Charlie, who had been rooting hard for Jackie to win, do everything he could think of to make him lose.

Chuck's story opened with a rugged, old Mississippi steamboat captain reading a letter from his wife. They had a quarrel twenty years before, just after their only child was born. She returned with the baby to her home town in New England. The letter explains that their baby, now a full-grown man, is on his way to see his father for the first time. He will arrive by train on Sunday and will wear a white carnation so his father will recognize him.

But the Sunday I arrive is Mother's Day and every man on the train is wearing a carnation in his buttonhole. Hopefully, my father, Steamboat Bill, approaches one muscular youth after another. But he doesn't find me until the train pulls out because I got off the train on the wrong side. He takes one look at me and groans. I have on a beret and plus fours. I have a ukulele under my arm and a "baseball mustache," so-called because it has nine hairs on each side. My airs and manners are those of a silly-ass boy from Back Bay.

My dismayed father marches me into a barbershop. He points to the absurd mustache, tells the barber, "Off!" The barber takes off the tuft with two strokes, one to a side. Steamboat Bill gets me a man's hat to replace the beret.

Now this is as much as Chuck Reisner needed to tell me about that story for me to buy it. With this for a start, all we needed to get the story rolling and churning was a wealthy menace with a pretty daughter. The menace has a modern river steamer that will ruin the business my father has done for years on the river with his old-fashioned back-wheeler.

The story continued this way:

Despite the stern disapproval of both of our fathers the girl

203

and I manage to meet secretly. When my father finds out about that it is the last straw. He orders me to go back to Boston. Sorrowfully I put on my beret and plus fours, pick up my ukulele, and go to the station. But as my train comes in I see my father being arrested. He is taken to the local jail, a log cabin which contains only two cells and the jailer's office.

Determined to rescue him, I let the train go again, put on my rough working clothes. In the cabin of my father's boat I hollow out a big loaf of bread and conceal in the hole hammers, saws, monkey wrenches, screwdrivers, and other tools. It is raining like mad as I go to jail. Even the loaf of bread gets wet. My father wants no part of me. But when the jailer's back is turned I point to the bread and make sawing and chiseling motions.

Meanwhile the soaked bread is expanding and sagging toward the ground under the weight of the escape tools. Then it falls apart and the hammer, screwdrivers, files, and monkey wrenches all clatter to the floor. The outraged jailer throws me into the other cell. The escape and the flood we planned were peppered with the natural gags I'd known we'd develop.

An unusual thing happened during the making of that picture, by the way. One of Joe Schenck's aides talked him into the idea that a flood would be a ruinous thing to have in a movie comedy. "You'll make a lot of enemies for this picture if you keep the flood in it," he told Joe. "Too many people have lost their dear ones in recent floods. They will resent us making a joke out of such a disaster.

When Schenck told me this, I pointed out that one of Chaplin's greatest successes was *Shoulder Arms,* a picture making fun of the war and everything connected with it.

"Chaplin made that movie in 1919, the year after the World War ended," I said. "Nobody objected to it. And that includes the gold-star mothers who lost their sons in the war."

But for once the easygoing Joe Schenck was adamant. When I became convinced he wouldn't change his mind I asked Fred Gabourie, my technical director, how much it would cost to remake our $100,000 worth of elaborate street sets if we had a hurricane instead of a flood in the picture. I had a hunch that Schenck might not object to a hurricane. Gabourie, a whiz at his job, said $35,000. And Schenck had no objections to my staging a hurricane. It turned out that the changes we made cost slightly less than that.

The location we had chosen was on the bank of the Sacramento River opposite Sacramento. The building fronts we had constructed there were on a street a block long. And a twister could cause the same sort of destruction as a flood. Either of them could do many things our script called for: blow buildings into the river, fill the little town jail with water almost up to the ceiling, and sink the sleek craft owned by the heavy, my girl's father.

Far more difficult than remaking the sets was the job of refashioning our gags. The best new gag we invented involved a breakaway hospital. We used a 120-foot crane set on a barge to pick up this whole structure, leaving only the floor.

It had occurred to me that there were usually many more people killed each year by cyclones and tornadoes than in floods. Just for fun, when the picture was over, I called the United States Weather Bureau in Los Angeles and asked for figures for the preceding year. I was told that in 1925 there were 796 persons killed in great windstorms and only 36 in floods. But I never mentioned that to Schenck, not wishing to rub it in. I usually could make Joe laugh, but I doubted that he would be amused to hear about the $35,000 mistake he had made.

When I went over to M-G-M I was again assured that every effort would be made to let me continue working with my team whenever possible. It turned out to be possible very seldom. I do not think that this was anyone's fault. Usually, when I needed the old gang, one of them would be busy on a Norma Shearer picture, another on a Lon Chaney picture, and so on. M-G-M even stole Fred Gabourie, my technical director, from me after I made just one picture on the lot. Before long he was head of the studio's whole technical department, a job he kept until he died.

This was all very flattering to my judgment, or perhaps I should say luck, in selecting superior men for my team. But it did not help me make pictures of the quality I had been able to turn out on my own lot. The worst shock was discovering I could not work up stories the way I'd been doing, starting only with the germ of an idea. I learned that when I brought Irving Thalberg my first idea for a Buster Keaton comedy.

Now it always helps, in telling a story to a film producer, if you have some particular actor in mind for a key role. It enables your listener to visualize the story more clearly as you tell it. So I started off by saying that I had the perfect woman for the lead, adding, "She is working right here on your lot."

"Who is that?" he asked.

"Marie Dressler," I told him.

The story itself was pretty much of a switch on *Steamboat Bill, Jr.,* except that Marie, as a rugged old aunt, would be playing opposite me instead of Ernest Torrence. The background was Fort Dodge shortly after the Civil War. A wagon train is about to leave for the West. In the rocker on the porch of her little shanty sits Marie Dressler. She is all ready and packed to go along. Before her house is a covered wagon, smaller than the others and drawn by one horse. Her mule is also saddled for the trip, and she has a milk cow in the stable which she also intends to take along.

As she rocks she takes out a letter from her purse and reads it. It is from her sister back East who begs Marie not to leave with the wagon train as it is too dangerous an undertaking for a lone defenseless woman. The sister is therefore sending her son, Ronald, to join her. He will arrive on May 18. This is the day, and Marie goes down to the station to meet the train, but Ronald is not on it. When asked by an old friend whether she is going along with the wagon-train party she explains she has to wait for her nephew. He shrugs, and the expedition leaves without her.

I arrive the next day with one carpetbag. I am obviously a weakling, and the absurdity of a scared-looking, little guy like me protecting the husky Marie Dressler from Indians, rapists, or even prairie dogs sets up the audience for a big laugh. I am full of heroic ideas, though, and I talk her into leaving with me at once. I am sure we can catch up with the wagon train.

When I got to this point, I explained to Thalberg, "That's all I have as yet. But I'd like to work on it." Now Irving Thalberg was only twenty-three then, four years younger than I, but already he had shown that he had the keenest appreciation of story values, both comic and tragic, of any executive in Hollywood. He admitted that my story had good points.

"But it's a little frail, Buster," he added. "There is really not much to it."

But he promised to give it some thought.

He was just being polite, of course.

This is the perfect illustration of my point, because Thalberg, as well as being a fine judge of light comedy and farce, also appreciated good slapstick whenever he saw it on the screen. No truck driver ever guffawed louder at my better sight gags than did that fragile, intellectual boy genius. Nevertheless, he lacked the true low-comedy mind. Like any man who must concern himself with mass production he was seeking a pattern, a format. Slapstick comedy has a format, but it is hard to detect in its early stages unless you are one of those who can create it. The unexpected was our staple product, the unusual our object, and the unique was the ideal we were always hoping to achieve.

Brilliant though he was, Irving Thalberg could not accept the way a comedian like me built his stories. Though it seems an odd thing to say, I believe that he would have been lost working in my little studio. His mind was too orderly for our harum-scarum, catch-as-catch-can, gag-grabbing method. Our way of operating would have seemed hopelessly mad to him. But, believe me, it was the only way. Somehow some of the frenzy and hysteria of our breathless, impromptu comedy building got into our movies and made them exciting.

There was nothing impromptu about the preparations for the first story I actually filmed at M-G-M. This was *The Cameraman*. In this I played a would-be newsreel photographer. William Randolph Hearst was a big stockholder in the company, and somebody had figured out that by using such a character we could legitimately publicize the newsreel company he owned, and in return his newspapers would give the picture an unusual amount of space. I had no objection because the idea also presented wonderful possibilities for good gags.

As the story starts I am a tintype photographer, the sort who makes pictures in a minute or two for ten cents each. This day I see Gertrude Ederle arrive at the Battery in New York, fresh from her English Channel swim. I join the crowd following her up Broadway to City Hall where Mayor Walker presents Gertrude with the key to the city.

There I fall in love with Marceline Day, who is working with the Hearst newsreel-camera unit. I immediately decide to become a newsreel cameraman. I feel sure I can get on the Hearst staff, which will enable me to meet, woo, and win that gorgeous-looking creature.

At a pawnshop I hock my tintype camera for $6.80, then go home to empty my piggy bank of $1.80 more. With the $8.60 I buy one of the first Pathé cameras ever made. It is so ancient a model that it is cranked from the rear instead of the side. With this equipment I consider myself ready to shoot any and all newsreel subjects. But when I go to the Hearst office and apply for a job everybody there but Marceline, the receptionist, laughs at me and my camera. Marceline, feeling sorry for me, confides that if I photographed a few news events as a free-lance and brought them in, she would try to sell them to her boss for me.

This is the story point we had reached when the *crème de la crème* of the M-G-M writing staff began descending on us in droves. Most of these men were very good writers and resourceful plotters. That was one of the troubles. They were too resourceful, and each naturally wished to contribute something. In all there were twenty-two staff writers helping us.

They complicated our simple plot with everything they could think of—gangsters, Salvation Army street bands, Tammany Hall politicians, longshoremen, and lady gem thieves.

And it wasn't only the twenty-two writers who were eager to help me out. The executives and studio big shots also turned into gagmen overnight, adding greatly to the confusion. With so much talk going on, so many conferences, so many brains at work, I began to lose faith for the first time in my own ideas.

Nevertheless, after eight head-busting months we did have a story written down, complete with camera directions for Sedgwick, who had been a top comedy director for years without any such instructions.

At long last we set off for New York to take some background shots. In the party were Sedgwick, Ed Brophy, our unit manager,

Marceline Day, myself, and our two cameramen, Elgin Lessley and Reggie Lanning.

In New York and other cities crowds always will hamper your work. But we had figured out how to camouflage to some extent what we were doing. Usually we would hire a big limousine, pull down its side curtains, and shoot with both cameras through the small window in the rear.

The first shot we attempted in New York was one of me, carrying my tintype camera, crossing the trolley tracks at Fifth Avenue and 23rd Street. As I was doing this, the motorman stopped his trolley in the middle of the crossing and yelled, "Hey, *Keaton!*" His passengers looked out of the windows and also began to shout things at me.

In no time at all I was surrounded by so many people that the nearest cop couldn't even get near me. Quickly the east-west trolleys were backed up for three blocks, also the north-south trolleys on Broadway and the double-decker buses on Fifth Avenue, not to mention the rest of the traffic flowing from six points of the compass.

When I was finally hauled back to the anguished Sedgwick, I pointed out to him the mocking irony of the line in the script describing this scene. It read: "No one in New York knows that this character exists." And when we tried to get a couple of other scenes at the Battery which the script called for, I was again mobbed.

Giving up for the day, we all went back to our suite in the Ambassador Hotel. None of us knew what to do, and in no time at all big Eddie Sedgwick was in bed, taking bromides and yelling for an ice pack.

We called Irving Thalberg in Hollywood and told him that we were unable to get the shots the present script called for. We did not have to remind him that so much of the story was built around these shots that without them we'd have no picture.

After both Sedgwick and Ed Brophy discussed this with Thalberg, I got on the telephone.

"Like Chaplin and Lloyd, I never worked before with a script written on paper," I said, "and I don't have to now. All I ask is that you let me throw away this script and the shooting schedule and permit Sedgwick and myself to decide what to shoot here."

Thalberg agreed. He had no alternative with us 3,000 miles away and burning up more time and money each day.

Given carte blanche we threw away the written script that had taken eight months to produce. In our version the crack Hearst cameraman became the villain, also my rival for the girl's affections. But the important job we did was simplifying the plot line from beginning to end. Our story also made it possible to shoot all but two of the New York scenes in Hollywood.

But to get the two scenes we could only make in New York we waited until Sunday. We also took the precaution of making them in the early morning hours when New York's good people are in church, and her bad people still in bed sleeping off their Saturday night wickedness. One scene was at the Fifth Avenue entrance to Central Park where the old horse-cabs have their stand. The other was in the lobby of the Ambassador Hotel and on the street in front of its entrance. In that scene I rush to the hotel on hearing that an admiral of high rank is leaving the hotel. I find a man, whose chest is covered with gold braid, going through the lobby and into the street. In great excitement I film his every step only to find out that he is not an admiral but the hotel doorman.

Some double exposures my tintype cameraman produced got big laughs in that picture. I took newsreel shots of a battleship going down the Hudson and also of the New York Police Parade. When developed, my film showed the battleship sailing down Fifth Avenue and New York's Finest marching bravely on the Hudson River.

Another scene in *The Cameraman* that movie-goers liked showed me photographing a ship's launching. In my eagerness to get the whole thing right I planted my camera on the cradle which slides the vessel into the water. As the ship is launched, my camera and I are launched with it.

During other misadventures I picked up an organ-grinder's monkey. Toward the end of the picture I rescued the girl from drowning, deserting my camera to do this. But circumstances enabled my rival to claim credit for this. However, my monkey kept turning the camera crank, and when the film in my camera was shown in the projection room it revealed me as the hero.

In the last scene the girl and I walked up Lower Broadway. She kept telling me how everybody admired me. Suddenly the windows on all floors of the skyscrapers we're passing open, and ticker tape and confetti by the bale are thrown out. Believing the acclaim is for me, I bow and blow kisses at all my admirers. But the last shot of the picture reveals that the excited welcome is really for a man riding right behind us, a fellow named Lindbergh who had just made a solo flight over the Atlantic Ocean.

This shot, like many others we used of New York in that picture, was taken from newsreel footage made of the actual events. Our work, except for the scenes taken on that one Sunday morning in New York, was all done at the studio or on nearby locations.

The sequence which furnished the longest laugh in the picture was found at Venice, California, which we dressed up—or down— to look like New York's Coney Island. Its gags were invented on the spot by Sedgwick, myself, and our two writers, Lew Lipton and Clyde Bruckman. Here is how the sequence went:

Marceline and I arrive at the beach and separate to undress in the bathhouse. The men's section is so crowded that two of us are being put into the same room which is about three feet wide and three feet deep, making it a tight squeeze for two men. Each bathhouse had six hooks on its walls. We removed four hooks, because a couple of men struggling to hang all of their clothes on one hook apiece could be very funny.

As usual we did not rehearse the scene. As I've said, rehearsed scenes look mechanical on the screen. Sedgwick, who had been an actor before turning to direction, wanted to do the bathhouse sequence with me. But I turned down the suggestion because he was so much bigger than I. I told him that the audience would expect a man of his size to throw me out of the bathhouse if irritated.

What I wanted was a fellow about my size who looked like a grouch but not the sort who dares start a fight. There were dozens of actors in Hollywood who fitted this description, but we were at the beach. That meant it would take hours to find the right one and get him to Venice.

I settled for Ed Brophy, our unit manager. He filled the bill on looks, although he had never done any acting. As it turned out, Brophy did so well that he has been making a first-rate living ever since acting that same irritable, worry-eaten, little character.

In that bathhouse scene we both were in a frenzy to get into our bathing suits and on the beach. Like myself, he was afraid that his girl might catch the eye of a lifeguard or some other husky chap and be picked up before we could get out there.

For our first gag I got my head caught in the suspenders he has just taken off. This as I tried to straighten up after unlacing my shoe. In taking off my tie I catch his elbow. I take off my coat which falls on him. He takes off his shoe and in coming up gets his head between my legs, upending me and sliding me off his shoulder. Meanwhile our clothes keep falling off the hooks on us. When we emerge from the bathhouse I have on a bathing suit four times too big for me while Brophy's is so small it is choking him to death.

The scene ran for four minutes, which is a very long time on the screen for a string of gags worked by just two men in a single ridiculous situation. Thalberg almost had hysterics when he saw that day's rushes in a projection room.

One day, quite a while after we finished *The Cameraman,* Thalberg asked me, "Now what was the story you wanted to do with Marie Dressler?"

But by then, as a reward for her great performance in *Anna Christie,* Marie was being starred. And at that time no one was using two stars in comedies like mine.

So I had to say, "It is too late for that story now." And he agreed that nobody but Marie would have been right for that role.

What I couldn't understand was why, after I proved my point, the big wheels at M-G-M would not allow me to have my own unit. I kept pleading, "Give me Eddie Sedgwick to direct, two or three writers, my own prop man, electrician, wardrobe woman, and a few technicians, and I will guarantee to deliver pictures as good or better than *The Cameraman.*"

I went into great detail about this, particularly with the gentle, soft-spoken, brilliant Thalberg. I tried to show him how much more effectively I could work with a unit of my own. "My prop man,"

I pointed out, "knowing how I work, will need few instructions. He can go out and buy whatever I need without my telling him. My cameraman will not stop grinding even if the director says 'Cut!' Knowing how I work, he will keep on because he has seen me take a fall or do something else on the spur of the moment. For instance, a package might accidentally fall off the shelf and give me a new notion. With each man knowing his job, much time and money will be saved. When we are ready to start each new picture the crew will have everything prepared and ready."

Most of the real heavy charges in movies come when you are in production. Any delay—a principal getting sick, bad weather, an accident to the equipment—can cost a fortune. So, once started, the quicker you get your picture finished and in the can the fewer the hazards.

Another obvious difficulty of working with different specialists on each picture was that they so often behave like prima donnas. Having less to gain through pleasing me than men on my team would, they were often more interested in getting outstanding results for their specialty instead of co-operating fully to get the story told in the quickest and best way possible. Not being on a team they rarely forgot that their next assignment depended on their work standing out, instead of being subordinated to the excellence of the picture as a whole. Under M-G-M's system each craftsman was more beholden to the head of his department than to me.

If they had been part of my regular unit I could have controlled them and kept them working as a team interested chiefly in the production itself. For example, sometimes, if a corner was not perfectly lighted we would not care enough about this to stop the camera, bring in more lighting equipment, and reshoot the scene. But the electrician who worried about being criticized by his chief didn't care how long he delayed us so long as he got his lighting exactly right.

The fact is that no picture ever became a smash hit because of its perfect lighting, wonderful sets, or exceptional camera work. The story was always the thing, with the star next in importance.

Thalberg, Mannix, and Louis B. Mayer all must have understood this. Yet they never did let me have my own unit. That would have lessened their power and control, I know, but only a little. I suppose the real reason was that they feared that if they yielded to me sooner or later every star on the lot would be demanding his own unit.

If I was not happy at M-G-M my 170-pound St. Bernard, Elmer, was. Each working day I brought him with me to the studio where he spent his time sunning himself on the porch of the bungalow assigned to me. Because Elmer was always there when I was, we called the bungalow "Keaton's Kennel."

Elmer had a very superior canine intelligence. Even our vet agreed to that, and as all dog-lovers know, sincere praise from a vet for any dog is praise indeed.

Early one morning the vet called me at the house. "Is Elmer back home yet?" he asked. I looked out of the back window and told him Elmer was out there all right.

"The reason I ask," explained the vet, "is that at one o'clock this morning I was awakened by scratching noises on my door. I got up, opened the door, and was astonished to find Elmer.

"As you know, Buster, the vet's is the last place any dog will come near—if he can help it. The odors of the animal hospital remind him of all the injections and terrible-tasting medicines he was forced to take there. 'What's up, Elmer?' I asked, and he came in limping. On examining him, I found a rose thorn in one of his paws. After extracting it, I opened the door, and he trotted out. After all, I figured that if he was smart enough to find his way here over three miles of road he'd be smart enough to get home. But I called just to make sure."

In the manner of large dogs of aristocratic lineage Elmer was indifferent to the cooings and caresses of members outside the family circle.

Our bungalow was located where the Irving Thalberg Memorial Building now stands, and all of the M-G-M stars, featured players, and Big Brass walked by daily. Elmer, usually with a yawn, permitted a few of them to pet him. But only for a moment or two, then he would get up and walk away in boredom.

Whenever Garbo was making a picture at M-G-M she had a light lunch in her dressing room, then walked the entire length of the studio, including the back lot where the large outdoor sets were located.

The first three or four times that Elmer saw the immortal Swede stroll by he observed her, I noticed, with unusual interest. One day he got up from his favorite spot on the porch and joined her. Each day after that Elmer would accompany Garbo on her mid-day strolls across the lot and back to the door of her dressing room. But whenever Garbo tried to pet Elmer he drew back and moved away. It was as though he considered such familiarity from a mere walking acquaintance in bad taste.

It went on for years that way, with Garbo loving her volunteer guard and strolling companion but never annoying him with so much as a pat on the jowls.

THE TALKIE
REVOLUTION

Until the coming of TV nothing ever rocked Hollywood like the talkie revolution. It all but destroyed the world market for American films. Thousands of the movie theatres in foreign countries were never wired for sound.

Most of the great silent stars were also put out of business by the talkie revolution. Women fans were dismayed to learn that John Gilbert, the man of their romantic dreams, had a squeaky voice. They also lost interest in Norma Talmadge, the screen's greatest lady, and scores of other fabulously paid silent stars whose real voices did not fit the personality which the public had imagined was theirs. Warner Brothers in 1926 became the first studio to exploit talking pictures. But it took the other studios several years to accept the unpleasant fact that talkies were not just a fad.

On finally waking up, the other studios tried to make up for lost time by rushing out platoons of Broadway performers who could "speak" to replace the silent screen stars, starlets, character people, and comics whose careers had been wrecked on the sound track.

But the talkies did not wreck my career. Quite to the contrary. The first talking picture I appeared in was an all-star musical, *The Hollywood Revue*. Everybody at M-G-M who could sing, dance, talk, whistle, or mumble appeared in this one. Look at the stardust-powdered cast: Conrad Nagel, Jack Benny, John Gilbert, Norma Shearer, Joan Crawford, Bessie Love, Charles King, Lionel Barrymore, Laurel and Hardy, Marie Dressler, Polly Moran, and last, and I hope not least, your Buster and mine. The hit of that glittering show was Cliff (Ukulele Ike) Edwards's number, "Singing in the Rain," the song which Gene Kelly repeated with such success just a season or two ago in *Les Girls*.

The Hollywood Revue was a walloping hit.

And *Free and Easy*, the first talkie I starred in, was among the company's biggest money-makers of the year. Louis B. Mayer was so pleased by the large earnings of *Free and Easy* that he rewarded me with a $10,000 bonus and a three-month vacation with pay. Adding my $3,000 a week salary for thirteen weeks, the bonus, I suppose, actually amounted to $49,000.

On our vacation my wife and I took a leisurely trip through Europe. After visiting England, France, and Germany we toured Spain with Gilbert Roland, who was born in Madrid but soon afterward was taken to Mexico City where he grew up.

Gilbert was one of the many romantic-looking Latins who got their chance in Hollywood following the sensational success of Rudolph Valentino. He is about the only one in the group still active.

One of the thrills of the trip for me was being hailed by the Spaniards as "Pamplinas," their nickname for me. I found out what "Pamplinas" means only recently when I appeared with José Greco on the Garry Moore TV program. While the brilliant flamenco dancer was rehearsing I asked him to translate the word into English. He couldn't, but held an animated conversation on the subject for about ten minutes with his manager and the members of his troupe.

This in Spanish, of course, which I understand about as well as I do Japanese. Finally Greco turned to me and explained, " 'Pamplinas' in English means 'a little bit of nothing.' "

" 'A little bit of nothing!' " I exclaimed. "Couldn't they call me 'a little bit of something?' That would be bad enough. But a little bit of nothing! After all——"

Greco told me that I was mistaken. He explained: "That's the finest compliment my countrymen could pay you." I could only reply, "It sure loses something in the translation."

My French nickname "Malec" for which there also is no literal English translation means about the same thing—"the hole in the doughnut" or "a blank piece of paper."

Another big thrill for me was going to the bullfights with a knowledgeable aficionado like Gilbert Roland. Until then I had seen only third-rate contests in such Mexican border towns as Tijuana and Juarez. Gilbert, on the other hand, had been studying this bravest of all sports since he was a little boy in Mexico. He was only too happy to explain the fine points to me. My wife did not go to the arena with us, as she thought bullfighting cruel. So Gilbert Roland and I attended the fights alone. We saw all of the fights we could, beginning with those at San Sebastian. Now I am not one of those actors who is embarrassed or annoyed when recognized by movie fans. To me, they are customers, and I try to behave toward them as though I were fully aware of that.

So I was anything but displeased when someone in that crowd at San Sebastian caught sight of me and passed the word along that "Pamplinas" was a fellow spectator. Soon you could hear the whisper "Pamplinas" passing all around that large amphitheatre. And in no time the entire arena was reverberating with shouts of "Pamplinas! Pamplinas!"

The nicest thing about getting this sort of big hello in Spain is that the fans demand so little of you. Perhaps this is not surprising in a country where dignity is held every man's birthright. All Spanish fans expect you to do is acknowledge their greeting by standing up and bowing. They don't claw at you or ask for your autograph. You sit down and also leave, unpawed, unpestered, and you are deeply touched that such considerate people have paid you a tribute.

Another appreciated honor that day was having the Number One matador dedicate the second bull he killed to their old deadpan "Pamplinas!"

I got the same heartwarming reception at other bullfights we attended. But the most memorable experience of this sort I had on the trip was in Toledo whose wooden bull ring was the most picturesque arena in all Spain.

It was a dreadful day for the matadors. All three had wretched luck, but the worst of it was reserved for the featured matador. The first bull he faced was so bad he was unable to put up a decent contest. His second bull could not be lured, bullied, or irritated into following his red cloth. There is nothing a matador can do to arouse the fighting spirit of a beast under such circumstances.

Now, those aficionados at Toledo knew this, of course, far better than I. Nevertheless that crowd was merciless. They screamed, whistled, hooted, and threw their cushions and everything else movable at the luckless matador. They demanded that the President of the Bullfight order him thrown out of the ring. But this was merely their first request. Before the afternoon was over they were pleading with the President of the Bullfight to have the man cast into a dungeon to be castrated by the village blacksmith.

At this fight, as at others, I had stood up, my heart swelling with pride and gratitude on being recognized. But when a howling mob of spectators surged down upon me as we were leaving I was not so sure that they were not going to wreak their vengeance on me. After all, they were, as far as I could gather, in no mood for hero worship. And I looked around for Gilbert Roland, who might have explained to me what was going on, but I had lost him in the crowd.

Meanwhile I was being lifted on the shoulders of a couple of husky young fellows who started carrying me to our hotel. Even then, with all kinds of shouting going on, I couldn't figure out whether they planned to kiss me or lynch me as a foreigner who had put the jinx on their show. I felt quite relieved when I was set down in one piece on the hotel's front steps.

Gilbert Roland then came running up. "What in hell did they do that for?" I asked him as we went inside.

Gilbert explained that the Toledans were in the habit each Sunday of carrying on their shoulders the matador who had most distinguished himself during the afternoon. He said, "They didn't care to return to town empty-handed. So they carried you back. You see now, Buster, what humble men these are. They'll settle for anybody, even you."

When we got to Granada the local Rotary Club invited us to a lunch in a beautiful restaurant. About a hundred persons were present and listened solemnly to the speeches their officers made to welcome us and to Roland's response.

After that many toasts were offered, by the presiding member, and drunk. Gilbert explained what each was for. But after we'd downed the last goblet of wine, he was silent.

"Don't hold out on me," I said. "What was that last toast for?"

"Oh, we were drinking to the death of the king," he replied casually.

I was horrified to hear I'd been drinking to the death of a man who had done me no harm, whom I did not know, and in whose country we were traveling.

"But I thought Alfonso was the most popular man in Spain!" I exclaimed to Roland. "Why do they want their king to die?"

Roland shrugged. "Alfonso *is* very popular. Nobody has anything against him *personally*. They are just sick of having to keep and support a royal family. They think it would help business a lot if they got rid of him and his whole gang any way they could."

"If that is the state of things in Spain," I said, "don't you think it might be smart to start heading home?"

Smilingly, Gilbert agreed, and that very day we started on the long trip North. And on April 14, 1931, the day we left Spain for France, the toothy, gay Alfonso also crossed the Portuguese border never to return to the country he had been born to rule.

That same year my matrimonial troubles began. Perhaps it would be more accurate to say they began in earnest that year. Like the wife of every other male movie star, my wife had previously had attacks of jealousy. I suppose this was natural. M-G-M, along with the other major studios, employed dozens of the world's most beautiful women. Some of them were very young and exceedingly eager to make a place for themselves in pictures. Some of them did not limit their use of sex appeal to get what they wanted to the hours they spent before the camera.

There are always benevolent characters in Hollywood, and I suppose every other town in the world, who unselfishly drop all of their own business the first chance they get to interfere in yours. My wife was forever hearing stories about my over-friendliness to this bright-eyed starlet or that leading lady.

Most of these stories had not a grain of truth in them. Most, I say, not all. The only comment I care to make on this is that I would like to see the healthy, normal man in my spot at M-G-M who could resist more feminine temptation than I did.

But Mrs. Buster Keaton kept seeing rivals everywhere. A good example is what had happened when I went on a duck-hunting trip early in 1930 with Buster Collier and Gilbert Roland. Marie Prevost, who was Collier's girl friend at the time, insisted on coming along. We were snowed in on that trip, and the Los Angeles *Examiner* heard about it and published the story under this headline:

MARIE PREVOST
SNOWED IN WITH
THREE COMPANIONS

There was no other girl along, but nothing I could say could convince my wife of that. Once or twice she threatened to leave me. I do not know yet whether these threats were made seriously or to scare me into being a nice little husband who was always at home in time for dinner and polite to her guests.

Then, one day in February 1932, all hell broke loose. An actress invaded my dressing room at M-G-M and announced that she had made up her mind that I should support her. When I refused, she ripped off my shirt and started to scratch and claw away at me. Ukulele Ike Edwards and Clarence Locan, an M-G-M publicity man, were there when this tigress walked in. But both of them ran for their lives when she steamed into action. Meanwhile, this gentlewoman was breaking my dressing-room windows and screaming like some crazy old witch. I had been too stunned by her daffy behavior to move. But when the lady picked up a pair of long shears and lunged at me with them I belted her in the jaw in self-defense.

At this point a couple of Culver City policemen arrived. They turned out to be unlucky cops. When they tried to drag her away she kicked one in the genitals and took a backhanded swipe at the other, giving him a black eye.

The next day I was summoned to Irving Thalberg's office. Eddie Mannix was with him. They showed me a report from the woman's doctor stating that when I hit her I broke her jaw.

"Now she wants $10,000 from you," said Mannix. "If she doesn't get it she'll bring the whole mess into court."

"The hell with her," I said. "I didn't hit her hard enough to break her jaw. And no one with a fractured jaw was ever able to yell as loud as she did at those two cops."

"If you guys are worried about this," I added, "let the company fork over the $10,000 that will shut her up."

"No," said Mannix, "you'll have to pay her. The name of M-G-M must not be on the check."

But he seemed to think it all right for the name of Buster Keaton to be on the check. They continued to argue, and in the end I made out the $10,000 check and handed it over.

Needless to say, it was a long, long time before I heard the last at home about this depressing incident. But eventually everything seemed to be patched up. I was told I was being forgiven only for the sake of the children.

Less than a year later I got a chance to buy the sort of boat I'd always wanted at a bargain price. It was a 98-foot ocean-going cruiser with a Diesel twin-screw engine, two master bedrooms, three smaller bedrooms, and a lounge which slept four more. It required a crew of five: captain, engineer, cook, steward, and deck hand. One of its two lifeboats had carried a six-cylinder engine. This dream ship had been built for the publisher of the Seattle *Times* at a cost of $102,000, but he had used it only once. On its maiden trip his wife and both of his children got terribly seasick, and in disgust he immediately put it up for sale. I got that slim, lovely, ocean-going yacht, which had seen only forty hours of service, for $25,000 cash. When the deal was set I went up to Seattle and sailed her to San Pedro Harbor—with some small assistance from the captain and crew, of course.

That weekend we took a large party of friends on a trip to Catalina Island. Among those on board was my boss, Louis B. Mayer. After looking the craft over, he said, "I don't know what you paid for this boat, Buster, but whatever it was, you can make a $10,000 profit right now by selling it to me."

We had almost reached Catalina before I realized our two boys weren't aboard.

"Where are the kids?" I asked Mrs. Keaton. "This would be great for them."

She explained that she had them at a friend's ranch for the weekend. "I was afraid that they might fall overboard." That seemed absurd to me. Jim and Bob had been given swimming lessons as soon as they could walk. And I told my wife that the idea of them having any such accident with the crowd we had aboard was ridiculous.

During the next week my wife disappeared, leaving no note or other word saying where she was going or when she would come back. Toward the end of the week I decided to give the boys a treat I had long been promising them; this was a weekend trip by airplane to Tijuana.

I took the boys' nurse along to take care of them. We traveled in a chartered plane, piloted by an aviator noted for his reliability. He carefully checked weather reports and equipment before each flight and refused to take up passengers if the slightest risk was involved.

The boys had the time of their young lives on the way down to San Diego, where we had to stop to get clearance papers before flying across the border. When we landed at San Diego the governess took Jim and Bob to the rest room.

After they were gone for ten minutes or so I went to the rest room to look for them. The attendant told me that my sons and their governess had just been taken away in a police car. I hurried to the nearest police station in a cab. My kids were there all right.

"What did they do now?" I asked the police official behind the desk.

"The boys haven't done anything," he explained. "But I just got a long-distance telephone call from a public official in Los Angeles requesting me to hold these boys to prevent you from kidnaping them."

"Kidnaping them?" I demanded. "How can a man kidnap his own children?"

"Damned if I know," he said, shaking his head. "But I have a lawyer on his way here to tell me why I'm holding them."

Before I had a chance to point out how silly this was the telephone on his desk rang. It turned out to be Eddie Mannix who said that my wife had phoned him in a panic.

"She's afraid you're going to hide the boys from her in Mexico," he said. "She's also dead set against the idea of taking them on a dangerous trip in an airplane. You know how women are."

He explained that he was coming down to Tijuana himself in the morning. Before he left he would talk to my wife and then see me when he got to San Diego.

"Okay," I said, "but at least tell this police official here to let me put the kids and the governess up at a hotel here. You can assure him I won't leave the United States without letting him know."

Next day we went home to find my wife still among the missing. That really drove me wild. What was wrong with her? What did she want of me? Why had she spoiled our weekend and caused all of that ridiculous trouble?

A story had even been published in the newspapers that charged me with trying to carry the boys into Mexico without her permission. I began drinking and continued drinking all of that day and part of the next. Meanwhile I heard not a word from my wife.

Late on Monday afternoon I went down to the studio. I was more than half full of whiskey and ready to explode with indignation. I saw an extra girl sitting outside of the casting office. She had just finished her day's work, she said. I didn't know her, had never seen her before, never saw her again, and do not know her name even now. I could not say today whether she was blonde, brunette, or a redhead.

"Have you a date tonight?" I asked her.

"No," she said.

"Do you want to come with me?"

"Yes."

I took her home with me and led her straight to the huge wardrobe in Mrs. Keaton's room. In this my wife had 150 pairs of shoes, most of which she had never put on since buying them. Also in the wardrobe were three fur coats and dozens upon dozens of frocks, house-coats, cocktail dresses, and evening gowns.

"Take whatever you want," I kept saying to the bewildered little extra. Whenever she hesitated, I would say, "Do you like these?" and yank a handful of clothes from the rack and pile them on the floor. And, "What about these nice things?" Then pile more on the floor.

Even through my alcoholic haze I could see that the girl, even as she accepted the clothes, was trying to humor me. I suppose she realized she would have to return them later on.

After a while, though, she started taking things from the rack too, possibly to placate me. But I didn't think the pile of stuff on the floor was growing fast enough. I grabbed more armfuls of dresses, underthings, stockings, and finally a mink coat.

When the pile of clothes on the floor was big enough to satisfy me, the extra girl said she didn't know where to take them. "Don't give it a thought, my dear," I told her, "I have the solution. You and I will go a-sailing on the high seas."

I telephoned the skipper of my cruiser and told him to get everything ready as we were about to start off on a trip, maybe down the coast of Old Mexico, possibly only to Catalina.

"Get fuel and provisions aboard and full steam up," I said.

By the time we got aboard it was eleven o'clock. "Okay, skipper," I told the captain. "Are we ready to go?"

"I can't move the boat, sir," he said, "without the owner's permission."

"Your troubles are over," I said, "I give you permission to heave ho."

"You don't seem to understand, sir."

"No, I do not."

"Mrs. Keaton is the owner of the boat, and some time ago she gave strict orders that I should take it out only with her permission."

It was some time before I could grasp the point. Then I recalled taking some fool's advice when buying the insurance for the boat. This fellow said that if I registered the cruiser in my wife's name I could save 20 per cent of the insurance premium. Actors, he told me, were considered unreliable types by the underwriters. Why their wives were considered better risks he didn't explain.

Technically, therefore, the cruiser did not belong to me but to my wife.

I argued with the captain, made whimpering noises, and tried to bribe him, but in vain. He remained as firm, steadfast, and purposeful as the boy on the burning deck.

Discouraged, I strolled over to Roland West's boat which was moored in the berth next to ours. West, a well-known screen writer and director, lived on his boat. He got out a bottle of whiskey, and I discussed the crisis with him.

"The skipper's right," he said.

"Can't I fire the captain?" I asked. "And hire someone else who doesn't know so much?"

By that time I was almost on the point of passing out. West explained that there were all sorts of papers and documents that had to be filled out before you could leave port in so large a craft.

"Well, even if I don't own the boat," I asked, mollified, "do you think I could sleep on it tonight?"

We went back to my boat to confer with the captain who made no objection. After getting aboard all of the clothes we had taken from my wife's wardrobe, the girl and I went to sleep in a cabin. And I do mean to sleep. Nothing else happened.

Somebody who did not have my real interests at heart must have telephoned my wife about some of the evening's booze-inspired goings on, because she arrived on the cruiser's dock about two o'clock that morning accompanied by her sister and two private detectives and an important public official.

One of the detectives came aboard with my wife and her sister. The other sleuth remained on the dock with the official, whose purpose in joining the raiding party I never learned. It was just as well that he did not venture aboard. He had been a guest at our house many times and until that moment I had considered him a friend. Whether I was drunk or sober, I would have pushed him overboard if he had even set foot on the cruiser. I was still sore for the shabby part he had played in the San Diego fiasco. His coming around now with my wife's raiding party was to me the last straw.

The two ladies and the detective, after establishing the facts on which an adultery charge could be based, busied themselves gathering up all of the clothes we had removed from the house.

"My lawyer will call on you in the morning," said my wife, and that was all she did say to me. She was hurt pretty badly, I guess. It is the only explanation I have for her subsequent actions.

The lawyer who called on me next morning was one of the best in the business. He brought the divorce action for my wife on July 25, 1932.

There is a community property law in California, but I refused to get a lawyer to safeguard my rights. The last thing I would claim is that I was smart about this; I was simply too stunned to put up any sort of fight.

The lawyer asked and obtained for Mrs. Keaton practically everything I had in the world. The list included our $300,000 home in Beverly Hills, two of our three cars, about $30,000 worth of other property I owned, $12,000 in cash which I had in the bank, the lawyer's counsel fees, custody of the boys and $300 a month for their support, plus $80,000 in insurance policies on my life.

I say I was too stunned and hurt to fight. With my whole home life swept away so unfairly I just told myself, "the hell with the money and everything else. Let her have everything she wants." It is also true that it never occurred to me that I possibly might not continue to be a big money-maker for as long as I wished.

About all I had left when my wife obtained an interlocutory decree on August 8 were my clothes and the third car. I did not even have a place to live.

After the divorce my wife immediately put the boys in an exclusive private school, the Black-Fox Academy in Hollywood, and took a long vacation in Europe. They were spoiled enough already, I felt, without acquiring the snobbery that often rubs off on boys in that sort of school.

The divorce decree allowed me visiting privileges, which I assumed meant I could take them out of the school for a weekend occasionally. But the first time I tried the head of the school told me that his strict orders were not to let me take them away overnight.

Shortly after the divorce, I borrowed $10,000 to buy something called a land yacht. I had read about it in a newspaper, and it seemed ideal for my purposes. I lived in it for about a year.

The land yacht originally cost $50,000, had been built for a railroad president by the Pullman Company. It had twin motors in the chassis of a Fifth Avenue bus, contained two drawing rooms, a galley, an observation platform, and slept eight persons.

After using this fancy house on wheels for eighteen months or so the railroad executive had died, and I bought it from his widow. Even then, during the depression, it was impossible to buy much of a house for that.

I had as much fun with my land yacht as a man can whose main purpose is to forget that his whole private world has fallen apart.

One weekend, for instance, Lew Cody and I drove the land yacht to San Francisco and parked it near the Palace Hotel's main entrance. Half of the hotel staff came running out, apparently believing some wild-spending Indian potentate had arrived. The general manager asked me if I wanted my usual suite.

"Not this time," I said. "Throw down a telephone from a second-story window that we can use, and we also will want all room-service privileges. To show you that our hearts are in the right place we will pay you the regular parking fee—fifty cents a day."

They laughed and agreed. That's San Francisco for you.

We stayed there for three days, later went on hunting and fishing trips in Arizona and other Western states. My land yacht got big newspaper space everywhere we took it. We also used it in a show put on for Franklin D. Roosevelt who had just been nominated as the 1932 Democratic presidential candidate.

The following year I went abroad to make two pictures. While I was away my wife obtained a court order changing our boys' last name from mine to hers. The first I heard about this was when I returned. I knew that the court order would be revoked if I appealed, for I had never been served with any papers in the case.

But it was something I wanted to think over. My wife's family had a lot of money—a great, great pile. My boys were the only children in the family, and it meant a lot to my in-laws to perpetuate their name. I knew my sons would be left all of this fortune someday if I did not make any legal moves to change their name back to Keaton. I did not want to do anything to lose them that chance of becoming rich. I was not sure that I would ever have a dime to leave them. For by that time I had been fired by M-G-M.

THE CHAPTER
I HATE TO WRITE

For quite a while before the breakup of my marriage I had not been happy about the way things were working out at the studio. Despite everything I could do, control of my comedies kept slipping out of my hands more and more.

Shortly after I started making pictures at M-G-M, Irving Thalberg's brother-in-law, Lawrence Weingarten, had been installed as producer of my pictures. But for quite a while he exercised little more authority over my crew, cast, and selection of story material than the fat cop on the corner. But just about the time I was divorced, Mr. Weingarten decided to stop being a rubber-stamp executive and take over as a producer with an iron will.

Larry Weingarten in the past quarter-century has produced an imposing number of important and successful dramatic pictures. Furthermore, with Thalberg dead these many years and most of the other old M-G-M brass gone, Larry is still there and getting along fine. With the number of high-level shake-ups the studio has undergone, this, needless to say, requires a good deal of talent of another sort.

Nobody can deny that Larry learned his trade somewhere along the line and learned it well. But his trade was never slapstick comedy, and that was what I was still doing whether he and the studio's top dogs realized it or not. Perhaps they were deceived because, when I began making full-length features, I had stopped throwing custard pies and also eliminated impossible gags like the one in which I dived through the cement walk and came up years later with a Chinese family.

If they had known I was still essentially a slapstick comedian they would not have bought for me the sort of stories they did. These purchases included two Broadway farces: *Parlor, Bedroom, and Bath* and *Her Cardboard Lover*. In *Her Cardboard Lover* I was assigned the role played on the stage by Leslie Howard, an Englishman with gazelle eyes and manners to match. M-G-M renamed it *The Passionate Plumber*, which was nothing compared to the names the critics called our movie version.

I suppose it isn't entirely fair to blame Larry Weingarten, Louis B. Mayer, or any other person for what happened to me in their studio during those dark days of the depression. The entertainment industry is always the first hit in bad times, and the movie moguls' financial aches and pains in the early thirties were compounded by the upheaval caused by the talkies.

Hard pressed on all sides, the kingpins of Hollywood were forced to make experiments. Many of these turned out disastrously, something which is inevitable when the experiments are inspired by fear and undertaken as a last resort. The experiment I know most about was the one made by Louis B. Mayer when he teamed up Jimmy Durante and myself in a series of features. There is no one in the world like Durante, bless him, but in my opinion we just did not belong in the same movies.

As the dynamo of the smash-em-up team of Clayton, Jackson, and Durante, Jimmy had electrified night-club, vaudeville, and musical-comedy audiences for years. Nothing could have been more hilarious than Jimmy pulling apart a piano or the team's

"Wood! Wood! Wood!" number in which everything constructed of wood, from a kitchen match to a full-sized canoe and an outhouse, was dragged on the stage. Jimmy also was successful, though to a lesser extent, on the radio and was great later in his own TV show.

But the moment he broke up the team at M-G-M's suggestion, Jimmy, depending almost entirely on his singing, piano playing, and priceless personality was unable ever to carry one successful picture. My guess is that without ingenious sight gags to work with he lacked the variety required of the star of a screen comedy running from seventy-five to ninety minutes. But the same thing is true of Ed Wynn and W. C. Fields, two of the greatest clowns of the century, in spite of the fact that they used brilliant sight gags—so my guess about Durante could well be wrong.

At any rate, as I see it, there was no way to mesh, match, or blend Durante's talents with mine. Yet Jimmy would have been great in the pictures that we did together if he had been allowed merely to do spots of comedy instead of playing a character all of the way through.

However, he was very good in the one picture we made together that had quality. I think this was because the character he played was very much like the real Jimmy Durante. The picture was *Speak Easily,* which was based on a Clarence Budington Kelland story and had a sound comedy plot.

From the time Jimmy and I were teamed up I heard rumors that Mr. Mayer was planning to build him up at my expense. This didn't worry me much, although I can't say I liked it. With my record of successful pictures, I felt I was a fixture at M-G-M. I couldn't imagine anyone there wanting to get rid of me. If Jimmy Durante could replace me it would be on his superior ability. Like a lot of men the world considers modest and humble I had unshakable confidence in my talent and ability to hold the place that I had staked out for myself.

The three pictures I made with Durante were *The Passionate Plumber, Speak Easily,* and *What, No Beer?* in that order. I made this last one—a 100 per cent turkey—right after my wife divorced me. I was trying to drink away my sorrow and woe every night. It was the only way I could get to sleep. But one weekend when

I absorbed unusually large quantities of whiskey I was unable to sleep at all.

I came to the studio that Monday so woozy from lack of sleep that I hardly knew what I was doing. Somehow or other I got the crazy idea that the one thing in the world that would wake me up was a bottle of beer. I'd tried coffee and everything else that I could think of, and none of them had helped.

Instead of waking me up, of course, the beer put me to sleep. I laid down on my studio couch for a cat nap. But my exhaustion was so complete that when the assistant director came to call me to the set he couldn't rouse me. Eddie Sedgwick, who was directing, summoned doctors who worked on me and then took me home.

There was no shooting that day. For the first time in my movie career I had delayed production and cost the studio a day's salary for everyone on the picture. I naturally assumed that nothing would be done about this single dereliction of mine. Every other star on the lot had caused them many such losses. I was also the only M-G-M star who had never failed to show up for work on time. Unlike Gilbert, Garbo, and most of the others I was never temperamental, never refused to do anything required of me, including the most hazardous stunts in my pictures.

Since talkies had made necessary the remaking of each picture in Spanish, French, and German, I was the only star at M-G-M who would do all three foreign versions when the original picture was finished.

I rarely heard of the other M-G-M stars agreeing to do more than one of these foreign versions. The remake chore, of course, was easier on me than on dramatic performers who spoke a great many more lines in each picture.

Eddie Sedgwick once said something interesting about this. He said that audiences everywhere knew I was an American and did not expect me to speak their language without making mistakes. Also, being a comedian, I could mispronounce words, and they might think it was on purpose and to get laughs, whereas if a romantic performer made such mistakes he would seem grotesque.

They had worked out an interesting technique for these foreign-language remakes. They used "idiot cards." On these the foreign words are spelled out in phonetic English and held up beyond camera range for the performer to consult as the scenes are shot. I never liked the idiot cards. I preferred memorizing one simple sentence or two or three, while the scenes I was not in were being made. I enjoyed learning how to roll my "r's" in speaking Spanish and French, and mastering the gutturals used in German. Once when we did a German version of a picture just after the French one, the Teutonic language expert said to me, "They told me you were an American. If that's true why are you speaking German with a French accent?"

My working on all foreign versions of my pictures saved the company a fortune, which was an additional reason, in my opinion, for the front office to overlook my beer-drinking error. And that seemed to be the way the big brass also felt. When the picture was finished M-G-M sent me to Arrowhead Springs to dry out in the sulphur caves there for four days—and picked up the check.

I came back feeling fine physically—and got a new shock. While I was away Larry Weingarten, without consulting me, had bought a dog·of a comedy from a director of small-budget comedies and also assigned this man to direct this new picture. I read the story, which was called *The Sidewalks of New York*, and told Larry it was impossible. The plot required me to cope with a gang of juvenile delinquents. I might have done that. What I couldn't cope with, I said, was the plot. But I couldn't convince him he had bought a lemon.

I felt this so strongly that I went over his head and appealed to Irving Thalberg to help get me out of the assignment.

Irving was usually on my side, but this time he said, "Larry likes it. Everybody else in the studio likes the story. You are the only one who doesn't."

In the end, I gave up like a fool and said, "What the hell?" Who was I to say I was right and everyone else wrong? I'd been wrong about my marriage, hadn't I? That was the way I reasoned.

So I mainly blame myself for what happened. The result would have been different if I had trusted my own judgment and not let them put me in parts I couldn't play. I cannot even claim I did not realize that the stories were wrong for me. I knew that when I did them. But somehow *The Sidewalks of New York* was finished and cut. At the preview it did not get a giggle, something which was blamed on me; I have no serious complaint about that. As I see it, the star gets the credit for turning in good pictures. Therefore, it is only fair that he be blamed for the bad ones he is in, including those he was bullied and hornswoggled into working in.

My drinking had steadily increased until I was putting away more than a bottle of whiskey a day. Drinking myself to sleep every night became a habit, and my weekends were all lost weekends.

It was my hard luck also to be engaged just then in a ridiculous controversy with Louis B. Mayer. A short while before the god-awful *Sidewalks of New York* was previewed, I'd been invited to act as mascot for the St. Mary's football team, then one of the best elevens in the country, during its big game of the season, the one with the UCLA Bruins. The invitation meant that I could sit on the bench with the team during the game. I was as thrilled as a child and said I would be there come hell or high weather.

I should have added "unless Louis B. Mayer has other plans for me." This proved to be the case. For some years Mr. Mayer had been indulging himself in a fairly harmless but annoying bit of hocus-pocus on Saturday afternoons in the alleged interest of the studio's public relations.

He liked to get his stars—and Mr. Mayer never thought of us as anything else but *his* stars—to make fake movie scenes for small groups of visitors from out-of-town. It could be a gang of welfare workers from Des Moines, a convention of beer salesmen, Lincoln (Nebraska) schoolteachers on a spree, or the members of a trade association. No matter what the group was or where it came from, Mr. Mayer liked to send instructions to the various companies that were working on the lot to plan some fake scenes for them. They had to be fake scenes, because in those early days of sound, a whisper on a sound stage recorded like a war whoop.

On the day before the great St. Mary's-UCLA game Mr. Mayer sent word through his secretary that I was to be in the studio at two o'clock next day to do my stuff for some sixty members of something or other.

I sent back word that much as I regretted it I could not be there. As I hung up I noticed that some of our crew had already begun to put up a set specially for the visitors and were furnishing it.

A few minutes later there was an ultimatum: "Mr. Mayer says to *be* there."

"I can't," I answered, and St. Mary's beat the Bruins that Saturday 14–7. I enjoyed being mascot, but on Monday when I arrived at the studio there was a letter on my dressing table. It read, "Your services at Metro-Goldwyn-Mayer Studios are no longer required."

It was signed, "Louis B. Mayer, General Manager and Vice-President."

Though my contract with the studio had several months to run I did not consult a lawyer about the matter. Once again I felt too sick and hurt and crushed to do anything at all about my legal rights. I certainly could have obtained a settlement even though technically M-G-M may have had the right to discharge me for causing the *What, No Beer?* company to miss a whole day's shooting.

Stupid not to have done this? Of course. But by that time I was drinking more than a bottle of whiskey a day which neither improved my mental processes nor lessened my sense of humiliation.

Shortly after I was thrown out I did something even more stupid. I had a chance to come back and refused to accept it. That happened this way:

While I was making my last picture or two at M-G-M the company was also producing its fabulous all-star picture *Grand Hotel* with most of the lot's great stars in the cast. Among them were Greta Garbo, Joan Crawford, John and Lionel Barrymore, Wallace Beery, and Jean Hersholt.

One day Edmund Goulding, who was directing it, sent for me. There was an important and serious role in the picture that he had a crazy hunch I could play. It was the part of the man who knows he is dying and wishes, in the last few months of his life, to make up for all of the fun and gay times he has missed.

As any actor would, I told Eddie his hunch was not crazy at

all. I was sure I could handle such a serious role. "In almost every picture I've made," I explained, "I make it a rule to become very serious about the fourth reel or so. That is to make absolutely sure that the audience will really care about what happens to me in the rest of the picture." I suggested he re-run some of my old pictures in a projection room and he would see that for himself.

I heard nothing more about this, and Lionel Barrymore, of course, got the role. Lionel, as usual, handled himself masterfully even though I would have played the part differently. I do not say better, mind you, just differently. Even being considered by Goulding for that straight dramatic role, however, was a compliment. It also started me thinking about that picture. After I saw it, I got one of the best travesty ideas of my life and told Eddie Sedgwick about it.

The scene for this take-off on *Grand Hotel* would be the Mills Hotel, the down-and-outers' hangout in New York, which then was renting its best rooms for fifty cents a night.

I planned to have Oliver Hardy play the part of the lustful, power-mad manufacturer which Wallace Beery played in the original. In our version, Hardy would be a manufacturer of front collar buttons who is trying to arrange a merger with Stan Laurel, a manufacturer of back collar buttons.

Polly Moran would play the secretary, Joan Crawford's role in the original, and in the scene in which Oliver Hardy seduces Polly I hoped to hit one of the comic high spots of the decade.

In *Grand Hotel* Jean Hersholt had the poignant role of the hotel clerk who is frantic with worry because his wife is having a baby. Henry Armetta would be our room clerk, but what is giving him the willies is the ordeal of his cat who is expecting kittens.

Jimmy Durante I saw as perfect in John Barrymore's role of the bogus count, but instead of making love to Greta Garbo as the aging ballerina, he would have Marie Dressler in his arms. Eddie and I almost got hysterical thinking of what Marie Dressler would do with her first scene. In this she would look into the full-length mirror, open her ankle-length ermine robe, exposing her battleship of a figure in ballet dancer's costume with slippers about a foot and a half long, and murmur, "I think I am getting too old to dance, and I fear that my public doesn't want me any more."

I, myself, would have Lionel Barrymore's role—with a few changes, of course. The doctor in my crucial scene would pronounce me suffering from hiccups and declare that I had but thirty or forty years to live.

"Only thirty or forty years?" I would exclaim. "That means I must not lose a single moment." And I'd order champagne and caviar, dancing girls, and a gipsy orchestra sent up to my suite at once.

"Let them release this parody of *Grand Hotel* six months after their big picture is released," I told Sedgwick, "and I'll bet anyone on the M-G-M lot anything from a Ford to a Cadillac that my take-off will outgross their all-star movie."

We also discussed the advantages. We could use many of the *Grand Hotel* sets, and most of the players were on M-G-M's contract list, so it would be neither troublesome nor expensive to line them up.

"I'll even use their script," I added.

One day, some time after I was fired by M-G-M, Eddie Sedgwick, grinning like some kid, came to see me. He said he had told Irving Thalberg about my *Grand Hotel* take-off and that Thalberg wanted to make it.

"He can't make it," I said. "It doesn't belong to M-G-M. It belongs to me."

"Irving knows that," Eddie replied. "That is what he wants to talk to you about."

"Where?"

"In his office, of course."

"I can't go back to M-G-M," I said. "Thalberg should know that. I'm in no shape to go back."

That wasn't my real reason, of course. After being kicked out that way I had made up my mind that I would never walk on that lot again until Louis B. Mayer invited me to. It was also true that I was in no shape to go back. In no mental shape, that is.

But I was a fool, and I admit it. For Irving Thalberg, with the chips down, was willing to fight for me. Aside from Norma Shearer, his wife, I think I was his favorite M-G-M star. He appreciated my work more than that of any of the Barrymores, Garbos, Crawfords, and Mickey Rooneys there.

Everything might have been different if I had gone back. Doing a picture I was so eager to do might have enabled me to stop drinking and re-establish myself as a man whose only business was making people laugh.

Eddie Sedgwick, like any successful director, was a master of persuasion. Yet he could not talk me that day into doing the sensible thing and eating humble pie.

So nothing ever came of that bright notion. If it had I think I would have won the bet of anything from a Ford to a Cadillac that our parody would have outgrossed the original, even though *Grand Hotel* earned millions for M-G-M in 1932, a year when the world was wondering if it could ever get back on its economic feet.

Losing out at M-G-M made me poison at the other major Hollywood studios. None of them seemed to want or need me. I don't know what wild rumors went around about my unreliability and alcoholism. But in that tightly knit one-industry town there were then seven major studios in a position to spend on a picture the sort of money that my comedies cost. No offers came from the other six: Paramount, Columbia, Warner Brothers, Universal, Fox, or RKO.

I was jubilant when I got an offer from Florida where Mickey Neilan had just made a picture called *Chloe* and wanted to make another with me. Lew Lipton, a comedy writer who had worked with me, was with Neilan, and this gave me added reassurance. I was going to be paid $3,000 a week, my M-G-M salary. Financing was being supplied by a group of Coca-Cola distributors and other businessmen. They had hopes of establishing Florida as a film-making center.

I was in very high spirits as I flew to St. Petersburg where Neilan and Lew Lipton met my plane. Getting 3,000 miles from the scene of my worst defeats was exhilarating. I was determined to stay off the booze, do a great job, and show everyone that I was anything but a dead duck.

I arrived in Florida in the spring of 1933, just when the hot weather was beginning to drive the tourists home. I had a story that seemed sound, and in no time we were ready to start shooting. But the weather made that impossible. I say this even after having made pictures on the Arizona desert where the heat was almost as oppressive. But in Arizona the air was dry. In soggy Florida it was not enough to put ice on top of the camera to keep the emulsion from melting off the film. We also had to keep cold air blowers going all the time on both sides of the camera. It was so hot down there that it was impossible for Molly O'Day, the leading lady, to keep the make-up on her face.

Yet we might have managed somehow if it hadn't been for the insects. They really finished us. Dragon flies, mosquitoes which seemed to have teeth, kept zooming in swarms between the actors and the camera. It was impossible for Neilan to get a clean shot even with the blowers going.

None of this discouraged our optimistic backers. But I told them the truth when I became convinced that they were only throwing their money away in trying to establish a year-round movie industry there. Among other things, I pointed out that for years they would have the additional heavy expense of transporting everything they needed, from costumes to actors, from New York.

They listened, paid off, and I was out of another job. The project had been widely publicized, so what I got from it was a couple of weeks' pay and another failure on my record.

The two worst years of my life were from 1933 to 1935. I really started to hit the bottle hard after returning from Florida, and in a short while I had a bad case of the d.t.s. I do not know why I say bad case, as I never have heard of a good case of delirium tremens.

Louella Parsons's husband, the late Dr. Harry Martin, who was an old friend of mine, sent me to Arrowhead Springs for renewed drying out and sulphur-cave treatments. I was accompanied by a young physician, associated with him, and a nurse.

When we returned, Dr. Martin was not satisfied with my condition and insisted that the nurse remain with me a couple of weeks longer to make sure I completed the cure. She had her orders of just the right amount of whiskey to give me so I wouldn't go nuts, also hypodermics to put me to sleep.

I was living in a little Culver City bungalow. It was a restful enough place with a rear porch facing the pleasant greens of the California Country Club's golf course, but it didn't rest me. Something about being so close to the studio I'd been kicked out of made me fret and brood.

I was able to endure just a week of living there. Then I told the nurse I wanted to go to Mexico. When she protested that her orders from Dr. Martin required her to stay close by me I told her she could come along.

I ran away to Mexico, but it did not solve anything, of course. About all that happened there was another marriage which got world-wide publicity because a full year had not elapsed since my interlocutory decree from my first wife became final. When that came through there was another marriage ceremony at Ventura, California. That second marriage of mine did not last long, which is the nicest thing about it I remember.

During those two bad years I made feature movies in Mexico, England, and France. None of them was any good, because in none of those three countries did the producer have money enough to finance a proper production. And the day had passed when the public would come to see a movie with inferior props, camera work, and generally poor production. In between these professional mishaps I kept on drinking like a fish. Once I was taken to a sanitarium in a strait jacket, and I twice was given the Keeley cure, or a reasonable facsimile. I will describe this cure briefly here, though with no great pleasure. It starts with three days during which the nurses and doctors do nothing but pour liquor into you, giving you a drink each half-hour on the half-hour.

I trust that any drunkards who happen to read this will not be misguided enough to rush off to the nearest sanitarium to get all of these free drinks. You get your favorite snort, all right, but never twice in a row. Instead they start you off on whiskey and on succeeding rounds give you gin, rum, beer, brandy, wine—before they get around to the whiskey again.

Needless to say, the Bacchus in you is revolted and rebellious long before your three-day round-the-clock drinking marathon is over. When you plead, "Oh, no! Take it away *please!*" all you get from your bartenders and barmaids in the white coats is a friendly smile.

"Please take it away," you repeat, "it hurts my stomach."

"Just one more," they say, for their purpose is to make the hurt in your stomach grow until it becomes unforgettable. And, being a weakling, you take that one more just as you did in a thousand barrooms.

The Keeley cure may have worked wonders for some alcoholics, but it did nothing for me that first time. When I got out I could think of too many excuses for drinking—the grandson of my grocer was having a birthday, or I had to celebrate good old St. Swithin's Day, the inauguration of Rutherford B. Hayes, or some other important occasion.

After taking that cure the second time, I was taken home and immediately went for a walk on the golf course. I walked over the entire eighteen holes, and, on reaching the clubhouse, I walked to the bar and ordered two manhattans. I drank them one after another. They not only tasted great, they stayed down.

That was in 1935 and, after proving to myself I could drink if I felt like it, stop if I felt like it, I did not touch a drop of whiskey or any other alcoholic drink for five years.

A PRATFALL CAN BE A BEAUTIFUL THING

Early in 1934, when I was flat broke, I received an offer of $15,-000 from a French producer to make a picture in Paris. The producer sent me nothing for traveling expenses, and to get there with my second wife I had to sell $350 worth of War Savings Bonds which I had been hanging onto ever since my Army days. It proved barely enough to get us to Europe in the cheapest way I could find: on a freighter traveling from Los Angeles to Glasgow, Scotland, via the Panama Canal.

After landing in Scotland we traveled to London and stopped overnight at the Grand Palace Hotel. There was a wonderful surprise waiting there for me, a letter from Joe Schenck with a $1,000 check in it. He wrote that this covered my share of the sale of some leftover equipment at the Keaton studio.

I could not remember any leftover equipment and suspected

this was Joe's tactful way of extending a helping hand. I was in no position to question this. It had come in the nick of time to pay pressing bills in Hollywood.

Somehow I have always found it impossible to borrow money from anyone. Perhaps the fact that I've paid my own way since I was four has something to do with this. Some sort of crazy pride even prevented me from asking friends to return money I had loaned them back in my $3,000-a-week days.

When I went broke, I had $15,000 in personal debts outstanding, not counting the tens, twenties, and fifties every star in show business is expected to hand out to down-and-outers as a matter of course.

Some of the friends I had loaned solid amounts to never got into a position where they could pay. It was that way with Arbuckle, who died owing me $2,500, and with Lew Cody, who died owing me $2,000.

But there were several others, including a cowboy star, a prominent comedian, and a pal who inherited a fortune, who could have paid me but never came near me.

One man who did pay up was Norman Kerry, whom Hollywood had written off as an irresponsible actor who drank too much. Kerry came to see me one day, and asked, "Do you remember the time about four years ago when I borrowed a thousand dollars from you?"

"I do, now that you mention it, Norman," I told him.

"Well, I just did a little acting job," he explained, "and got $1,000 for it. But I cannot give it all to you. I need some of it to live on. Would it be all right if I only gave you $900 and keep the rest for myself?"

My old friend, Norman Kerry, died recently, but I'll never forget him or the day he gave me a nine-to-one split on the first thousand dollars he had seen in many months.

I also am one man who can throw a sincere kiss to the Internal Revenue Bureau for consideration in time of need. At the height of my troubles the Bureau informed me I owed $18,000. But after I showed them my books and convinced them that my current income was only a shadow of what it had been they offered to clean the slate for $4,000.

Throughout all my troubles I was buoyed up by one thing: the conviction that no matter what else happened I could always get work in show business in some capacity. Another advantage I had over other once-rich brokes was being able to live without luxuries.

I enjoy having expensive things, but it did not bother me when I had to turn my Cadillac in for a Ford and wear ready-made suits instead of custom-tailored jobs and live without servants in a cheap bungalow court. After I made the picture in Paris I made another in London. But these two pictures, as I said, were too cheaply made to re-establish my reputation. After that I had to take anything I could get. And what I got was a contract to make comedy short subjects for Educational Films. When this expired I was signed for a similar deal by Columbia Pictures. It meant a living, for I was paid $2,500 each for them and made about six a year.

These two-reelers, shot in three days each, were what picture people call "cheaters," meaning movies thrown together as quickly and cheaply as possible. All of the energy and ingenuity of the director is concentrated on the saving of money. New props and scenery were never used if old ones would do. The supporting casts couldn't support themselves, and the scripts were cooked up as quickly and carelessly as a hobo's mulligan stew. For they brought in no revenue to the company, were just thrown in free with Columbia's features.

Several times I urged Harry Cohn, president of Columbia, to let me spend a little more time and money. I explained that on a larger budget I could turn out two-reelers that he could sell instead of giving them away as part of a package.

Cohn, whose company was doing great without my suggestions, was not interested. And making those "cheaters" was the way I supported myself and my family from 1935 to 1940. Occasionally I got a day's work at some other major studio in a feature.

I did get one fascinating four-week assignment in 1939 when Twentieth Century-Fox made *Hollywood Cavalcade*, a story about making comedies in the old silent days. It starred Don Ameche and Alice Faye, with Alice playing a Broadway show girl who comes to Hollywood believing she has been hired to play in dignified dramas. Instead she finds herself playing leads in Keystone Komedies.

My deal called for me to act in this and also to work as the director's comedy consultant. Not surprisingly, there were some pie-throwing episodes in the picture. "Alice Faye will catch one from you," Alan Dwan, the director, told me, "and you can also teach her and the others the secrets of the art."

I had not thrown a custard pie for years and lost no time in getting in some practice when not busy on the set.

I started by drawing a circle on the wall in white chalk. This was the approximate size of Alice Faye's lovely blonde head. I used a wooden plate as my practice "pie." When this proved too light I kept on driving nails into it until it weighed about as much as the custard pies Roscoe, Al St. John, and I had so much fun throwing at one another in the old days. I practiced throwing the plate from various distances. I have always considered myself the world's champion custard-pie thrower, and slowly my old marksmanship returned.

I had the studio's bakers make the pie according to our original 1917 recipe. No custard is used, and, with a blonde the target, the filling is a mixture of blackberries, flour, and water, garnished with whipped cream. When a brunette is the one to be smeared, a lemon-meringue filling is substituted for the blackberries, which shows up better on the screen against a dark complexion.

Two crusts are cooked, one inside the other, until brittle. The double crust prevents crumbling when your fingers slide across the bottom in delivering the confectionary.

Tin plates are never used because of the danger of cutting the recipient's eye, something that could happen when the plate slides sideways at the crucial moment of impact. The shortest throw, across a distance of from three to six feet, is called a shot putt, and this was the custard-pie surprise I was to heave at sweet-faced Alice Faye.

I worried about her flinching. Besides spoiling the shot, this would mean hours of delay while Alice took a shower, got a whole new make-up job, a hairdo, and was fitted for a duplicate clothes outfit.

I decided not to warn her when the great moment approached.

After talking it over with Dwan, we placed George Givot, who was playing the villain, between Alice and me. Givot faced me, but Alice, standing right behind him, was faced in the opposite direction. Givot was told that he should turn the girl around slowly as I started to say my line, which was, "We will see who gets the girl!" He would hold her in front of him, using her as a shield. After timing this, using another girl for Alice, I suggested that if the word "Now" was added, it would give me time to deliver the pie at just the right split second.

When we made the shot, Givot turned Alice around too quickly, which forced me to speed up my throw. Consequently the pie hit her harder in the face than should have been necessary.

You never saw a more stunned-looking girl in your life than Alice Faye that day. We required no retake, but Alice did not thank me for that. As the camera was being moved to the next location I saw her go over to a table on which the pies for other scenes were waiting to be used. Alice picked one up, weighed it in her hand, then tried several others. When she found one she liked she headed toward me on the run. I leaped up and ran, but Alice chased me off the sound stage and clear out of the studio holding all the while that menacing custard pie in her hand.

I think I proved I was still the champ custard-pie thrower during that picture when I caught George Givot squarely in the face with a pie from a distance of twenty-seven feet.

Only a few years ago I had another chance to demonstrate the art of custard-pie throwing on Ed Wynn's TV program. I had been guest star several times on Ed's show, but this was an impromptu appearance. As everybody knows, Ed is a lifelong collector of funny hats. One day I found one I thought he would like and brought it to the CBS Playhouse where he was broadcasting. I found him in his dressing room, being made up. After admiring the hat and thanking me for it, Ed asked, "Where do you keep your stage wardrobe?"

"Home," I replied, "but why?"

"I have no finish for tonight's show. I thought if you come on you might think of something. How fast can you get home and change into your stage clothes and get back?"

I told him, "It will take me ten minutes to drive there, ten to drive back, and five minutes more to dig up the stage outfit and get into it."

Ed looked at his watch, saw he had thirty-three minutes before going on, and said, "You can just make it. That's if you hurry." He quickly explained that he had lined up four of the old Keystone Cops to demonstrate custard-pie throwing.

"Why I never thought of getting the champ," he added, "I'll never understand. Even now I don't know how to use the pie-throwing for the finish. But hurry—and try to think of a finish for me."

I raced home, hustled into my old outfit—pork-pie hat, slap shoes, and baggy pants, and was back in time. But not in time, of course, to write any dialogue or to explain to the cameraman where I was going to move and what I was going to do next. And without that—a camera rehearsal—everybody, particularly in the control room, can get very confused on a TV show.

But there was no time to worry about that.

Everybody loved the finish I improvised—except Chester Conklin, Hank Mann, his brother Heinie, and Snub Pollard, the four Keystone Cops involved. They had been looking forward to throwing the custard pies and did not like my taking over the job. They had to be sweet-talked into accepting the change I had dreamed up.

As many TV fans will recall, Ed Wynn always ended his show by coming out in nightgown and nightcap, carrying a candle, and getting into bed.

This night I followed him on, sat on the side of his bed, and warned him, "Now, Ed, if you're going in for this style of comedy and getting mixed up with characters like Keystone Cops, you've got to learn to throw pies. I'm going to give you your first lesson tonight."

I went off stage, got Hank Mann, and stood him near the head of the bed. Then I got a pie from the stack on a tea table.

"Now, anyone can do this one," I explained to Ed Wynn, demonstrating as I talked. "It is called the walking thrust. All you need to do is walk up to him and push it in his face. But before you start away, give it a slight twist. That's in the interests of efficiency. The slight turn makes the dough portion of the pie cling to the victim."

"Just a second," I said, "till I get a clean Cop."

When I had the next Keystone Cop lined up I continued my lecture to Wynn, saying, "Any time you have to throw one of these things from three to six feet you shot putt it—like this. But, my friend, the secret, when you have to throw the pie more than eight feet, is to have exactly enough dough in the pie so it will remain perpendicular, that is, sail flat as it comes off your fingers."

With the third Cop ready, I continued my explanation with, "However, if you wish to be more artistic, you use the renowned ancient Roman discus throw which is by far the most beautiful delivery of all." In demonstrating this I spun halfway around, turning the pie as I whirled, and let go hitting the Cop square in the face.

Now I paused for a moment, as though awed by the significance of the final contribution I was to make to Ed's education in slapstick. "The last one, of course, is the most difficult," I told him. "And, Ed, it will take you years to learn to throw like *this!*

"For this one is the custard-pie throw that everyone misses with most often. It is really the same sort of overhand throw that the catcher makes to second base from behind the plate.

"As you can observe, Ed, you pull back your arm just as far as it will go, then bring the pie in all of the way from East St. Louis —and let 'er go!"

Traveling all the way across the stage as that custard pie did, you need luck to catch your target square. But luck was with me that night, the fourth and final Cop catching it right in the face.

"I got the finish I wanted," Ed Wynn whispered to me. "You saved the show for me tonight."

So many good things happened to me during 1940 that I see that year now as the one in which my life started on the upgrade once more. I also started drinking again—which wasn't one of the good things, of course.

For some time my friends had been assuring me that beer never hurt anyone. That is very easy to believe if you enjoy drinking beer as much as I do. The trouble with drinking beer is that it is such a short step to drinking whiskey.

And each time I started drinking whiskey, I again could always find occasions to celebrate. It might be somebody's birthday, anybody's, even the cat's, or a holiday, St. Patrick's Day, St. Swithin's, Arbor Day, Mother's Day, Father's Day. If not, somebody was easily found who had just got out of the hospital, got married or divorced, lost his mother-in-law and wanted you to drink with him because he was happy or wanted to forget his sorrows. Refusing seemed positively rude.

Even so, in my opinion, you are all right as long as you can drink and wake up without a hang-over. You are still all right if you can fight off the tearing desire for an eye opener.

That's always been the killer in my life, that eye opener that brings such relief but doesn't last long enough, and leads you into taking another and another until you find yourself waking up with a hang-over all over again.

Keep it up awhile, and whenever a couple of little things go wrong you find yourself saying the hell with it and getting drunk to help you forget. And that's the final step that brings you to the police station or the psychopathic ward.

I was to go on many a bender in the next fifteen years though without ever getting into as bad shape as back in 1932 and 1933 when the roof fell in on me.

Oddly enough, I never got drunk while I was working. Always I was far too interested in what I was doing to take a chance on missing out on any of it. When idle and with no work in prospect, I could get as bagged as anyone else.

And now for the good things that happened to me during 1940. I'll start with the best of them, my marriage to Eleanor Norris, the dancer, on May 29 that year. I had been divorced five years. She was twenty-one, I forty-four. On hearing of our plans, a couple of my middle-aged friends took the liberty of advising Eleanor against marrying a man more than twice her age. They said no good could come of it. Their concern by the way was not for her, but for me.

Having been brought up to respect her elders, Eleanor listened to the two middle-aged wise men, and we continued our plans for the wedding. I, myself, had one fairly good reason for hesitating about making that pretty young girl my bride. For a good many years I had been going steady, as they say, with a beautiful woman who had been a star at M-G-M with me. We had been sweethearts for quite a long time, and I doubted whether she would take the news that I was marrying a younger girl in any truly Christian spirit.

Well, I saw no point in either hurting her feelings or getting my head broken. I spent a good deal of time trying to solve the dilemma. Eventually I recalled that my long-time girl had always shown a considerable interest in wrestlers. As an experiment I took her to a couple of wrestling shows at the Hollywood Stadium.

To my great joy she appeared utterly fascinated by one curly-haired young grappler. Getting his manager to one side I told him that my companion was deeply interested in his boy and slipped him her telephone number to pass along to the muscular youth. Before Eleanor and I were married ourselves, my other girl and the wrestler dated, fell in love, and eloped. Eleanor and I have been married happily now for nineteen years, but you can bet I've never become sappy enough to take *her* to any wrestling matches.

Another big 1940 event in my life came on the day that I decided to quit making cheaters at Columbia. I just got to the point where I couldn't stomach turning out even one more crummy two-reeler.

The next morning I drove over to M-G-M and saw my old friend, Eddie Mannix. I told him how I felt about what I'd been doing and asked him if he could put me on the payroll as a gagman and comedy constructionist.

"I can put you on at a $100 a week."

"It's a deal," I told him.

I am always surprised when people ask me if I didn't feel it was a comedown to take a job like that at such a small salary at the studio where I'd been a $3,000-a-week star. The answer is "No." I had not the slightest sense of humiliation. For one thing, I'd had ten years to forget my old grievances. For another, I never had the sort of pride many actors are afflicted with. Like me, many of them had once been stars. They said they preferred to starve to death rather than accept a small-paying job. I do not know whether any of them starved or not, but the Hollywood hills are certainly always swarming with them.

When Eddie put me on at a $100 a week I thought it was darned nice of him. We could live on that, and I was sure M-G-M would raise my pay the moment I started giving them gags and comedy ideas they could use. And that's what happened: before long I was getting $300 a week.

I also knew that whenever an acting job came my way the company would give me time off for it. And I again got such jobs occasionally, usually for a day's work, at a $1,000 a day. I had one of those one-day jobs that very fall in *The Villain Still Pursued Her.* This was a screen version of *The Drunkard,* the old stage melodrama which was revived in Los Angeles more than fifteen years ago and is still running there. I played a waiter who dropped a tray of dishes, something almost anyone will do for nothing. But the producer wanted a familiar face in that little bit and picked mine as the movie face hardest for fans to forget.

Though my principal job at M-G-M was as a trouble shooter who rushed in with gags whenever needed, I got a bit to do once in a while on the studio's pictures. And the company, I must say, was most generous with their bonuses for this work.

I did my best work on the Red Skelton pictures, though, generally speaking, my suggestions were far more graciously received by M-G-M's dramatic performers than by my fellow comedians. Perhaps this is not surprising, but it sure surprised me. I cannot imagine Chaplin, Lloyd, Harry Langdon, or myself rejecting or resenting a first-rate gag just because another comic suggested it. But then, as I've mentioned, our approach to our work was quite different from theirs.

I now discovered that they never saw a script until it was completed. It was almost routine for them to return the first version to the studio with the notation, "This stinks." The studio would then assign a couple of new writers whose effort, more often than not, would be returned as "Not up to par!" or with some similar comment. When an acceptable script was whipped up, the comedian asked, "When do we start and what do I wear?"

I have been told that Phil Silvers, Jerry Lewis, and Jackie Gleason are among the comedians now popular who work from the beginning on their stories, and I hope it is true. But I never worked with any of the three. One of the equally famous comics I did work with hardly could wait to finish a scene. He had a big-stakes poker game going on in his dressing room which he was much more interested in than his picture. The men he played with dressed, acted, and talked like mobsters. Another great comic would not even watch the scenes in his pictures that he did not appear in. He was more interested in getting back to his dressing room so he could write jokes for his radio show. And so it went.

To say that any of these enormously popular comics was not a really funny man would be ridiculous. Writers, directors, advisers, and material can help you get to the top. What no outsider can supply is the rare talent to make people laugh. This the comic was born with and developed himself, or he would never have gained recognition in the first place. It just seems to me that for a man with such a rare and irreplaceable talent not to use it fully is like throwing away your birthright.

Among the M-G-M star comics I failed to click with were Abbott and Costello. I also got nowhere with the Marx Brothers. But I still think that an opening gag I devised for the Marxes' *A Day at the Circus* was as sure-fire and amusing as anything I ever dreamed up for my own pictures. In this shot, Harpo was selling gas-filled balloons. Standing next to him is a midget on a sideshow platform. When a customer buys a balloon and hands Harpo a ten-dollar bill, he hands over the other balloons to the midget to hold for him while he fishes in his pockets for change. But the midget is not heavy enough to hold onto the balloons which rise in the air, carrying him off his feet. Harpo, who has given the customer his change, grabs the midget's ankle just as he is flying beyond reach, takes back the balloons. Then, without looking at the midget, he makes a slapping gesture as though he blamed the midget for not weighing enough.

After this shot Harpo walks past a camel. It has two baskets hanging on its back. A man with a pitchfork is filling these with straw. Harpo can see this but not the keeper on the other side of the camel who holds the reins attached to the animal's halter.

Some of the straw falls out of the basket nearest Harpo. He picks the straw up and throws it back into the basket. Meanwhile the keeper he cannot see is looking in his pockets for a match. Harpo finds a single straw on the ground and throws this into the basket just as the keeper bends over to strike the match on his trousers, accidentally pulling on the halter and causing the camel to sink to his knees.

Amazed at this apparent proof that there is a last straw that breaks the camel's back, Harpo takes back the single straw just as the keeper straightens up, loosening the rein on the camel who rises to his feet. Now Harpo is delighted: the ancient aphorism is based on truth.

When I acted this out for the Marx Brothers, Groucho asked with a sneer, "Do you think that's *funny?*" Harpo and Chico just stared at me in disgust.

Perhaps the reason I worked so much more effectively with Red Skelton is because he is the contemporary comedian whose working methods are closest to what ours were in the silent days. The first Skelton movie I worked on was the one in which Esther Williams made her screen debut. The picture was called *Swimming Beauty* but without my consent. I suggested that a more effective box-office title would be *The Fatal Breast Stroke*, but Mr. Mayer was stuffy about it and said *Swimming Beauty* was as far as he cared to go in summoning up carnal images in our customers' lively imaginations. Another Esther Williams picture that I wanted to retitle was one in which she did a great deal of riding. I tried to get M-G-M to call that one *The Bride Wore Spurs*, but failed again to win over the brass.

I can hardly think of one star on the M-G-M lot whom I did not work with during my years as a trouble shooter there, or one top director or producer.

In various pictures I showed Lana Turner how to get a laugh spilling a cup of coffee on Mickey Rooney, tutored Van Johnson how to get his bicycle's sprockets tangled up in Judy Garland's dress, and helped Clark Gable work himself into a state of bewildered frustration.

The Gable picture was a whale of a yarn called *Too Hot to Handle*. In this Clark, one of the best-liked and easiest-to-work-with stars in Hollywood, was playing a lazy, cynical newsreel cameraman. Though assigned to cover the Japanese-Chinese war, this character had no intention of risking his neck at the front.

One scene I worked on produced as natural a gag as I ever saw. In this Gable was faking a scene showing the horrors of war. He had a four-year-old boy sitting on the ground, playing with gravel. Gable made a paper airplane and was trying to photograph this in such a way that its shadow—the supreme symbol of destructiveness in war—would cross the little boy's face.

To heighten the effect of a helpless little victim caught in a bombing attack, he had placed some dirt and debris on the limbs of the tree under which the child was at play. When he shook the tree—at the right moment—the debris would fall on the tiny victim. For an additional effect he had a bucket full of dirt on the end of a wooden board. That end rested on the ground; the middle of the board was propped on a rock, which left the other end a foot or so above ground. This was close to Gable's foot, and by stepping on it he could send the bucket of dirt flying into the air and make it come down all over the little boy under the tree. If this worked, he could ship the film home as an incident during a bombing attack and stall off going to the front.

In the scene a slightly older boy was watching Gable's elaborate faking of the horrors of war with admiring smiles. He was continually annoying Gable by getting in his way. Gable kept moving this second boy out of his way, finally perching him on a nearby wall.

What was needed here was a laugh provoked by something going wrong. I figured out that it would be funnier if this second boy climbed on the tree over the smaller child so he could see everything better. Then when the tree was shaken the branch would break under the boy's weight, causing him to fall on Gable just as he was making his shot, and that's the way it worked out.

M-G-M also remade my old picture *The Cameraman* as *Watch the Birdie*, with Red in my part. But the great scene in the bathhouse got nothing like the laughs our version had. I believed this was because they made a mistake I had avoided. This was using Mike Mazurski, the huge, ex-wrestler as the other man in that undressing scene. In my opinion, the audience just did not believe that Mazurski would not have thrown Red Skelton out the moment he got annoyed enough. I think that M-G-M made another error in that picture in having Red Skelton sneezing repeatedly all over Mazurski which was a disgusting thing to watch.

In 1948 Jack Cummings, one of the great M-G-M directors, called me in to look at Red Skelton's *The Southern Yankee,* which had received disappointing receptions when previewed. This is, of course, a situation which makes a man feel like the Marines coming to the rescue.

I told Cummings he had a whale of a story but, in my opinion, they had made a couple of mistakes. One was having Red behave like an imbecile in the opening scenes. As the comedian and leading man, Red lost the audience's sympathy by behaving too stupidly. If you act as screwy as he was doing, the people out front would not care what happened to the character you were playing. They reshot those scenes, toning down Red's nutty behavior and also eliminating some of the noise that marred the opening scene.

I also contributed the gag in which Red was shown walking between the Union Army and the Confederate Army, with both armies cheering him madly. The reason was that Red was wearing half of a Union Army hat and uniform on the side facing the Northern soldiers and a Southern hat and uniform on the other. In addition he had sewed together the flags of the two opposing sides so that the boys in blue saw a Union flag and the Southerners only the flag of the Confederacy.

Both sides cheer him wildly until a sudden gust of wind reverses the flag, showing both sides the game he is playing. As Red turns around to straighten the flag they discover his half-and-half uniform.

During the nine or ten years I worked as a gagman at M-G-M I discovered, among other things, how little faith some of the industry's most-respected directors and producers had in their own judgment.

One director who had brought in many fabulous successes canceled one of the *Thin Man* series, which he had been all ready to shoot, after he got my opinion of the story.

"This is a very amusing script," I told him, "but you have one tricky problem. That is keeping your audience interested in your leading lady. This is because you show her as so frivolous and screwloose that you will lose all sympathy for her."

That was *all* I said. It should not have been too difficult for this gifted director and a crack M-G-M screen writer to rewrite this character. Instead he completely lost faith in the story, ordered it taken off the schedule, and had an entirely different story written for the *Thin Man* series.

Some time later I had another revealing experience with another experienced director at Twentieth Century-Fox. That studio had borrowed me to help work on the W. C. Fields sequence in *Tales of Manhattan.* As this old director slipped me a script of the picture he was shooting, he whispered, "Take this home and read it, but don't let *anyone* see you walking out with it under your arm." I was able to give him some advice next day that he accepted and used in the picture, but the studio never knew he had let me read the script. And it wasn't that he wanted all of the credit for himself. He was afraid that if the news got around that he required an outside opinion from an old friend it would injure his reputation.

Making any sort of movie is tense, nerve-racking work. This was particularly true in a big studio like M-G-M which was so bedeviled by office politics and conflicts for power on all of its higher levels. One of the top directors there once asked me to read the script of the film he was shooting. When I suggested that in one scene he move the camera to avoid having a shadow fall across, he shouted in a rage, "Damn it! Don't tell me where to put my cameras."

I shut up and let him make the scene his own way. I mention it here only as another instance of cracking nerves in the higher ranks of the movie world.

Though TV revived my career as an actor, I take no satisfaction in the way so many of these men were driven into involuntary retirement by the coming of the same medium. Each of them, at his peak, produced fine entertainment.

ALL'S WELL
THAT ENDS WELL

Charlie Chaplin's mind is so frisky and intuitive that it is difficult to surprise him. Yet I have caught him off guard at least twice.

The first time was on a night away back in 1920 when Charlie and I were drinking beer in my kitchen. He was going on at a great rate about something new called communism which he had just heard about. He said that communism was going to change everything, abolish poverty. The well would help the sick, the rich would help the poor.

"What I want," he said, banging the table, "is that every child should have enough to eat, shoes on his feet, and a roof over his head!"

Naturally, this amazed me, and I asked, after thinking about it a minute or two, "But, Charlie, do you know anyone who doesn't want that?"

Charlie looked startled. Then his face broke into that wonderful smile of his, and he began to laugh at himself. I myself have gone through life almost unaware of politics, and I only wish my old friend had done the same. He must know by now that communism, wherever it has been practiced, bears not the slightest resemblance to the benign system he described to me forty years ago.

I do not really think Charlie knows much more about politics, history, or economics than I do. Like myself he was hit by a make-up towel almost before he was out of diapers. Neither of us had time while growing up to study anything but show business. But Charlie is a stubborn man, and when his right to talk favorably about communism was challenged he simply got bullheaded about it.

As this was written there were rumors that Charlie would like to get back to America. I hope he makes it. Even more I hope he keeps his promise to start making pictures again.

For nobody ever made so many people laugh as did Charlie with his little tramp. And there never was a time in history when more people needed something like Charlie's tramp to help them forget their fears and troubles.

Chaplin's troubles began when he started to take himself seriously. That was after he had produced *A Woman of Paris*. Most people forget it now, but this was the first time suggestion was used on the screen to convey an idea.

When Charlie wanted to tell his audience that his heroine, played by Edna Purviance, was taking a train he did it with a shadow of a cardboard train and a six-foot section of a first-class railway coach. To tell the audience that she was the mistress of the Paris man-about-town, whom Adolph Menjou portrayed, Charlie merely had Menjou use his own key in entering her home and then take a clean collar from a bureau.

That made motion-picture history. But the avalanche of praise for Charlie's brilliant directing also turned his head, I am afraid. It was his misfortune to believe what the critics wrote about him. They said he was a genius, something I would be the last to deny, and from that time on Charlie Chaplin, the divine clown, tried to behave, think, and talk like an intellectual.

The second time I took Charlie unawares was on the day in

1951 when he sent for me to discuss doing a scene with him for *Limelight*, the last picture he made in this country.

He seemed astonished at my appearance. Apparently he had expected to see a physical and mental wreck. But I was in fine fettle. I'd just been in New York for four months doing an average of two TV guest shots a week. So I was prosperous and looked it.

"What *have* you been doing, Buster?" he asked. "You look in such fine shape."

"Do you look at television, Charlie?" I asked.

"Good heavens, no," he exclaimed. "I hate it. I will not permit it in my house. The idea of actors letting themselves be shown on that lousy, stinking, little screen!"

"Don't you even have it in the kids' rooms, Charlie?"

"There last of all. Oona has enough trouble as it is with the lively little bouncers. They are darlings, but mischievious. There would be no controlling them at all if we let them see all that tripe on television. Should be done away with. It is ruining the whole country." Then he said again, "But Buster, tell me, how do you manage to stay in such good shape. What makes you so spry?"

"Television," I said.

He gasped, choked, got red, then said, "Now about this sequence we're going to do together."

The subject of TV was not mentioned again during the three days we did the sequence in *Limelight* in which I played the near-blind pianist and he the fiddler.

TV had brought me back as an actor. By 1949, except for an occasional day's work—which seemed to me to be getting more occasional all of the time—I had not put on grease paint for the cameras in almost five years. The summer theatres had put in no bids for my services since 1941 when I toured in *The Gorilla*. My most important engagement had been a four-week date as star of a famous Paris circus, back in 1947.

So it was one of the thrills of my life when I got a chance in December of 1949 to do my own weekly TV show on KHJ, the Los Angeles *Times* broadcasting station.

By then I had almost given up hope of getting another real chance as an actor. I emphasize the word *almost*, because no one with actor's blood in his veins ever really admits to himself he is through, no matter what he says to other people. No, I did not really believe it in my heart, even after so many years of little success, no home runs, and plenty of errors.

The Buster Keaton Show was a success, but only on the West Coast where it gradually worked its way up to the position of Number One Comedy Program. In those days the only way to sell a Hollywood show to a national network was with kinetoscopes, and these were dismal things to look at eight or nine years ago. And my show was never sold to a sponsor as a coast-to-coast attraction. I think the story would have been different if I had waited for just two more years. But I had never, of course, wanted less to wait for anything.

The important thing, though, was how these appearances on local television shows steamed up the interest of producers in other fields. I did about twenty-three Buster Keaton TV shows in 1950 and seventeen more in 1951. The same day I turned in the final 1951 show Eleanor and I left for Paris to play a return engagement at the Paris circus. The date was so successful that I was booked for another four-week engagement during the following year.

European circuses do not play under canvas but in arenas which are more like vast theatres in the round than anything else. You perform in the center of the arena which you approach through the same wide passages used by the elephants and other animals. In 1947, two years after the war ended in Europe, there had been no German acrobats, clowns, jugglers, or trapeze performers in the show as the feeling in the French capital was still too bitter against the recent enemy. But the Germans were back in Paris by 1950.

I found another great thrill in appearing in person before a European audience. Many of those who came to see me seemed to remember my pictures fondly. I did a dueling sketch which I had originally performed in *The Passionate Plumber*.

My salary was $3,500 a week. However, a French law that we ran into stopped foreigners from taking more than half of their earnings out of the country. This restriction gave Eleanor and me the excuse to live like regal personages at the George V Hotel— without even feeling extravagant.

For my return engagement in 1950 I used a sketch from my last silent picture, *Spite Wife*, doing it with Eleanor. Previously she had done no acting, had worked only as a dancer. But she did so well in those first appearances that I have never needed another woman partner.

The sketch is the one we have done many times since on TV. Also in my appearances with summer-stock companies as Erwin, the mystical-minded horse handicapper, in *Three Men on a Horse*.

The sketch shows us coming home on our wedding night, a little drunk but far more exhausted from fatigue. Eleanor collapses and falls on the floor. The rest of the sketch concerns my efforts to put her in bed. Eleanor weighs 110 pounds, and she has never put on an extra ounce. I thank heaven for that because that act, which runs between sixteen and seventeen minutes, requires me to stumble about carrying her in my arms. We also did this sketch for twelve weeks that year in Italian theatres.

In 1951 I did a less strenuous sketch called "A Park Bench." But what developed during the engagement was far more strenuous in its way than anything we had been through in quite a while.

While we were on the high seas my agent's European representative, without informing me, had booked me for a two-week engagement at the *Cirque Royale* in Brussels. This was to follow immediately after the Paris booking. The salary was $600 less than I was getting from the French showman.

In European circus circles they have not as yet heard about Macy's not telling Gimbels. In any event, when the French showman learned about the Brussels engagement at less money he hit the roof. He seemed to think I was robbing him by letting him pay our round-trip expenses from Hollywood and then working for less money for a circus that had contributed nothing for our expenses.

He suggested I get off the hook by reducing my salary to the Brussels figure. When I refused, he offered to book me for two weeks more on the condition that I cancel the Belgian engagement. This, of course, I could not conscientiously do, and monsieur's next move was to go to the police.

When we returned to our hotel that night we found the

gendarmes in our suite. They were itemizing everything we owned, down to and including the toothbrushes and Eleanor's hair net.

I appealed to the American consul for help. He recommended the services of a White Russian woman attorney. She spoke four languages and may have talked to our French boss in all four but could not convince him that he should release our personal belongings. The fiasco ended only when I agreed to reduce my Paris salary to the Brussels figure.

The incident brought me world-wide publicity. I imagine many persons said, "Poor old Buster Keaton! After being such a great star he is down to playing in European circuses."

But they were a little too late with their sympathy. I was enjoying my busiest and best-paid year since Louis B. Mayer fired me from M-G-M. While we were in Brussels, Douglas Fairbanks, Jr., came over to hire me to play a straight dramatic role in one of the TV shows he films in London. It was a flattering offer, being for a straight dramatic role. I was paid $1,500 for my five days' work on it.

We toured the English and Scottish provinces after that in the sketch in which I put Eleanor to bed.

On coming home I became, I think, the year's No. 1 guest star. I appeared on three Ed Sullivan shows in a row, five Ed Wynn shows, three Arthur Murray shows. Conrad Nagel and Faye Emerson, who had their own shows then, were others who used me as guest star. That was the year we were kept in New York for four months just doing guest shots. I averaged two shows a week, with the lowest pay $750 a shot (when rehearsal was necessary) and $2,000 per Sunday from Sullivan.

Summer theatre owners also got into the pleasant custom of booking me in for star appearances in three old Broadway successes: *The Gorilla, Merton of the Movies,* and *Three Men on a Horse.*

Between one thing and another I was pretty much in business as an actor once more. And Robert Smith, a screen writer, was talking to Paramount about doing a screen biography of me. Doing a one-day job in such a picture as *Sunset Boulevard*—in which I worked with old pals like Erich von Stroheim—came to seem more of a lark than a happy opportunity to grab a fast thousand bucks.

Late in November I was among the ten silent stars who were presented with gold placques at the first annual George Eastman Festival of Film Arts at Rochester, New York. Only six of us—Mary Pickford, Lillian Gish, Mae Marsh, Harold Lloyd, Richard Barthelmess, and myself—were able to attend. The other four old stars who couldn't come were Norma Talmadge, Gloria Swanson, Ronald Colman, and Charlie Chaplin. Jesse Lasky made the presentations, and similar placques were given to five famous directors and five cameramen whose work from 1915 to 1925 contributed much to the advancement of motion-picture entertainment.

Two weeks later I almost died.

One afternoon in December I started hemorrhaging. This was the aftermath of coughing too much while suffering from a cold. Medication did not ease the attack, and our physician, Dr. John F. Fahey, instructed Eleanor to take me to the hospital if the hemorrhages did not stop by eight o'clock. Because I am a World War I veteran, he suggested the Veterans Administration Hospital at Sawtelle as it was superbly equipped to treat such an emergency.

The hemorrhaging continued while Eleanor was driving me to Sawtelle. Taken to the emergency room I was rushed straight to the operating room where teams of from five to eight physicians worked over me. They were unable to stop the bleeding for twenty-seven hours. During that night I had to be given blood transfusions continually to replace the blood I was losing.

The next morning Eleanor was advised to summon my boys, my sister and brother. The doctors said it was impossible to tell how long I had to live. However, Eleanor was also told that if I could survive the next five or six days I possibly might pull through.

I will spare my readers further harrowing details, except to say that when Eleanor saw me during that critical period I had so many tubes coming out of my nostrils and other parts of my body I looked to her like an octopus.

But after two weeks in the hospital I was able to get up and stand on my feet. Dr. Avedon, the staff physician in charge of my case, told me I had the constitution of an ox.

"You can live to be a hundred years old," he said, adding, "that is if you never take another drink and cut out eating highly seasoned foods."

I thought it over, decided that it was worth while sacrificing liquor, light wines, and beer, chili con carne, and all of the rest if it would prolong my life.

While I was in the hospital the deal with Paramount to make a screen biography of my life was completed. The writer, Robert Smith, came to the hospital one day and waved a check at me. He said (according to what I read in the newspapers later on), "Here is $50,000 of Paramount's money. That's for the screen rights to your life story, Buster. Are you going to lie there and die, or are you going to get up and spend it?" The idea of having my biography filmed did not bring me out of the hospital, of course, but it helped.

And it was a strange and wonderful experience working with Donald O'Connor who played Buster Keaton in Paramount's *The Buster Keaton Story*. Donald was first-rate in that movie, I thought, though he kept confessing to newspaper people that he could not do my teacup roll. That's the one in which, while carrying a tray with a teacup on it, I tumble and do a somersault without upsetting the cup. One other thing Donald could not figure out was that old trick of Pop's, the one in which my father put one leg up on a table, then the other, and seemed to be sitting on nothing, hanging in the air, until he crashed to the floor.

After *The Buster Keaton Story* was made, Paramount sent me on a tour of the country to exploit the picture. For years I'd heard stories about the inefficiency of the major studios, and often I had been in a position to observe examples of it. But they are not inefficient when they send you out on one of those trips: they work you like the town pump. They keep you busy night and day, plugging the picture in newspaper interviews, on the radio, and TV.

When we returned from the tour Eleanor and I used Paramount's money to buy the home of our dreams. This is far out in the San Fernando Valley and stands on an acre and a quarter of ground. The house is a modern farmhouse with six spacious rooms furnished in early American. Paramount bought the house, but it was furnished by "Truth and Consequences," "This Is Your Life," "It Could Be You," and other TV programs on which I made guest appearances. Eleanor's endless books of S & H stamps also helped furnish the place. Our swimming pool is of natural stone, and we decorate its borders with colored stones collected in each place we visit. The pool was paid for with some of the money I got for the TV commercials I have been doing for the last couple of years for Alka-Seltzer, Northwest Orient Airlines, and other firms.

Today the most exciting moments of my life come when I step out on my own property and walk around it, accompanied by Elmer III, my amiable 180-pound St. Bernard. Sometimes Jenny, our cat, also comes along. There were nine walnut trees in the garden when we bought the house, and I since have put in all sorts of fruit trees, including lemon, orange, tangerine, lime, plum, peach, apple, crab apple, and apricot. We grow three kinds of grapes—Tokay, Concord, and Thompson seedless—and also have raspberry and boysenberry bushes, and an artichoke bed. Each spring I grow radishes, cabbages, turnips, beefsteak tomatoes, and lettuce. I built a chicken yard in the rear of our land and a miniature railroad that carries peanuts, soda pop, sandwiches, popcorn to guests seated around a small garden house near the pool. For the accommodation of visiting grandchildren, nephews, movie producers, and TV sponsors we installed a bunkhouse.

If there is a better place in the world to be—when I'm not in front of an audience or a camera—someone else will have to name it.

Now, in closing, I try to think of a few of the thrills of my lifetime which I have not mentioned here. One came the day my two sons—then sixteen and fourteen years old—knocked on my door to shake hands and say "Hello." Jim, the older one, had just got his driver's license, and the first ride he took with his brother was to my house. I had not seen them since they were in Black-Fox Academy.

From that day on I had my own boys back again. And any worry I had about the growing up spoiled was eased during

277

World War II. They served in the Navy as frogmen and also did demolition work in one-man submarines. Bob had the lobe of his ear knocked off by a sniper.

These days when they come to see me they bring along their wives and their children. Jim has four of them: Jimmy thirteen, Mike eleven, Missy nine, and Marc three. Bob has two: Bobby eight, and Tommy three.

Today my boy, Jimmy, is in charge of the still section of the publicity department at Twentieth Century-Fox. Bob wanted no part of the picture business. He and a war buddy ran a couple of garages for some years. They were great fellows for devising special bodies for custom-made cars and stuff like that. But Bob gave that up a short while ago to go into business in Reno. As I mentioned all six of my sons' children call me Grandpa Buster.

With one thing and another I seem to have missed very little in not being a millionaire. I did miss it twice, now that I think about it again after a couple of hundred-odd pages. Once, of course, was because of my folly in not holding onto my screen properties.

But even before that, Roscoe Arbuckle, Al St. John, and myself, all narrowly escaped becoming multi-millionaires over night—thanks to a hardheaded businessman's logical thinking and shrewdness.

The business associate was our studio manager, Lou Anger.

When the Arbuckle Company moved to the Coast in 1918, we worked at the Hockheimer Studios in Long Beach. We did some of our wild chases back of the studio. There was a gravel pit there on the side of a big hill. Before long Roscoe and I got very interested in the man who was carting away gravel in his horse-drawn dump truck.

We became friendly with this guy, and Roscoe asked him a lot of questions about the business—how much the horse and wagon cost, their maintenance, how much he paid the owner of the pit for the gravel, and what he got per load from his customers.

I forget the figures on his profits that he gave us, but it sounded like a potentially lucrative undertaking. Roscoe was so impressed that he asked the owner how much he wanted for the property. He was told he could buy twenty-four acres, including the site of the gravel pit, for $2,400. Roscoe discussed this deal with me and St. John, and we agreed to put up $600 each for the property. We planned to buy a good many horses and dump trucks of our own and turn the one-man operation into a thriving large-scale business.

We needed just one more investor with $600 to throw into this sure thing. Somebody suggested Lou Anger, and we rushed to tell him the good news. Lou went out with us, looked at the gravel pit, and then asked a few shrewd questions of each of us in turn. Questions like: "Do you know anything about gravel?"

Roscoe said, "No." So did St. John and I.

"Do you know anything about horses?"

"Why no, but——" Roscoe started to say, but Lou was already asking Al and myself the same question and getting "No" from both of us.

"Do you know anything about dump trucks?"

Each of us shook our heads.

"Now," said Lou, "do you know anything about motion pictures?"

"I think so," replied Arbuckle. When Lou turned to each of us, we ventured to say we thought we did too.

"O.K., boys. Then if you have $600 apiece to invest, invest it in movies, the one business you know something about."

As he walked away, Roscoe said, "Isn't it great to have a fellow like Lou Anger around to save us from making foolish investments?"

Al and I agreed heartily.

Soon after that I was drafted.

After I came back to Hollywood, Roscoe and I were having dinner one evening when he told me he wanted to take me for a ride.

"Where are you going?" I asked him.

"Never mind, Buster, you'll find out when we get there."

I could tell very soon, of course, where he was heading. As we neared the site of the Hockheimer Studios, he said, "Do you recognize that hill? That's dear old Signal Hill."

"Wasn't that the hill in back of the old Hockheimer lot?" I asked.

He said it was, indeed, and drove around it so I could count the oil wells the Shell Oil Company had started drilling on the property on March 23, 1920, and the oil had since come in. By 1921 there were some five hundred derricks going, two years later more than 1,000. This makes the area, which is slightly more than two miles square, one of the most intensively developed oil fields on earth.

Roscoe shook his head that night and said, "And to think I thanked Lou Anger for talking us out of buying twenty-four acres of that oil-soaked real estate!"

Where I get a great feeling is that now, twenty-five years after I've made my last important picture, I am still recognized and given special privileges wherever I go. This is particularly true in Europe. When I check in at the Ritz or the George V or the Savoy, the clerk will give me the best room available just because I'm Buster Keaton. I've never had to tip a headwaiter to get a good table anywhere. I don't have to be announced in the leading cafés of Europe.

Now even a beloved businessman, a millionaire many times over, like Joe Schenck gets no recognition. He has to tip the room clerk and the headwaiter lavishly to get the best in the house.

I think the reason I never lost my humility before audiences is because I have always felt it is the performer's job to make everything he is doing understandable. After all the audience's duty ended when they paid to get in.

I think I have had the happiest and luckiest of lives. Maybe this is because I never expected as much as I got. What I expected was hard knocks. I always expected to have to work hard. Maybe harder than other people because of my lack of education. And when the knocks came I felt it was no surprise. I had always known life was like that, full of uppercuts for the deserving and undeserving alike.

But it would be ridiculous of me to complain. I find it impossible to feel sorry for myself. I count the years of defeat and grief and disappointment, and their percentage is so minute that it continually surprises and delights me.

When José Greco said my name in Spanish meant "A little bit of nothing," I said, "A little bit of *nothing!* Not even a little bit of something?" He replied, "That's the finest compliment my countrymen could pay you."

And I do think he's right.

To get back to that twelve-year-old mind nonsense, I sometimes resent the whole idea that humor, for example, has more to do with the human mind than with the emotions. If it were mental, the most brilliant people would have the keenest sense of humor. And this is not true.

All of us have our absurd side. The brighter people often cannot see that. But the Irish gravedigger, the ward-heeling politician, and the Jewish pants peddler often see it where the Einsteins don't.

Isn't it true that the geniuses of the world are those who channel all of their energies in one specialty?

Not long ago a friend asked me what was the greatest pleasure I got from spending my whole life as an actor. There have been so many that I had to think about that for a moment. Then I said, "Like everyone else, I like to be with a happy crowd."

And that is the comedian's greatest privilege and pleasure, I think: to have been with so many happy crowds whom he has made laugh with his pratfalls and other clowning antics.

Since 1920, when I was first starred in the movie *The Saphead,* I've enjoyed another reward as a dividend. This comes whenever people smile on seeing me and call out my name. I have told how that happened in Spain. And it has happened almost everywhere that I've traveled.

It happened in New York the night in 1922 that the *Chauve-Souris* opened. It was a gala night, and the whole house literally swarmed with celebrities. But I was the only one summoned backstage by Nikita Balieff, the Russian show's master of ceremonies. The women kissed me, and the men pumped my hand.

My wife and I were puzzled until I pointed out that none of our big Hollywood stars were in the audience. But mentioning this occasion now reminds me that when Douglas Fairbanks, Sr., came back from one of his triumphal world tours he told Joe Schenck, "Who do you think is the Number One movie star in Russia? Buster Keaton, that's who."

There was just one discouraging thing about this. Russia would never pay more than $5,000 for a print of any movie. And once it got the print it duplicated it so it could be shown everywhere—

Omsk and Tomsk, Yalta to Vladivostock. Which meant it might have been more profitable for me and my employers to be Number One star in Upper Monrovia or East Budapest.

This thrilling acclaim was given me in London, Paris, Mexico City, and practically everywhere else I have traveled. I was recognized and hailed when things were going great for me and also in the years when I began to think I was forgotten. There was a day in 1950 when we arrived in Genoa where Eleanor and I were to start a twelve-week musical-comedy tour in Italian theatres.

I was standing on the deck looking down at a gang of stevedores working on the dock thirty feet below. One of them recognized me, nudged his neighbor, and pointed. All at once the whole gang stopped working to yell, "Booster! *Booster* Keaton!" They waved in wild excitement, and I waved back, marveling, because it was fifteen years or more since they could have seen my last M-G-M picture.

And if there is sweeter music this side of heaven I haven't heard it. Dr. Avedon said I could live to be a hundred years old. I intend to do it. For who would not wish to live a hundred years in a world where there are so many people who remember with gratitude and affection a little man with a frozen face who made them laugh a bit long years ago when they and I were both young?

BUSTER KEATON FILMOGRAPHY

COMPILED BY RAYMOND ROHAUER

This chronological listing of Buster Keaton's appearances on film—theatrical and television releases—does not contain his credits as screen writer, contributor to comedy sketches, or director for some MGM shorts made in the 1930s.

The Keaton films from the silent era, as well as some of the later films and compilations, are distributed by Rohauer Films, Inc., 44 West 62nd Street, New York, NY 10023.

1. 4/23/1917   THE BUTCHER BOY   2 reels
Comique Film Corp./Paramount
Dir.: Fatty Arbuckle
Cast: Fatty Arbuckle, Buster Keaton, Al St. John, Josephine Stevens, Arthur Earle, Agnes Neilson, Joe Bordeau

2. 5/21/1917   A RECKLESS ROMEO   2 r.
Comique Film Corp./Paramount
Dir.: Fatty Arbuckle
Cast: Fatty Arbuckle, Buster Keaton, Al St. John, Alice Lake, Corinne Pacquet, Agnes Neilson

3. 6/25/1917   THE ROUGH HOUSE   2 r.
Comique Film Corp./Paramount
Dir.: Fatty Arbuckle
Cast: Fatty Arbuckle, Buster Keaton,
Al St. John, Alice Lake

4. 8/20/1917   HIS WEDDING NIGHT   2 r.
Comique Film Corp./Paramount
Dir.: Fatty Arbuckle
Cast: Fatty Arbuckle, Buster Keaton,
Al St. John, Alice Mann, Arthur Earle

5. 9/20/1917   OH, DOCTOR   2 r.
Comique Film Corp./Paramount
Dir.: Fatty Arbuckle
Cast: Fatty Arbuckle, Buster Keaton,
Al St. John, Alice Mann

6. 10/29/1917   FATTY AT CONEY ISLAND   2 r.
Comique Film Corp./Paramount
Dir.: Fatty Arbuckle
Cast: Fatty Arbuckle, Buster Keaton,
Al St. John, Alice Mann, Agnes Neilson,
James Bryant, Joe Bordeau
Also known as CONEY ISLAND

7. 12/10/1917   A COUNTRY HERO   2 r.
Comique Film Corp./Paramount
Dir.: Fatty Arbuckle
Cast: Fatty Arbuckle, Buster Keaton,
Al St. John, Alice Lake, Joe Keaton

8. 1/20/1918   OUT WEST   2 r.
Comique Film Corp./Paramount
Dir.: Fatty Arbuckle
Cast: Fatty Arbuckle, Buster Keaton,
Al St. John, Alice Lake

9. 3/18/1918   THE BELL BOY   2 r.
Comique Film Corp./Paramount
Dir.: Fatty Arbuckle
Cast: Fatty Arbuckle, Buster Keaton,
Al St. John, Alice Lake, Charles Dudley,
Joe Keaton

10. 5/13/1918   MOONSHINE   2 r.
Comique Film Corp./Paramount
Dir.: Fatty Arbuckle
Cast: Fatty Arbuckle, Buster Keaton,
Al St. John, Alice Lake, Charles Dudley,
Joe Bordeau

11. 7/8/1918   GOOD NIGHT, NURSE   2 r.
Comique Film Corp./Paramount
Dir.: Fatty Arbuckle
Cast: Fatty Arbuckle, Buster Keaton,
Al St. John, Alice Lake, Kate Price,
Joe Bordeau, Joe Keaton

12. 9/15/1918   THE COOK   2 r.
Comique Film Corp./Paramount
Dir.: Fatty Arbuckle
Cast: Fatty Arbuckle, Buster Keaton,
Al St. John, Alice Lake, Glen Cavender

13. 6/10/1919   A DESERT HERO   2 r.
Comique Film Corp./Paramount
Dir.: Fatty Arbuckle
Cast: Fatty Arbuckle, Buster Keaton,
Al St. John, Alice Lake
This is probably a re-issue title for OUT
WEST, released at this time because Kea-
ton was just returning from the Army and
no new film of his was available.

14. 9/7/1919   BACK STAGE   2 r.
                Comique Film Corp./Paramount
                Dir.: Fatty Arbuckle
                Cast: Fatty Arbuckle, Buster Keaton,
                Al St. John, Molly Malone, John Coogan,
                Alice Lake

15. 10/26/1919 THE HAYSEED   2 r.
                Comique Film Corp./Paramount
                Dir.: Fatty Arbuckle
                Cast: Fatty Arbuckle, Buster Keaton,
                Molly Malone

16. 1/11/1920   THE GARAGE   2 r.
                Comique Film Corp./Paramount
                Dir.: Fatty Arbuckle
                Cast: Fatty Arbuckle, Buster Keaton, Molly
                Malone, Harry McCoy, Daniel Crimmins

17. 8/1/1920   THE ROUND-UP   7 r.
                Famous Players-Lasky/Paramount
                Dir.: George Melford
                Cast: Fatty Arbuckle, Tom Forman
                Keaton appeared as an Indian extra in this
                Western.

18. 9/7/1920   ONE WEEK   2 r.
                Buster Keaton Prod./Metro
                Dir.: Buster Keaton and Eddie Cline
                Cast: Buster Keaton, Sybil Seeley,
                Joe Roberts

19. 10/18/1920 THE SAPHEAD   7 r.
                John L. Golden & Winchell Smith/Metro
                Dir.: Herbert Blache
                Cast: Buster Keaton, William H. Crane,

Beulah Booker, Edward Connelly, Odette
Tyler, Irving Cummings, Carol Holloway

20. 10/27/1920   CONVICT 13   2 r.
Buster Keaton Prod./Metro
Dir.: Buster Keaton and Eddie Cline
Cast: Buster Keaton, Sybil Seeley
Joe Roberts, Eddie Cline, Joe Keaton

21. 11/17/1920   THE SCARECROW   2 r.
Buster Keaton Prod./Metro
Dir.: Buster Keaton and Eddie Cline
Cast: Buster Keaton, Joe Roberts,
Sybil Seeley, Joe Keaton

22. 12/22/1920   NEIGHBORS   2 r.
Buster Keaton Prod./Metro
Dir.: Buster Keaton and Eddie Cline
Cast: Buster Keaton, Virginia Fox,
Joe Roberts, Joe Keaton, Eddie Cline,
James Duffy

23. 2/10/1921   THE HAUNTED HOUSE   2 r.
Buster Keaton Prod./Metro
Dir.: Buster Keaton and Eddie Cline
Cast: Buster Keaton, Virginia Fox,
Joe Roberts, Eddie Cline

24. 3/11/1921   HARD LUCK   2 r.
Buster Keaton Prod./Metro
Dir.: Buster Keaton and Eddie Cline
Cast: Buster Keaton, Virginia Fox,
Joe Roberts

25. 4/12/1921   THE HIGH SIGN   2 r.
Buster Keaton Prod./Metro

Dir.: Buster Keaton and Eddie Cline
Cast: Buster Keaton, Virginia Fox,
Joe Roberts

26. 5/18/1921 **THE GOAT** 2 r.
Buster Keaton Prod./Metro
Dir.: Buster Keaton and Mal St. Clair
Cast: Buster Keaton, Joe Roberts, Virginia
Fox, Mal St. Clair

27. 10/6/1921 **THE PLAY HOUSE** 2 r.
Joseph M. Schenck/First National
Dir. by Buster Keaton and Eddie Cline
Cast: Buster Keaton, Virginia Fox,
Joe Roberts

28. 11/10/1921 **THE BOAT** 2 r.
Comique Film Corp./First National
Dir.: Buster Keaton and Eddie Cline
Cast Buster Keaton, Sybil Seeley,
Eddie Cline

29. 12/17/1921 **THE PALEFACE** 2 r.
Comique Film Corp./First National
Dir.: Buster Keaton and Eddie Cline
Cast: Buster Keaton, Joe Roberts

30. 2/15/1922 **COPS** 2 r.
Comique Film Corp./First National
Dir.: Buster Keaton and Eddie Cline
Cast: Buster Keaton, Virginia Fox,
Joe Roberts, Eddie Cline

31. 6/12/1922 **MY WIFE'S RELATIONS** 2 r.
Comique Film Corp./First National
Dir.: Buster Keaton and Eddie Cline

Cast: Buster Keaton, Kate Price, Monty Collins, Wheezer Dell, Tom Wilson

32. 6/26/1922   SCREEN SNAPSHOTS—#3   1 r.
Pathe Exchange
Produced by Jack and Louis Lewyn
Keaton is one of several stars shown news-reel fashion in informal settings.

33. 7/21/1922   THE BLACKSMITH   2 r.
Comique Film Corp./First National
Dir.: Buster Keaton and Mal St. Clair
Cast: Buster Keaton, Virginia Fox, Joe Roberts

34. 8/3/1922   THE FROZEN NORTH   2 r.
Buster Keaton Prod./First National
Dir.: Buster Keaton and Eddie Cline
Cast: Buster Keaton, Bonny Hill, Freeman Wood, Joe Roberts

35. 9/28/1922   DAY DREAMS   2 r.
Buster Keaton Prod./First National
Dir.: Buster Keaton and Eddie Cline
Cast: Buster Keaton, Renee Adoree, Joe Roberts

36. 10/19/1922   THE ELECTRIC HOUSE   2 r.
Buster Keaton Prod./Associated-First National
Dir.: Buster Keaton and Eddie Cline
Cast: Buster Keaton, Virginia Fox, Joe Roberts, Joe Keaton, Myra Keaton, Louise Keaton

37. 12/21/1923   THE BALLOONATIC   2 r.
                   Buster Keaton Prod./Associated-First
                   National
                   Dir.: Buster Keaton and Eddie Cline
                   Cast: Buster Keaton, Phyllis Haver

38. 3/6/1923   THE LOVE NEST   2 r.
                   Buster Keaton Prod./Associated-First
                   National
                   Dir.: Buster Keaton
                   Cast: Buster Keaton, Joe Roberts,
                   Virginia Fox

39. 7/25/1923   THREE AGES   6 r.
                   Buster Keaton Prod./Metro
                   Dir.: Buster Keaton and Eddie Cline
                   Cast: Buster Keaton, Margaret Leahy,
                   Wallace Beery, Joe Roberts, Lillian
                   Lawrence, Horace Morgan

40. 11/19/1923   OUR HOSPITALITY   7 r.
                   Buster Keaton Prod./Metro
                   Dir.: Buster Keaton and Jack Blystone
                   Cast: Buster Keaton, Natalie Talmadge,
                   Joe Roberts, Leonard Clapham, Craig
                   Ward, Joe Keaton, Buster Keaton, Jr.

41. 4/21/1924   SHERLOCK, JR.   5 r.
                   Buster Keaton Prod./Metro
                   Dir.: Buster Keaton
                   Cast: Buster Keaton, Kathryn McGuire,
                   Ward Crane, Joseph Keaton, Horace
                   Morgan, Jane Connelly

42. 10/13/1924   THE NAVIGATOR   6 r.
                   Buster Keaton Prod./Metro-Goldwyn
                   Dir.: Buster Keaton and Donald Crisp

Cast: Buster Keaton, Kathryn McGuire,
Frederick Vroom, Noble Johnson,
Clarence Burton

43. 3/16/1925   SEVEN CHANGES   6 r.
Buster Keaton Prod./Metro-Goldwyn
Dir.: Buster Keaton
Cast: Buster Keaton, Ruth Dwyer,
Snitz Edwards, T. Roy Barnes, Frankie
Raymond, Jules Cowles, Erwin Connelly

44. 11/1/1925   GO WEST   7 r.
Buster Keaton Prod./Metro-Goldwyn
Dir.: Buster Keaton
Cast: Buster Keaton, Kathleen Myers,
Howard Truesdale, Ray Thompson

45. 8/30/1926   BATTLING BUTLER   7 r.
Buster Keaton Prod./MGM
Dir.: Buster Keaton
Cast: Buster Keaton, Sally O'Neil,
Snitz Edwards, Francis McDonald, Mary
O'Brien, Tom Wilson, Eddie Borden,
Walter James

46. 12/31/1926   THE GENERAL   8 r.
Buster Keaton Prod./United Artists
Dir.: Buster Keaton and Clyde Bruckman
Cast: Buster Keaton, Marion Mack, Glen
Cavender, Jim Farley, Frederick Vroom,
Charles Smith, Frank Barnes, Joe Keaton

47. 9/10/1927   COLLEGE   6 r.
Buster Keaton Prod./United Artists
Dir.: James W. Horne
Cast: Buster Keaton, Ann Cornwall, Flora
Bramley, Harold Goodwin, Buddy Mason,

Grant Withers, Snitz Edwards, Florence
Turner, Carl Harbaugh

48. 5/12/1928   STEAMBOAT BILL, JR.   7 r.
Buster Keaton Prod./United Artists
Dir.: Charles F. Reisner
Cast: Buster Keaton, Ernest Torrence, Tom
Lewis, Marion Byron, Tom McGuire

49. 9/15/1928   THE CAMERAMAN   8 r.
MGM
Dir.: Edward Sedgwick
Cast: Buster Keaton, Marceline Day,
Harold Goodwin, Harry Gribbon, Sidney
Bracy, Edward Brophy, William Irving,
Vernon Dent

50. 4/6/1929   SPITE MARRIAGE   9 r.
Edward Sedgwick/MGM
                        Part sound (music & effects)
Dir:. Edward Sedgwick
Cast: Buster Keaton, Dorothy Sebastian,
Edward Earle, Leila Hyams, William
Bechtel, John Byron, Hank Mann, Pat
Harmon
Originally filmed silent; later partial sound
added.

51. 9/23/1929   THE HOLLYWOOD REVUE   112 m.
OF 1929 .
Harry Rapf/MGM   Sound
Dir.: Charles Reisner
Cast: Jack Benny, Conrad Nagel, John
Gilbert, Norma Shearer, Joan Crawford,
Bessie Love, Cliff Edwards, the Bronx
Sisters, Laurel & Hardy, Lionel Barrymore,

Anita Page, Nils Asther, Marion Davies,
William Haines, Buster Keaton, Marie
Dressler, Polly Moran, Charles King, Gus
Edwards, Karl Dane, George K. Arthur,
Ann Dvorak, Gwen Lee

In this revue of many acts, Keaton does an
Oriental dance routine in "Dance of the
Sea" and appears briefly in the finale
"Singin' in the Rain."

52. 3/22/1930   FREE AND EASY   93 m.
                 Edward Sedgwick/MGM
                 Dir.: Edward Sedgwick
                 Cast: Buster Keaton, Anita Page, Trixie
                 Friganza, Robert Montgomery, Fred
                 Niblo, Edgar Dearing, David Burton,
                 Edward Brophy, Gwen Lee, John Miljan,
                 Lionel Barrymore, William Collier, Sr.,
                 William Haines, Dorothy Sebastian, Karl
                 Dane, Jackie Coogan, Cecil B. De Mille,
                 Arthur Lange, Joe Farnham

53. 3/22/1930   ESTRELLADOS   93 m.
                 (Spanish version of FREE AND EASY)
                 Director unknown—possibly Sedgwick
                 Cast: Buster Keaton, Raquel Torres, Don
                 Alvarado, Maria Calvo, Emile Chautard
                 Filmed in parallel with the English speak-
                 ing version, but replacing most of the speak-
                 ing parts with Spanish actors.

54. 4/28/1930   VOICE OF HOLLYWOOD #10 1 r.
                 Louis Lewyn/Tiffany
                 Dir.: Louis Lewyn
                 Cast: Robert Woolsey, Al St. John, Nancy
                 Wilbur, Johnny Walker, Lew Cody, Cliff

Edwards, Buster Keaton, the Meglin
Kiddies

In this sound compilation of acts, Lew
Cody, Cliff Edwards and Buster Keaton do
short takes in front of a lion's cage.

55. 8/30/1930   DOUGHBOYS   81 m.
Buster Keaton/MGM
Dir.: Edward Sedgwick
Cast: Buster Keaton, Sally Eilers, Cliff
Edwards, Edward Brophy, Victor Potel,
Arnold Korff, Frank Mayo, Pitzy Katz,
William Steele

56. 8/30/1930   DE FRONTE, MARCHEN   81 m.
(Spanish version of DOUGHBOYS)
Director unknown
Cast: Buster Keaton, Conchita Montenegro,
Juan de Landa, Romualdo Tirado

57. 3/27/1931   WIR SCHALTEN UM AUF   2 r.
HOLLYWOOD
(German version of THE HOLLYWOOD
REVUE OF 1929)
Dir.: Frank Reicher
Made in Germany, with some of the speak-
ing parts and sketches re-enacted with Ger-
man actors (e.g., Heinrich George, Nita
Parlo), but big musical and production
numbers taken intact from the American
original. Since Keaton's skit was a non-
speaking one, it was used as is.

58. 4/3/1931   THE STOLEN JOOLS   2 r.
Pat Casey/Paramount and National
Screen Service

Dir.: William McGann
Cast: Wallace Beery, Buster Keaton, Jack
Hill, Allen Jenkins, J. Farrell McDonald,
Edward G. Robinson, George E.
Stone,
Eddie Kane, Laurel & Hardy, Our Gang,
Polly Moran, Norma Shearer, Hedda
Hopper, Joan Crawford, William Haines,
Dorothy Lee, Edmund Lowe, Victor
McLaglen, El Brendel, Charlie Murray,
George Sidney, Winnie Lightner, Fifi
D'Orsay, Warner Baxter, Irene Dunne,
Wheeler & Woolsey, Richard Dix, Claudia
Dell, Lowell Sherman, Eugene Pallette,
Stu Erwin, Skeets Gallagher, Gary Cooper,
Wynne Gibson, Buddy Rogers, Maurice
Chevalier, Douglas Fairbanks, Jr., Loretta
Young, Richard Barthelmess, Charles
Butterworth, Bebe Daniels, Ben Lyon,
Barbara Stanwyck, Frank Fay, Jack Oakie,
Fay Wray, Joe E. Brown, Gabby Hayes,
Little Billy, Mitzi Green

This short, presented by National Variety
Artists to raise funds for a tuberculosis san-
atorium, concerns a stolen pearl necklace
belonging to Norma Shearer. Keaton plays
one of four Keystone Kops who appear at
the very beginning.

Released in England in 1932 as THE SLIP-
PERY PEARLS.

59. 4/3/1931   PARLOR, BEDROOM   73 m.
                   AND BATH
                   MGM
                   Dir.: Edward Sedgwick
                   Cast: Buster Keaton, Charlotte Greenwood,
                   Reginald Denny, Cliff Edwards, Dorothy

Christy, Joan Peers, Sally Eilers, Natalie
Moorhead, Edward Brophy

60. 4/3/1931   BUSTER SE MARIE   80 m.
(French version of PARLOR, BEDROOM
AND BATH)
Dir.: Claude Autant-Lara
Cast: Buster Keaton, Mona Goya, André
Luguet, Mireille, Françoise Rosay,
Georgette Rhodes, Jeanne Helbling,
Lya Lys, Rolla Norman

61. 4/3/1931   CASANOVA WIDER   73 m.
WILLEN
(German version of PARLOR, BEDROOM
AND BATH)
Dir.: Edward Brophy
Cast: Buster Keaton, Paul Morgan, Marion
Lessing, Egon von Jordan, Francoise Rosey,
Leni Stengel, Gerda Mann, George Davis,
Wolfgang Zilzer

62. 9/26/1931   THE SIDEWALKS OF   75 m.
NEW YORK
Buster Keaton/MGM
Dir.: Jules White and Zion Myers
Cast: Buster Keaton, Anita Page, Cliff
Edwards, Frank Rowan, Norman Phillips,
Jr., Frank La Rue, Oscar Apfel, Syd Saylor,
Clark Marshall

63. 2/6/1932   THE PASSIONATE   73 m.
PLUMBER
Buster Keaton/MGM
Dir.: Edward Sedgwick
Cast: Buster Keaton, Jimmy Durante,
Irene Purcell, Polly Moran, Gilbert Roland,

Mona Maris, Maude Eburne, Henry
Armetta, Paul Porcasi

64. 2/6/1932   LE PLOMBIER AMOUREUX 72 m.
(French version of THE PASSIONATE
PLUMBER)
Dir.: Claude Autant-Lara
Cast: Buster Keaton, Jimmy Durante,
Irene Purcell, Polly Moran, Mona Maris,
Jeanette Ferney, Barbara Leonard, Maude
Eburne, Del Val, George Davis

65. 8/13/1932   SPEAK EASILY   80 m.
MGM
Dir.: Edward Sedgwick
Cast: Buster Keaton, Jimmy Durante, Ruth
Selwyn, Thelma Todd, Hedda Hopper,
William Pawley, Sidney Toler, Lawrence
Grant, Henry Armetta, Edward Brophy

66. 1/8/1933   HOLYWOOD ON   1 r.
PARADE #A-6
Louis Lewyn/Paramount
Dir.: Louis Lewyn
Cast: Richard Arlen, Frances Dee, Clark
Gable, Tallulah Bankhead, Buster Keaton,
Lew Cody
In this compilation of walk-ons and minor
acts, Buster Keaton plays host to Lew Cody
on his big land cruiser.

67. 2/10/1933   WHAT! NO BEER?   70 m.
MGM
Dir.: Edward Sedgwick
Cast: Buster Keaton, Jimmy Durante,
Roscoe Ates, Phyllis Barry, John Miljan,

Henry Armetta, Edward Brophy, Charles
Dunbar, Charles Giblyn

68. 1/5/1934   LE ROI DES CHAMPS-   70 m.
ELYSEES
Nero Film/Paramount. Released in France
Dir.: Max Nosseck
Cast: Buster Keaton, Paulette Dubost,
Colette Darfeuil, Madeline Guitty, Jacques
Dumesnil, Pierre Pierade, Gaston Dupray,
Paul Clerget, Frank Maurice, Pitouto,
Lucien Callamand

69. 3/16/1934   THE GOLD GHOST   2 r.
Educational/20th Century-Fox
Dir.: Charles Lamont
Cast: Buster Keaton, Dorothy Dix, William
Worthington, Lloyd Ingraham, Warren
Hymer

70. 5/31/1934   ALLEZ OOP   2 r.
Educational/20th Century-Fox
Dir.: Charles Lamont
Cast: Buster Keaton, Dorothy Sebastian,
Harry Myers, George Lewis

71. 1/11/1935   PALOOKA FROM PADUCAH 2 r.
Educational/20th Century-Fox
Dir.: Charles Lamont
Cast: Buster Keaton, Joe Keaton, Myra
Keaton, Louise Keaton, Dewey Robinson,
Bull Montana

72. 2/22/1935   ONE RUN ELMER   2 r.
Educational/20th Century-Fox
Dir.: Charles Lamont

Cast: Buster Keaton, Lona Andre, Dewey
Robinson, Harold Goodwin

73. 3/15/1935 HAYSEED ROMANCE   2 r.
Educational/20th Century-Fox
Dir.: Charles Lamont
Cast: Buster Keaton, Jane Jones,
Dorothea Kent

74. 5/2/1935 TARS AND STRIPES   2 r.
Educational/20th Century-Fox
Dir.: Charles Lamont
Cast: Buster Keaton, Vernon Dent,
Dorothea Kent, Jack Shutta

75. 8/9/1935 THE E-FLAT MAN   2 r.
Educational/20th Century-Fox
Dir.: Charles Lamont
Cast: Buster Keaton, Dorothea Kent,
Broderick O'Farrell, Charles McAvoy,
Si Jenks, Fern Emmett, Jack Shutta

76. 10/25/1935 THE TIMID YOUNG MAN   2 r.
Educational/20th Century-Fox
Dir.: Mack Sennett
Cast: Buster Keaton, Lona Andre, Tiny
Sandford, Kitty McHugh, Harry Bowen

77. 12/7/1935 LA FIESTA DE SANTA   2 r.
BARBARA   Color
Louis Lewyn/MGM
Dir.: Louis Lewyn
Cast: Buster Keaton, Chester Conklin,
Gary Cooper, Harpo Marx, Maria
Gambarelli, Warner Baxter, Leo Carillo,
Adrienne Ames, Robert Taylor, Mary
Carlisle, Edmund Lowe, Toby Wing, Ida

Lupino, Irvin S. Cobb, Ted Healy

This was essentially a boating party going to a Mexican carnival. All of the above stars are seen briefly on the boat or at the carnival, but the music and revelry are the main attraction.

78. 1/2/1936   THE INVADER   61 m.
Released in the U.S. as AN OLD SPANISH CUSTOM
British & Continental/MGM
Dir.: Adrian Brunel
Cast: Buster Keaton, Lupita Tovar, Esme Percy, Lyn Harding, Webster Booth, Andrea Malandrinos, Hilda Moreno, Clifford Heatherley
Made and originally released in England. First U.S. distribution by J. H. Hoffberg.

79. 1/3/1936   THREE ON A LIMB   2 r.
Educational/20th Century-Fox
Dir.: Charles Lamont
Cast: Buster Keaton, Lona Andre, Harold Goodwin, Grant Withers, Barbara Bedford, John Ince, Fern Emmett, Phyllis Crane

80. 2/21/1936   GRAND SLAM OPERA   2 r.
Educational/20th Century-Fox
Dir.: Charles Lamont
Cast: Buster Keaton, Diana Lewis, Harold Goodwin, John Ince, Melrose Coakley, Bud Jamison

81. 8/21/1936   BLUE BLAZES   2 r.
Educational/20th Century-Fox
Dir.: Raymond Kane

Cast: Buster Keaton, Arthur Jarrett, Rose Kessner, Patty Wilson, Marlyn Stuart

82. 10/9/1936   THE CHEMIST   2 r.
Educational/20th Century-Fox
Dir.: Al Christie
Cast: Buster Keaton, Marlyn Stuart, Earl Gilbert, Don McBride, Herman Lieb

83. 11/20/1936   MIXED MAGIC   2 r.
Educational/20th Century-Fox
Dir.: Raymond Kane
Cast: Buster Keaton, Eddie Lambert, Marlyn Stuart, Eddie Hall, Jimmie Fox, Walter Fenner

84. 1/8/1937   JAIL BAIT   2 r.
Educational/20th Century-Fox
Dir.: Charles Lamont
Cast: Buster Keaton, Harold Goodwin, Betty Andre, Bud Jamison, Matthew Betz

85. 2/12/1937   DITTO   2 r.
Educational/20th Century-Fox
Dir.: Charles Lamont
Cast: Buster Keaton, Barbara Brewster, Gloria Brewster, Harold Goodwin, Lynton Brent, Al Thompson, Bob Ellsworth

86. 3/26/1937   LOVE NEST ON WHEELS   2 r.
Educational/20th Century-Fox
Dir.: Charles Lamont
Cast: Buster Keaton, Myra Keaton, Louise Keaton, Harry Keaton, Al St. John, Lynton Brent, Diana Lewis, Bud Jamison

87. 6/16/1939   PEST FROM THE WEST   2 r.
Columbia
Dir.: Del Lord
Cast: Buster Keaton, Lorna Gray, Gino
Corrado, Richard Fiske, Bud Jamison,
Eddie Laughton

88. 8/11/1939   MOOCHING THROUGH   2 r.
GEORGIA
Columbia
Dir.: Jules White
Cast: Buster Keaton, Monty Collins, Bud
Jamison, Jill Martin, Lynton Brent, Jack
Hill, Stanley Mack

89. 10/13/1939   HOLLYWOOD CAVALCADE   96 m.
Darryl Zanuck/20th Century-Fox Color
Dir.: Irving Cummings
Cast: Alice Faye, Don Ameche, J. Edward
Bromberg, Alan Curtis, Stuart Erwin, Jed
Prouty, Donald Meek, George Givot, Chick
Chandler, Russell Hicks, Robert Lowery,
Ben Weldon

Guest stars appearing as themselves: Buster
Keaton, Ben Turpin, Chester Conklin, Al
Jolson, Mack Sennett, the Keystone Kops.

90. 1/19/1940   NOTHING BUT PLEASURE   2 r.
Columbia
Dir.: Jules White
Cast: Buster Keaton, Dorothy Appleby,
Beatrice Blinn, Bud Jamison, Richard
Fiske, Robert Sterling, Jack Randall

91. 3/22/1940   PARDON MY BERTH   2 r.
                  MARKS
                  Columbia
                  Dir.: Jules White
                  Cast: Buster Keaton, Dorothy Appleby,
                  Richard Fiske, Vernon Dent

92. 6/28/1940   THE TAMING OF   2 r.
                  THE SNOOD
                  Columbia
                  Dir.: Jules White
                  Cast: Buster Keaton, Dorothy Appleby,
                  Elsie Ames, Richard Fiske, Bruce Bennett

93. 7/18/1940   NEW MOON   85 m.
                  MGM
                  Prod. & dir.: Robert Z. Leonard
                  Cast: Jeanette MacDonald, Nelson Eddy,
                  Mary Boland, George Zucco, H. B. Warner,
                  Grant Mitchell

                  Originally made with Buster Keaton in the
                  cast. When the film was screened for the
                  stars and the studio bigwigs, it was discov-
                  ered that Keaton stole too many scenes and
                  the featured stars would have suffered by
                  comparison; hence the film was re-edited
                  to cut out Keaton's part. However, the edit-
                  ing was not perfect, and he can be glimpsed
                  in a few scenes left in the final version.[1]

94. 9/20/1940   THE SPOOK SPEAKS   2 r.
                  Columbia
                  Dir.: Jules White
                  Cast: Buster Keaton, Elsie Ames, Dorothy
                  Appleby, Don Beddoe, Bruce Bennett

[1]As told to R. Rohauer by Nelson Eddy.

95. 10/11/1940   THE VILLAIN STILL   65 m.
PURSUED HER
Franklin-Blank Prod./RKO
Dir.: Eddie Cline
Cast: Buster Keaton, Hugh Herbert, Anita
Louise, Alan Mowbray, Richard Cromwell

96. 11/1/1940   LI'L ABNER   78 m.
Vogue/RKO
Dir.: Albert S. Rogell
Cast: Buster Keaton, Granville Owen,
Martha O'Driscoll, Mona Ray

97. 12/13/1940   HIS EX MARKS THE SPOT   2 r.
Columbia
Dir.: Jules White
Cast: Buster Keaton, Elsie Ames, Dorothy
Appleby, Matt McHugh

98. 2/21/1941   SO YOU WON'T SQUAWK   2 r.
Columbia
Dir.: Del Lord
Cast: Buster Keaton, Eddie Fetherstone,
Matt McHugh, Bud Jamison, Hank Mann,
Vernon Dent, Edmund Cobb

99. 9/18/1941   GENERAL NUISANCE   2 r.
Columbia
Dir.: Jules White
Cast: Buster Keaton, Elsie Ames, Dorothy
Appleby, Monty Collins, Bud Jamison,
Lynton Brent, Nick Arno, Harry Semels

100. 11/20/1941   SHE'S OIL MINE   2 r.
Columbia
Dir.: Jules White

Cast: Buster Keaton, Elsie Ames, Monty Collins, Eddie Laughton, Bud Jamison

101. 3/26/1943   FOREVER AND A DAY   104 m.
Anglo-American Prod./RKO
Prod. & directed by René Clair, Edmund Goulding, Cedric Hardwicke, Frank Lloyd, Victor Saville, Robert Stevenson & Herbert Wilcox
Cast: Anna Neagle, Ray Milland, Claude Rains, C. Aubrey Smith, Dame May Whitty, Gene Lockhart, Ray Bolger, Edmund Gwenn, Lumsden Hare, Stuart Robertson, Claude Allister, Ben Webster, Alan Edmiston, Patrick Knowles, Bernie Sell, Halliwell Hobbes, Helen Pickard, Doris Lloyd, Lionel Belmore, Louise Bissinger, Clifford Severn, Charles Coburn, Alec Craig, Ian Hunter, Jessie Matthews, Charles Laughton, Montague Love, Reginald Owen, Sir Cedric Hardwicke, Noel Madison, Ernest Cossart, Peter Godfrey, Buster Keaton, Wendy Barrie, Ida Lupino, Brian Aherne, Edward Everett Horton, Isobel Elsom, Wendell Hulet, Eric Blore, June Duprez, Mickey Martin, Queenie Leonard, May Beatty, Merle Oberon, Una O'Connor, Nigel Bruce, Anita Bolster, Marta Gale, Roland Young, Gladys Cooper, Robert Cummings, Herbert Evans, Kay Deslys, Richard Haydn, Emily Fitzroy, Odette Myrtil, Elsa Lanchester, Sara Allgood, Vangie Beilby, Robert Coote, Art Mulliner, Ivan Simpson, Pax Walker, Lola Vanti, Bill Cartledge, Charles Hall, Percy Snowden, Donald Crisp, Ruth

Warrick, Kent Smith, June Lockhart, Lydia
Bilbrook, Billy Bevan, Herbert Marshall,
Victor McLaglen, Harry Allen, Ethel
Griffies, Gabriel Canzona, Joy Mary
Gordon, Evelyn Beresford, Moyna MacGill,
Arthur Treacher, Anna Lee, Cecil
Kellaway, Stuart Hall, Barry Heenan,
Barry Norton, Philip Ahlin, Daphne Moore

A wartime paean to the noble British spirit
instigated mainly by Sir Cedric Hardwicke.
Keaton plays Hardwicke's assistant—they
are two plumbers installing a bathtub. Stars
contributing their talent included most of
the British colony in Hollywood. The story
traces the building of a stately home by C.
Aubrey Smith in 1804 and what happens to
the subsequent generations who live in it.

102. 9/29/1944 SAN DIEGO, I LOVE YOU   73 m.
Universal
Dir.: Reginald Le Borg
Cast: Jon Hall, Louise Allbritton, Edward
Everett Horton, Eric Blore, Buster Keaton,
Irene Ryan, Rudy Wissler, Gerald Perreau

Keaton plays a bus driver whom Louise
Allbritton persuades to take a wild ride on
a whim.

103. 6/1/1945 THAT'S THE SPIRIT   87 m.
Universal
Dir.: Charles Lamont
Cast: Peggy Ryan, Jack Oakie, June
Vincent, Gene Lockhart, Johnny Coy,
Andy Devine, Arthur Treacher, Irene
Ryan, Buster Keaton, Victoria Horne,
Edith Barrett

Keaton has a bit role in a fantasy about a man whose spirit is allowed to come back to Earth.

104. 9/28/1945   THAT NIGHT WITH YOU   84 m.
Universal
Dir.: William A. Seiter
Cast: Franchot Tone, Susanna Foster, Louise Allbritton, David Bruce, Jacqueline de Wit, Irene Ryan, Barbara Sears, Anthony Caruso, Julian Rivero, Teddy Infuhr, Janet Ann Gallow, Buster Keaton, Thomas Fadden, Howard Freeman
Zany farce about a girl who tells a producer that she's the result of his one-day marriage many years before. Keaton plays a short-order cook.

105. 5/18/1936   GOD'S COUNTRY   70 m.
Action Pictures/Screen   Color
Guild Prod.
Dir.: Robert Tansey
Cast: Robert Lowery, Helen Gilbert, Buster Keaton
Outdoor film; Keaton is an animal lover

106. 8/2/1946   EL MODERNO BARBA AZUL 90 m.
Alsa Films (Mexico). Never released in the U.S.
Dir.: Jaime Salvador
Cast: Buster Keaton, Angel Garasa, Virginia Seret, Luis Bareiro, Fernando Sotto
Keaton is a prisoner of Mexicans who send him to the Moon.

107. 5/11/1949 THE LOVABLE CHEAT   74 m.
Skyline Pictures/Film Classics, Inc.
Dir.: Richard Oswald
Cast: Charles Ruggles, Peggy Ann Garner,
Richard Ney, Alan Mowbray, Iris Adrian,
Minerva Urecal, Buster Keaton
A classic Balzac story of an inveterate gambler who keeps stalling creditors with charmingly inventive tales. Keaton has a bit role.

108. 6/23/1949 IN THE GOOD OLD   102 m.
SUMMERTIME   Color
MGM
Dir.: Robert Z. Leonard
Cast: Judy Garland, Van Johnson, Buster Keaton, Spring Byington, S. Z. Sakall

109. 7/16/1949 YOU'RE MY EVERYTHING   94 m.
20th Century-Fox
Dir.: Walter Lang
Cast: Dan Dailey, Anne Baxter, Anne
Revere, Stanley Ridges, Shari Robinson,
Henry O'Neill, Selena Royle, Alan
Mowbray, Robert Arthur, Buster Keaton,
Phyllis Kennedy, Chester Jones
Musical comedy about the early days of sound in Hollywood. Keaton plays a butler.

110. 8/4/1950 SUNSET BOULEVARD   110 m.
Paramount
Dir.: Billy Wilder
Cast: William Holden, Gloria Swanson,
Erich von Stroheim, Nancy Olson, Fred
Clark, Jack Webb, Lloyd Gough, Ruth
Clifford

Appearing as themselves: Cecil B. De
Mille, Hedda Hopper, Buster Keaton,
Anna Q. Nilsson, H. B. Warner, Ray Evans,
Jay Livingston, Sidney Skolsky
Keaton is seen in a card game with Gloria
Swanson, Anna Q. Nilsson and H. B. Warner.

111. 9/7/1950   UN DUEL A MORT   3 r.
Films Azur (France). Never released in U.S.
Dir.: Pierre Blondy
Cast: Buster Keaton, Antonin Berval
This short captures on film a skit which
Keaton used for years at the Cirque Me-
drano in Paris. He is a comic duellist.

112. 4/22/1951   SCREEN SNAPSHOTS: 1 r.
MEMORIES OF FAMOUS
HOLLYWOOD COMEDIANS
Columbia
Directed and compiled by Ralph Staub
Narrated by Joe E. Brown
Cast: Fatty Arbuckle, Zasu Pitts, Laurel &
Hardy, W. C. Fields, Charley Chase, Andy
Clyde, Buster Keaton, Louise Fazenda, Ben
Turpin, Marx Brothers, Olsen & Johnson
A compilation of deleted scenes and off-
screen candid footage of many stars.

113. 10/15/1952 PARADISE FOR BUSTER   39 m.
Wilding Pictures, for Deere & Co.
(Shot in 16 mm private company film)
Dir.: Del Lord
Cast: Buster Keaton
In this industrial short, Keaton plays in
pantomine an unsuccessful bookkeeper
who inherits an old rundown farm and

turns it into a well-stocked lake used by fishermen.

114. 10/22/1952   LIMELIGHT   143 m.
Celebrated Films/United Artists
Dir.: Charles Chaplin
Cast: Charles Chaplin, Claire Bloom,
Sydney Chaplin, Andre Eglevsky, Melissa
Hayden, Charles Chaplin, Jr., Wheeler
Dryden, Nigel Bruce, Norman Lloyd,
Buster Keaton, Marjorie Bennett,
Geraldine Chaplin, Michael Chaplin,
Victoria Chaplin
Keaton plays a piano accompanist to Chaplin's performance as a clown.

115. 6/14/1953   L'INCANTEVOLE NEMICA   86 m.
Orso Film (Italy). Not released in U.S.
Dir.: Claudio Gora
Cast: Silvana Pampanini, Robert
Lamoureux, Carlo Campanini, Raymond
Bussieres, Buster Keaton
Buster appears in a brief sketch.

116. 7/14/1054   DOUGLAS FAIRBANKS, JR. TV: 30 m.
PRESENTS: THE AWAKENING
Based on Gogol's "The Overcoat," Keaton
plays a timid individual beset by troubles.
(NBC)

117. 10/13/1954 BEST OF BROADWAY: TV: 60 m.
THE MAN WHO CAME TO DINNER
Dir.: David Alexander
Cast: Buster Keaton, Sylvia Field, Zasu

Pitts, Frank Tweddell, Margaret Hamilton, Merle Oberon, Monty Woolley, Howard St. John, Joan Bennett, Reginald Gardiner, Bert Lahr, Catherine Doucet, William Prince

Adaptation of the Kaufman and Hart play. Keaton plays Dr. Bradley.

(CBS)

118. 10/10/1955 EDDIE CANTOR   TV: 30 m.
THEATER: WORLD OF
ALONZO PENNYWORTH
Keaton plays Alonzo Pennyworth, a bashful travel agent who himself has never been anywhere and who is doing badly romantically as well (with Christine Larsen).

(ABC)

119. 12/21/1955 SCREEN DIRECTORS' PLAYHOUSE:
THE SILENT PARTNER   TV: 30 m.
Dir.: George Marshall
Cast: Bob Hope, Joe E. Brown, Buster Keaton, Zasu Pitts, Jack Elam

Keaton plays a show biz has-been who watches the Academy Awards show on TV in a bar, and sees Bob Hope give a special medal to a producer who used to be his old partner.

120. 3/6/1956 MARTHA RAYE SHOW TV: 60 m.
Guests: Buster Keaton, Paul Douglas, Harold Arlen.
In a sketch, Keaton and Martha Raye do a parody of LIMELIGHT.

(NBC)

121. 9/17/1956   PRODUCERS' SHOWCASE:
                 THE LORD DON'T PLAY   TV: 90 m.
                 FAVORITES
                 Prod.: Hal Stanley
                 Cast: Buster Keaton, Robert Stack, Kay
                 Starr, Dick Haymes, Louis Armstrong,
                 Nejla Ates, Mike Ross, Arthur Q. Bryan
                 Musical about a small traveling circus that
                 gets stranded in a Kansas town around
                 1905.

122. 10/17/1956 AROUND THE WORLD   148 m.
                 IN 80 DAYS   Color
                 Michael Todd Co./United Artists
                 Dir.: Michael Anderson
                 Cast: David Niven, Cantinflas, Robert
                 Newton, Shirley MacLaine, Charles Boyer,
                 Joe E. Brown, Martine Carol, John
                 Carradine, Charles Coburn, Ronald
                 Colman, Melville Cooper, Noel Coward,
                 Finlay Currie, Reginald Denny, Andy
                 Devine, Marlene Dietrich, Luis Miguel
                 Dominguin, Fernandel, Sir John Gielgud,
                 Hermione Gingold, Jose Greco, Sir Cedric
                 Hardwicke, Trevor Howard, Glynis Johns,
                 Buster Keaton, Evelyn Keyes, Beatrice
                 Lillie, Peter Lorre, Edmund Lowe, Victor
                 McLaglen, Tim McCoy, A. E. Mathews,
                 Mike Mazurki, John Mills, Alan Mowbray,
                 Robert Morley, Edward R. Murrow, Jack
                 Oakie, George Raft, Gilbert Roland, Cesar
                 Romero, Frank Sinatra, Red Skelton,
                 Ronald Squire, Basil Sydney, Harcourt
                 Williams, Ava Gardner
                 Keaton plays a conductor on a train be-
                 tween San Francisco and Ft. Kearney.

123. 6/5/1958   PLAYHOUSE 90:   TV: 90 m.
                  THE INNOCENT SLEEP
                  Dir.: Franklin Schaffner
                  Cast: Buster Keaton, Hope Lange, Dennis
                  King, John Ericson, Hope Emerson
                  Keaton plays a town character who is struck
                  deaf and dumb at a trial in which he is
                  accused of having killed his father.
                                                    (CBS)

124. 12/24/1958 DONNA REED SHOW: TV: 30 m.
                  A VERY MERRY CHRISTMAS
                  Cast: Donna Reed, Buster Keaton, Carl
                  Betz, Shelley Fabares, Paul Petersen
                  Keaton plays a philanthropist who provides
                  the money for the annual party at the chil-
                  dren's ward in a hospital, and who is talked
                  by Donna Reed into playing Santa.

125. 2/7/1960   SUNDAY SHOWCASE: TV: 60 m.
                  AFTER HOURS   Color
                  Dir.: Alex March
                  Cast: Buster Keaton, Christopher Plummer,
                  Sally Ann Howes, Robert Emhardt, Philip
                  Abbott, Natalie Schafer, Paul McGrath,
                  John Fiedler
                  A comedy of mistaken identity in which
                  Keaton plays Santa Claus.

126. 3/29/1960   WHEN COMEDY WAS KING 81 m.
                  Ro-Co Prod./20th Century-Fox
                  Produced and selected by Robert Youngson
                  Cast: Charlie Chaplin, Laurel & Hardy,
                  Buster Keaton, Harry Langdon, Ben
                  Turpin, Fatty Arbuckle, Wallace Beery,
                  Gloria Swanson, Mabel Normand, etc.

A compilation of great moments from many films from the silent era. No new footage.

127. 6/17/1960   THE ADVENTURES OF   107 m.
HUCKLEBERRY FINN   Color
MGM
Dir.: Michael Curtiz
Cast: Tony Randall, Eddie Hodges, Archie Moore, Patty McCormack, Neville Brand, Buster Keaton
Keaton has a small role as a lion tamer.

128. 9/15/1960   THE DEVIL TO PAY   28 m.
Education Research Films, for National Association of Wholesalers
           (Private use only; 16 mm)
Dir.: Herb Skoble
Cast: Buster Keaton, Ralph Dunne, Ruth Gillette, Marion Morris, John Rodney
Keaton plays the devil.

129. 1961   THE HISTORY OF   TV: 30 m.
MOTION PICTURES:
THE SAD CLOWNS
Produced and narrated by Saul J. Turrel & Paul Killiam. Edited by Bill Everson
Cast: Charlie Chaplin, Harry Langdon, Buster Keaton
Compilation of clips from their silent films.

130. 12/15/1961   TWILIGHT ZONE: TV: 30 m.
ONCE UPON A TIME
Dir.: Norman Z. McLeod
Cast: Buster Keaton, Stanley Adams, Milton Parsons, Jesse White, Gil Lamb, James Flavin, Michael Ross

Keaton plays a janitor who in 1890 fools around with a time machine and propels himself into 1962.

131. 1962   TEN GIRLS AGO   Length
                    Am-Can Productions (Canada) unknown
                    Filmed in 1962 but never released
                    Dir.: Harold Daniels
                    Cast: Dion, Austin Wills, Jan Miner,
                    Jennifer Billingsley, Risella Bain, Buster
                    Keaton, Bert Lahr, Eddie Foy, Jr.
                    A rock-and-roll story filmed hurriedly and
                    amateurishly, with three old-timers provid-
                    ing comedy relief. This was the last picture
                    on which Bert Lahr worked.

132. 4/20/1962   THE SCENE STEALERS TV: 60 m.
                    March of Dimes
                    Cast: Buster Keaton, Jimmy Durante,
                    Ed Wynn

                    The three comedians get involved in re-
                    hearsals of the March of Dimes Show and
                    mess things up.

133. 9/28/1962   ROUTE 66:   TV: 60 m.
                    JOURNEY TO NINEVEH
                    Dir. unknown
                    Cast: Buster Keaton, George Maharis,
                    Martin Milner, Joe E. Brown, Gene
                    Raymond, Jenny Maxwell, John Astin,
                    John Davis Chandler, John Durren
                    Keaton plays the town jinx.

134. 12/20/1962   THE GREAT CHASE   79 m.
                    Saul J. Turrell & Paul Killiam/Janus Films
                    Prod. and editor: Harvey Cort

Cast: Douglas Fairbanks, Sr., William S.
Hart, Mack Sennett, Mabel Normand,
Buster Keaton
Compilation of scenes involving chases
from many silents, with narration and
sound effects. Keaton is seen in scenes from
THE GENERAL.

135. 1/19/1963   MR. SMITH: TV: 30 m.
                    THINK MINK
                    Dir. unknown
                    Cast: Buster Keaton, Jesslyn Fax,
                    Fess Parker, Sandra Warner
                    Keaton and Fax play a couple who discover
                    how to breed mink much faster by feeding
                    them her special stew.

                                            (ABC)

136. 2/12/1963   THIRTY YEARS OF FUN   85 m.
                    20th Century-Fox
                    Produced and written by Robert Youngson
                    Cast: Charlie Chaplin, Buster Keaton,
                    Laurel & Hardy, Andy Clyde, Billy Bevan,
                    etc.
                    Compilation of vintage scenes from com-
                    edy classics. Keaton is seen in excerpts
                    from COPS, DAY DREAMS and THE
                    BALLOONATIC.

137. 3/25/1963   THE TRIUMPH OF   22 m.
                    LESTER SNAPWELL   Color
                    Eastman Kodak Co.   16 mm
                    (Private company film)
                    Dir.: James Calhoun
                    Cast: Buster Keaton
                    Keaton traces the highlights of the devel-

opment of the camera in his comic style in this industrial film.

138. 4/26/1963 TODAY SHOW   TV: 120 m.
Special guest: Buster Keaton
Host Hugh Downs devotes most of the show to a Keaton tribute. Clips from his old films are viewed several times.
(NBC)

139. 11/7/1963 IT'S A MAD, MAD, MAD   192 m.
WORLD
Stanley Kramer/United Artists
Dir.: Stanley Kramer
Cast: Spencer Tracy, Milton Berle, Sid Caesar, Buddy Hackett, Ethel Merman, Mickey Rooney, Dick Shawn, Phil Silvers, Terry-Thomas, Jonathan Winters, Edie Adams, Dorothy Provine, Rochester, Jim Backus, Ben Blue, Alan Carney, Barrie Chase, William Demarest, Peter Falk, Paul Ford, Leo Gorcey, Edward Everett Horton, Buster Keaton, Don Knotts, Carl Reiner, Moe Howard, Larry Fine, Joe DeRita, Joe E. Brown, Andy Devine, Sterling Holloway, Marvin Kaplan, Charles Lane, Charles McGraw, Zasu Pitts, Madlyn Rhue, Arnold Stang, Jesse White, Lloyd Corrigan, Stan Freberg, Ben Lessy, Bobo Lewis, Mike Mazurki, Nick Stewart, Sammee Tong, Norman Fell, Nicholas Georgiade, Jimmy Durante, Allen Jenkins, Stanley Clements, Tom Kennedy, Harry Lauter, Doodles Weaver, Chick Chandler, Barbara Pepper, Cliff Norton, Roy Roberts, Eddie Ryder, Don C. Harvey, Roy Engel, Paul Birch,

Dale Van Sickel, Jack Benny, Jerry Lewis
Keaton plays a crook.

140. 12/17/1963   THE SOUND OF   75 m.
LAUGHTER
Union Films
Dir.: John O'Shaughnessy
Cast: Bing Crosby, Bob Hope, Danny Kaye,
Buster Keaton, etc.

Compilation of early sound comedy films.
Keaton is seen in excerpts from ONE RUN
ELMER and GRAND SLAM OPERA.

141. 4/28/1964   THE GREATEST SHOW   TV: 60 m.
ON EARTH: YOU'RE ALL RIGHT, IVY
Dir.: Jack Palance
Cast: Buster Keaton, Jack Palance, Stuart
Erwin, Lynn Loring, Ted Bessel, Joe E.
Brown, Joan Blondell, Barbara Pepper

Keaton, Brown and Blondell are three veteran performers now reduced to menial
work in a circus.

(ABC)

142. 5/8/1964   BURKE'S LAW: WHO   TV: 60 m.
KILLED HALF OF GLORY LEE?
Cast: Gene Barry, Buster Keaton, Gary
Conway, Regis Toomey, Joan Blondell,
Nina Foch, Anne Helm, Betty Hutton,
Gisele McKenzie

Keaton is one of the suspects in a case involving a rigged elevator accident.

(ABC)

143. 6/6/1964   HOLLYWOOD PALACE   TV: 60 m.
Host: Gene Barry

Guests: Buster Keaton, Gloria Swanson,
offering a spoof of "Cleopatra."

(ABC)

144. 11/11/1964 PAJAMA PARTY   85 m.
                  American International   Color
                  Dir.: Don Weis
                  Cast: Annette Funicello, Tommy Kirk,
                  Elsa Lanchester, Donna Loren,
                  Buster Keaton
                  Teenage beach fun mixed with a little
                  science fiction. Keaton plays a villainous
                  Indian chief.

145. 1/17/1965   THE MAN WHO   TV: 60 m.
                  BOUGHT PARADISE
                  Dir.: Ralph Nelson
                  Cast: Buster Keaton, Robert Horton, Angie
                  Dickinson, Paul Lukas, Ray Walston,
                  Hoagy Carmichael, Dolores Del Rio, Cyril
                  Ritchard, Walter Slezak
                  In a foreign country, fugitives from the law
                  live at Hotel Paradise. Keaton plays a knife-
                  wielding lawbreaker.

(CBS)

146. 2/11/1965   DONNA REED SHOW: TV: 30 m.
                  NOW YOU SEE IT, NOW YOU DON'T
                  Dir.: Gene Nelson
                  Cast: Donna Reed, Buster Keaton,
                  Ann McRea, Carl Betz, Bob Crane,
                  Paul Petersen
                  Family comedy.

(ABC)

147. 4/15/1965   BEACH BLANKET BINGO   98 m.
American International   Color
Dir.: William Asher
Cast: Frankie Avalon, Annette Funicello,
Deborah Walley, Paul Lynde, Buster
Keaton
Keaton has a cameo role as himself.

148. 6/5/1965   FILM   22 m.
Evergreen Theater/Grove Press   16 mm
Dir.: Alan Schneider
Cast: Buster Keaton
A brooding pantomime drama with Keaton
as the only character.

149. 7/14/1965   HOW TO STUFF A   90 m.
WILD BIKINI   Color
American International
Dir.: William Asher
Cast: Annette Funicello, Dwayne
Hickman, Brian Donlevy, Mickey Rooney,
Beverly Adams, Buster Keaton, Frankie
Avalon, Irene Tsu
Another rock'n'roll beach frolic. Keaton's
cameo role is that of a witch doctor.

150. 8/18/1965   SERGEANT DEADHEAD   90 m.
American International   Color
Dir.: Norman Taurog
Cast: Frankie Avalon, Deborah Walley,
Cesar Romero, Fred Clark, Gale Gordon,
Reginald Gardiner, Buster Keaton,
Eve Arden
Keaton plays a private at a missile base
who pushes some wrong buttons at a cru-
cial moment.

151. 10/2/1965   THE RAILRODDER   21 m.
                  National Film Board (Canada)   Color
                  Dir.: Gerald Petterton
                  Cast: Buster Keaton
                  Keaton on a railroad handcart as a guide for
                  a trip through glorious Canadian scenery.

152. 10/30/1965   BUSTER KEATON   55 m.
                  RIDES AGAIN
                  National Film Board (Canada)
                  Dir.: John Spotton
                  Cast: Buster Keaton, Eleanor Keaton
                  Documentary about the making of the film
                  THE RAILRODDER.

153. 1/8/1966   THE SCRIBE   30 m.
                  Film-Tele Prod. (Canada), for   16 mm
                  Construction Safety Association   Color
                  of Ontario
                  Dir.: John Sebert
                  Cast: Buster Keaton
                  In this industrial safety film, Keaton plays
                  a reporter at a construction site doing a
                  story on safety. This is the last film he
                  worked on.

154. 10/16/1966   A FUNNY THING   99 m.
                  HAPPENED ON THE   Color
                  WAY TO THE FORUM
                  United Artists
                  Dir.: Richard Lester
                  Cast: Zero Mostel, Phil Silvers, Buster
                  Keaton, Jack Gilford, Michael Crawford,
                  Annette Andre, Patricia Jessel, Michael
                  Hordern
                  In this spoof of ancient Rome, Keaton plays

Erronius, a man searching for his children who were taken away by pirates.

155. 1/18/1967   DUE MARINES E UN   89 m.
GENERALE
Released in the U.S. as
WAR ITALIAN STYLE
Italian Intl/American International
(Made in Italy)
Dir.: Luigi Scattini
Cast: Franco Franchi, Ciccio Ingrassia, Martha Hyer, Buster Keaton, Fred Clark

Keaton plays a German general whom two Italian Marines at first outwit, but then get to like.

156. 1968   THE GREAT STONE FACE   93 m.
Funnyman Prod.
Dir.-editor: Vernon P. Becker
Narrated by Henry Morgan

Compilation film using stills and excerpts from his silent films to trace Keaton's career. Keaton is seen in lengthy bits from, among others, FATTY AT CONEY ISLAND, COPS, DAY DREAMS, THE BALLOON-ATIC, and THE GENERAL.

157. 9/9/1970   FOUR CLOWNS   97 m.
20th Century-Fox
Prod./writer/editor: Robert Youngson
Narrated by Jay Jackson

Compilation film of excerpts from the work of Buster Keaton, Charley Chase, and Laurel & Hardy. The lengthiest Keaton sequence is the chase from SEVEN CHANCES.

158.   11/3/1974   **THE THREE STOOGES**   116 m.
                   FOLLIES
                   Columbia
                   Dir.: unknown
                   Cast: The Three Stooges, Vera Vague,
                   Buster Keaton, etc.
                   Compilation of Columbia shorts from the
                   1930s and 1940s, most of them featuring
                   The Three Stooges. Keaton is seen in
                   NOTHING BUT PLEASURE, one of his
                   1940 releases.

159.   10/11/1975 **THREE COMEDIES**   60 m.
                   Jay Ward Productions
                   Prod.: Raymond Rohauer
                   Exec. Prod.: Jay Ward and Bill Scott
                   Compilation film made up of three Buster
                   Keaton shorts, with narration and musical
                   score: THE HIGH SIGN, THE PALE-
                   FACE and ONE WEEK.

160.   11/1/1982   **BUSTER**   97 m.
                   Also known as THE GOLDEN AGE OF
                   BUSTER KEATON (1975)
                   Jay Ward Productions
                   Prod.: Raymond Rohauer
                   Exec. Prod.: Jay Ward and Bill Scott
                   Compilation film using clips from many
                   Buster Keaton shorts and features, narrated
                   by Bill Scott.

Related Quality Paperback Books from Da Capo Press

Jazz In the Movies:
New Enlarged Edition
  by David Meeker

On Movies
  by Dwight Macdonald
  New Introduction by John Simon

Adventures with D. W. Griffith
  by Karl Brown

Cagney:
The Actor as Auteur
  by Patrick McGilligan
  New Introduction by
  Andrew Sarris

Before My Eyes
  by Stanley Kauffmann

John Ford
  by Joseph McBride and
  Michael Wilmington

. . . available at your bookstore